I0541716

A PERFECTLY
DESIGNED
IMPERFECT
WORLD

A THEODICY of DESIGN

A PERFECTLY DESIGNED IMPERFECT WORLD

*Understanding God's Architecture
for Spiritual Growth*

MICHAEL G. CARROLL

GRAND
PRAIRIE
PRESS

Copyright © 2024 by Mike Carroll

All rights reserved. No part of this book may be reproduced or transmitted in any form or by any means, electronic or mechanical, including photocopying, recording, or by any information storage and retrieval system, or internet program or system, without written permission from the author.

Editing
Katherine Colwell
Rebecca J. Cook

Book Design and Publishing Services
Connie King, Constance King Design

GRAND
PRAIRIE
PRESS

grandprairiepress@gmail.com
Tuscola, Illinois

ISBN 979-8-218-46211-6
Printed in USA

Dedicated to My Loving and
Supportive Wife Rebecca

CONTENTS

PREFACE

A THEODICY IS A defense of God against the negative implications for God created by the problem of evil.

The problem of evil is, at its most simple, the anti-God implications from the following argument: If God is all-powerful, God could prevent evil in the world; If God is wholly good, God would want to prevent evil in the world; but evil exists in the world.

The logical implication is that, because evil exists in the world, God doesn't exist. Or, if God exists, such God is not all-powerful and/or wholly good. It presents a paradox for Christians, what some call Christianity's biggest problem today since it's also been called the rock upon which modern atheism stands.

Theodicy is any argument seeking to defend God by countering the logical anti-God implications of the problem of evil. Theodicy also refers to the theological/philosophical discipline of studying the problem with a view of defending God.

This work presents a theodicy based upon an understanding of how God designed the experience of life so that we can come to freely choose, but are not compelled, to know, appreciate and love God and others (otherwise known as growth in spiritual maturity).

Being a philosophical question, the problem of evil is usually argued with the dense and technical jargon of academic-speak—primarily within the domains of philosophy and theology—and, thus, is not easily accessible to the lay person. One of this book's main goals is to make theodicy more accessible to the lay reader. Here's one simple example of how I plan to accomplish that task: a Yogi Berra quote. Yogi, a Hall of Fame baseball catcher, was equally famous for his head-scratching Yogisms, what some called malaprops.

Yogi once said: "If the world were perfect, it wouldn't be." What? He then went on to clarify: "I believe you have to take the good with the bad, otherwise how do you know when things are good? If the world were perfect, how would you know?"

Yogi's saying is deeply insightful, suggesting we cannot know and appreciate the good without the bad. This reveals an understanding of the structure of ambiguity within life where we can only learn and grow through the experience of opposites, which is essential in understanding why evil necessarily exists within creation.

Disclaimer: I am not a philosopher or theologian. I am a lawyer by education and experience, and a recently retired Judge. I was drawn to the world of theodicy over twenty years ago and found it fascinating. For these last twenty years I have studied the problem of evil, reviewing main arguments for and against God, considered traditional Christian responses, all the while studying Scriptural explanations for evil. To it all, I applied my life lessons, legal education, and experience to create an intellectually defensible and Scripturally sound justification for God allowing evil within creation.

I don't consider my lack of technical, credentialed qualifications a draw back. On the contrary, by being forced to wade through the complicated arguments and counterarguments on the issue, I feel I can convert them to ordinary language with supporting stories and thought exercises to buttress my argument.

My hope for this book is that it be helpful to serious and thoughtful readers interested in the study of God and evil.

PROPOSITION

DARKNESS HAS NO MEANING but for the Light that provides contrast. And Light gains meaning and appreciation by the existence of Darkness. Each bathes the other in contrast. How would we ever know one without the other? How would we know good without evil?

God designed the experience of life with enough positive indicators and inducements to discover God's purpose for life and for every person, but not so much as to make this discovery certain and predetermined. God's purpose includes love. Since love must be freely chosen, our discovery of God's purpose for life and each of us cannot be forced or predetermined.

In the world, the lived experience remains radically free and ambiguous, with all the anxiety and doubt that freedom and ambiguity entail. This design is necessary for us to come to know, appreciate, and love God, each other and life—in other words, to mature in Christ.

INTRODUCTION

God saw all that he had made, and it was very good.
Genesis 1: 31

*Religion offers an architecture of meaning in which
people may find shelter and hope.*
Neil MacGregor, *Living With Gods*

*It is now imperative that Tibetan Buddhists be able to
explain clearly their tenants and beliefs to others using reason.
Simply quoting from Buddhist scripture does not convince people who
did not grow up Buddhists of the validity of the Buddhist doctrines.
If we try to prove points only by quoting scripture, these people
may respond: 'Everyone has a book to quote from.*
Tenzin Gyatso, the 14th Dalai Lama, *Wall Street Journal* (7-7-2017)

A s concerns the title—A Perfectly Designed Imperfect World—it is, admittedly, provocative, probably outrageous and, to those who have suffered greatly, even obscene. But, if God is all-powerful and perfectly good—as most Christians believe—then, *logically, God made no mistakes in creation.*

And yet creation *seems so horribly imperfect* in terms of *evil* experiences in the world with its wars, death and disease—physical and mental—misery, pain and suffering, and injustice.

These negative, unwanted experiences of evil frustrate, if not outright destroy, our desired positive experiences. As Hasker (2008) argues, "evil is seen as the 'privation of good,' as the absence of some good state of affairs that would reasonably be expected to obtain." (p. 75) For example:

1

injustice robs us of our desire for fairness and justice, pain and suffering frustrates our desire for pleasure and well-being, and death and dying denies a desire for more life.

Negative experiences are the *imperfections* in our life that seem to mar if not outright destroy our desire for a *perfect life,* and we struggle to understand why God would allow this to happen to us.

Evil experiences are typically classified as those caused either by fellow humans (moral evil) or nature (natural evil). And they exhibit a range in terms of the amount, variety, breadth and depth and severity. For simplicity, reference will be to the two extreme ranges of evil: ordinary evil, at one end of the spectrum and horrendous evil[1] at the other.

Ordinary, everyday simple evil, say the pain of a broken bone in our leg, often is understandable; that is to say, we can see the good reason it accomplishes. With a broken leg bone, for example, its pain and suffering serves to keep us off that leg until we attend to its repair and healing. Movement can aggravate the injury and if there were no pain and suffering we might move about. Thus, the pain and suffering of a broken leg bone helps prevent further injury.

In terms of horrendous natural evil, at the epic scale that could be an earthquake/tsunami event, like the 2004 Asian tsunami that killed around 250,000 people. In terms of horrendous moral evil, that could be the Holocaust where around six million Jews were exterminated by Nazis in World War II. At the individual level of horrendous evil, that could be the kidnapping and murder of a baby (moral evil) or a storm such as a tornado causing death to a child (natural evil). Horrendous evils defy our understanding and seem to serve no good purpose.

* * *

There are three reasonable understandings of the relationship between God and evil that we can draw from the amount, variety, breadth and depth of evil we find in the world.

---

1 Horrendous evils include evils that are excessive in scale such as intense pain and suffering, disproportionate in spread, heinous and seemingly gratuitous, that is, serving no good justifiable reason we can imagine.

1. Any evil in the world, whatsoever, means it's *not possible* that Christianity's God of Perfect power and love exists, because God could (being all-powerful) and would want to (being wholly good) design a perfect world. (This is known as the *logical problem of evil*.)

For example, going back to our broken leg bone, a critic could complain that God could have made bones that didn't break. One skeptic asked: *But why didn't God make our bones out of something stronger like titanium?* To which, philosopher Richard Swinburne reportedly replied: *It could be worse; God could have made our bones out of glass.*

Here we can see that the argument that there should be no pain and suffering in the world (felt as evil) is premised on the idea that a perfect world created by a perfect God should never include any pain and suffering[2]. This viewpoint, in turn, is premised on the notion that God made the world for our pleasure, happiness and wish-fulfillment and not for any higher goal (good reason) that God has in store for us.

2. Even if *some evil in the world can be justified* as serving a good reason (say, the pain of a broken leg), the great amount, variety, breadth and depth, and severity of evil in the world makes it *improbable* that Christianity's God exists. (This is known as the *evidential problem of evil*).

Here, a Christian could see, as Swinburne did, that God made our bones out of fairly durable material; maybe not titanium but at least not glass. And they could reasonably conclude that God had a good reason to justify some pain and suffering. This viewpoint is premised upon the notion that God created the world for God's good reason/s and not our selfish, narrow and immediate goals in life.

3. God has a good reason, or reasons, to allow evil in the world, such that even someone enduring intense pain and suffering from horrendous evil is necessary to achieve God's good reason/s. (Proving this is the task of *theodicy*, with theodicy being both the discipline of

---

2 Pain and suffering is often a substitute term for evil. Almost all evils cause pain and suffering. For example, if someone experiences injustice, that causes mental and, possibly, physical suffering. Since evil is described as a negative, unwanted experience in life, any evil should produce pain and suffering.

studying the problem of evil with a goal of defending God, as well as any argument in favor of God.)

Here, in possibility 3, we have the hard problem of evil. That is, while we might be able to understand and justify ordinary evil, we have great difficulty understanding and justifying horrendous evil.

The current status of the issue, in terms of the above three possibilities, is that the logical problem of evil (1) has been solved to the satisfaction of many, if not most, philosophers. That is, a logical argument exists that it's *possible* Christianity's God exits despite evil in the world because of some assumed good reason of God. However, it appears there's very little consensus that the evidential problem of evil (2) has been solved. That is, most philosophers don't agree that anyone has presented a persuasive argument that, given horrendous evil, it's *probable* Christianity's God exists. This is the task of theodicy, to logically counter (2) and support the argument for God (3) that, despite horrendous evil, it can be logically shown that it's *probable* Christianity's God exists.

[Note: the task is to show that it's *probable* God exists, not that God's existence is guaranteed beyond doubt. Being a philosophical question, the problem of evil (and the issue of God's existence) does not lend itself to mathematical certainty and/or scientific verification or falsification. Some Christians might find this depressing, this inability to prove God's existence through human logic; however, they should be comforted by the fact that atheists cannot, for the same reasons, disprove God's existence. As will be argued later, God's purpose and good reason/s depend upon doubt. If God's reality were objectively certain, then neither love nor moral consequential behavior would be possible. Since love and morally consequential behavior are a large part of God's good reason/s for creation, then I urge Christians to embrace the fact and challenge of doubt, uncertainty and ambiguity in our march of faith—even though they create anxiety, which, also, serves God's purpose.]

* * *

The problem of evil is a philosophical/theological problem concerning God and evil that has been debated even before Christ was born. The problem of evil creates a logical paradox, with its solution (if any) requiring a logical response. This doesn't mean a Christian can't have an answer for the problem of evil that fails to meet the test of logic. Indeed, the problem of evil might defy our logical abilities to understand God's reasons. That is certainly the inference from Job's tragic plight and complaint to God.

However, finding a logical solution to the problem of evil is important as *evil in the world counts against God*. That is, the inferences we can reasonably draw about evil in the world, especially horrendous evil, automatically seems to count against God's reality and/or essence as all powerful and wholly good. This places the burden of proof upon Christians to answer or solve the problem of evil. Failure to provide a logically compelling reason for horrendous evil has significantly contributed to the decline of faith, at least in the western civilization.

Some, if not many, theologians have called the problem of evil *the largest obstacle to Christianity today*. It has also been called *the rock upon which modern atheism stands*.

This book attempts to present a logically persuasive argument that it's *probable* Christianity's God exists despite evil, including horrendous evil, existing in the world. By *logically persuasive*, I mean the argument will meet the four requirements for a good theodicy: logical coherence; scriptural coherence; scientific coherence; and common sense coherence.

[Note: this work, while adhering to academic rigor, is primarily aimed not at academics but the average, critically thinking Christian—even atheists or agnostics who are interested into the reason for existence and why it's designed as it currently exists. As such, every attempt is made to make the often complex, arcane worlds of theology and philosophy accessible to the non-academic, lay reader with definitions along the way (at the end of the book), thought experiments, everyday examples from my life, even humor and popular culture references.]

* * *

Briefly, let's begin with two basic premises that guide my theodicy: (1) God designed the experience of life for God's good reasons and not our selfish, desired good reasons; and (2) "perfection"—whether viewed from the perspective of God's good reasons or our selfish good reasons—requires imperfection.

Definitions matter, and here we need to think about what a "perfect world" would be. One popular image is a world where a person is happy and full of bliss from sensual pleasures and where a person's every wish is granted. Assuming that is the case, then consider the following as two examples that indicate *perfection is either overrated or misunderstood.*

A modern television parable: In a 1960 *Twilight Zone* television episode entitled *A Nice Place to Visit*, a small-town hoodlum awakens after being shot to find himself in what he believes to be heaven. The man he meets upon awakening—played by Sebastian Cabot—seems to be his guardian angel, agreeing to satisfy the hoodlum's desire for a perfect life.

Upon re-entering life, the hoodlum assumes he is in heaven because his flawed, imperfect life suddenly changes for the better. Overnight, his every wish and desire is fulfilled: women, money, booze, always winning at gambling. He is living the perfect life he always desired, perfect in the sense his every wish is fulfilled. He is not frustrated in any way, faces no obstacles, no negative, unwanted experiences. He is constantly and continually happy and full of sensual bliss.

At first the hoodlum is thrilled, but then, after awhile, he gets bored.

He misses risk, the unknown, excitement, spontaneity, joy, of beating the odds. In frustration, he summons, then complains, to Cabot that heaven is overrated, to which Cabot replied: "Who said you were in heaven?"

Ouch.

Perfect golf: Another way to illustrate the point is through a thought experiment involving sports, say golf. You've always dreamed of a perfect round. Let's say that one day you wake up and the world has changed. You have your dream. Every time you hit the ball it goes into the hole, no matter how far away from the hole you are, no matter how poorly you swing, no matter even if you don't sincerely try. Even if you kick it with your foot, or bounce it off your head, every shot goes in the hole. You can't help it. Every day you shoot 18, all holes-in-one.

At first, it might be euphoric. You never lose. If your partners have the same power, they never lose either. Everyone always shoots 18. Every day. Forever. But soon it would get boring and lose all meaning, joy, adventure and spontaneity. It ceases being fun and you quit the game, wanting to escape this new golf hell.

You realize golf's great treasure is in the challenge, in marshalling one's talent and effort against all the obstacles confronting you: the weather—rain and wind, cold and dreary; the stress of the shot or the pressure of competition; the tired muscles that don't always move as you want them to move; the depression over a missed shot and the need to mentally rebound—to get it together; the unfairness of a bad bounce or the arbitrariness of a lipped-out putt because the ball hit a spike mark caused by *some idiot* dragging his feet across the green.

These and other *imperfections* are what you struggle against. Without them, there would be no joy in hitting a pure shot, of improving your game, of overcoming adversity through hard work, effort, confidence, discipline, sacrifice and force of will.

Negative experiences necessary for appreciating positive experiences: We can easily see in these two fairly simple examples that—even viewed from the perspective of thinking that God designed the world for our pleasure and happiness—a perfect world (defined as constant wish fulfillment and narcissistic happiness) is quite sterile, bereft of meaning, value and heft over and against which to measure and treasure the great joys of positive experiences.

Living in a utopian world of perfection where only one force, one unambiguous experience—like constant happiness—is at work, can never produce knowledge, appreciation, maturity, moral consequentiality, or the capacity for love. Such a world would be shallow, lacking great texture and depth. It would not be a world where dynamic, creative life unfolds, or where love is possible.

One solution to this seeming paradox of an imagined perfect life being actually imperfect, is to consider the notion that perfection requires imperfection. In that regard, I think it's best to consider the notion of perfection not from the perspective of life's purpose being centered around human desires (an anthropocentric perspective). Rather, we should assume life is centered on God's good reason/s (a theocentric perspective). This involves, first, believing in God, and second, understanding God's good reason for life's imperfections (e.g., evil) as being necessary to achieve God's plan or goal/s with creation.

If we think God created our experience of life to make us constantly happy and full of sensual pleasures, then it's only logical to conclude God clearly failed.

I argue that thinking of perfection in terms of what God is trying to achieve (God's plan for us) through God's design of life is the best way to both understand the logic behind creation and to rationally defend God against atheism's argument that evil negates the existence of a loving, all-powerful God.

* * *

Part One will develop the problem of evil in its two main forms—the logical argument and the evidential argument—that Christians face in defending their faith against the arguments of a rising, and often militant atheism.

As indicated, the problem of evil counts against Christianity's God existing. The burden is always on the faithful to overcome the reasonable inferences of the problem of evil in some persuasive fashion. And those *reasonable inferences* are: God, being omnipotent, *could have* created a world with no evil, or at least no horrendous evil; and God, being wholly good, *would want to* create a world with no evil, or at least no horrendous evil. But, the problem is that despite these reasonable inferences evil, including horrendous evil, exists.

Various popular arguments have been advanced over millennia in defense of God. They will be more fully developed in Part Two of this work. Briefly, popular, traditional arguments include interpreting Adam and Eve's Fall as the reason for humanity's eviction from paradise and into an imperfect world containing evil. This argues evil is humanity's fault.

Another explanation is that fallen angels, such as Satan, have despoiled God's creation. This argues fallen angels are responsible for evil.

Yet another popular understanding of how/why evil is within creation is that God has reasons but God's reasons are beyond our ability to understand/comprehend. They are beyond our ken. This argument is supported by the plight of Job and the answers from God that Job received, suggesting we cannot know God's reason for evil.

These arguments (and others to be discussed) have Scriptural support, and any of them, admittedly, might be the answer to the problem of evil.

However, true or not, most of these traditional responses to the questions posed by evil within the world don't seem to meet the rigorous requirements of a good theodicy.

There is also the excellent argument that defending God has nothing to do with logic at all. Rather, God's plan is for us to access God through love, spiritually, by being seized by God's love made manifest by Christ on the cross.

Once again, this attractive argument may be ultimately true—probably is true—however, it does not provide us with a logical ladder to God's reason for evil. Theodicists[3] assume God would want us to have some rational insight into why life contains so much pain and suffering, otherwise why give us the gift of logical reasoning.

Part Two also includes a description of logical defenses to the arguments from evil, together with a brief historical tour of theodicies presented to date.

The section ends with a listing of sixteen possible good reasons for God allowing evil in the world. The sixteenth is this book's contribution: that evil allows the emergence of certain human abilities (such as the ability to learn or know) made possible by the shaping and channeling effect of certain innate mechanisms (such as free will and ambiguity) that God wove into life and our experience of life, all of which leads to the possibility of love and Christian moral behavior.

Part Three presents the book's theodicy. It is not necessarily a new one. Rather, it builds upon existing free will theodicies that stress the various good reasons that human free will creates: e.g., Christian maturity; moral consequentiality; love.

---

3 Theodicists are people who practice theodicy. Atheodicists practice atheodicy which is both the discipline of, and any answer in favor of, arguing that, given evil, it's not possible, or at least not probable, that Christianity's God exists.

A good example of free will theodicy is *open theism*: a belief that God, as love, and out of love, and for love, granted creatures a freely self-determining will, because "love must be freely chosen." (Boyd, p. 23)

If, as open theism argues, God's goal is love, then free will is the method to achieve that goal, and evil is the necessary cost of that method. Evil is the necessary cost because God's creatures, being free, can choose and act other than God wishes they would choose and act.

The premise that humans possess a self-determining free will, therefore, goes a long way toward understanding evil within a creation designed by an omnipotent and wholly good God.

[Note: however, there exists serious doubt—primarily within science but also within theology—that humans possess free will. Part Three will fully discuss whether or not human free will exists.]

I emphasize this structure of human free will but build upon it, adding other structures of being[4] that God wove into the warp and woof of creation so as to achieve God's goal for the world and for each of us. Those structures are *ambiguity, anxiety, doubt and self-consciousness*. Each structure is necessary to achieve God's plan and, combined, I argue they are sufficient.

Each structure of being will be fully defined and discussed along with how each is necessary for God to achieve God's plan for us. I will also discuss how each structure can create and/or cause and/or constitute evil, but argue that God's plan cannot be achieved otherwise. Then I discuss whether or not these structures and their operation upon human behavior are supported by current scientific thinking in various fields. Finally, I will defend each structure as consistent with Scripture.

---

4 What do we call our faculty for free will? I choose, for want of a better term, to call it a structure of being. That implies it was designed into the human experience of life by God. Another term I might use—sorry, don't mean to confuse you and will try to stick with common terms—is life processes, a term I believe Tillich prefers. Structures of being are human abilities we possess (and/or structures that exist in the world that shape, channel and limit our behavior), whether we like to possess them or not. Take free will. Sartre says we are not only free but "condemned to be free." These are innate abilities within us or the world, deny them as much as we want. The other structures of being—anxiety, doubt, ambiguity, and self-consciousness—are also innate to our experience of living in the world.

I build upon free will theology, such as open theism that stresses love as God's good reason and the theodicies that stress how evil builds Christian character and present opportunities for good moral action (e.g., Hick and Swinburne).

I build upon these excellent works under the assumption that, as promising and convincing as they present, they are incomplete, having explanatory shortcomings (e.g., horrendous evil, natural and moral) and lack a detailed grand schema (of God's architecture) of how all the dynamic moving parts of the lived experience work to God's good.

I argue that God's overall architecture, with its structures of being or life processes (such as free will) enables human abilities such as knowledge, appreciation, moral maturity and love, all of which leads to accomplishment of God's plan for creation and each one of us.

Is it a new theodicy, an advance forward of existing theodicies, or merely a synthesis? I see it as both a synthesis of and an advance forward of existing free will theodicies in defending God. At a minimum, I think it's at least a grand tour of theodicy and an excellent primer for the critically thinking Christian who wants to be both better equipped to defend God against atheistic broadsides and be comforted in spirit that their faith is intellectually defensible.

* * *

This is a Christian theodicy for a couple of reasons. First, the essence of God which creates the problem of evil—Perfection: perfect in love and perfect in power—are the attributes Christians believe God possesses. Second, I am a Christian. Third, I am not as familiar with other faiths—e.g., their doctrines, Holy works, traditions—so I cannot speak to their views of God's attributes nor their understanding of evil. Hopefully, this will help all faith traditions that believe in a loving God.

The other reason I focus specifically on Christianity is that Christianity appears to be in *serious decline* and has been for some decades if not centuries, most specifically in highly developed and educated North America and Europe (the "West").

A 2021 Gallup poll revealed that church membership has fallen below 50% for the first time in U.S. history. A 2020 Pew research poll showed that 64% of U.S. citizens call themselves a Christian today, down from 90% fifty years ago. 30% of citizen indicate "none" or no religious affiliation while 6% identify as "other religions." Predictions are that by 2070, assuming the same current rates of change, only 46% of U.S. citizens will identify as Christian, "nones" will increase to 41% while "other religions" will rise to 13%.

There have been several studies of this phenomenon with many theories. One theory is that with the rise of science, its discoveries and its empirical method, unprovable myths have slowly eroded and magical happenings that defy scientific laws are increasingly seen as incredulous. Another theory, based upon the atheistic argument that *religion never invented anything*, is that science, technology and human ingenuity have invented things. Thus, our lives are largely better today—e.g., longer life, better health, disease cures, better shelter, stable food supply, more leisure time, etc.—than say hundreds of years ago when faith in God was the world's dominant force. So we look more to science and technology than the pulpit for solutions to our problems. Then there's the government which increasingly expands its reach to solve the problems and needs of its populace.

Whatever the reasons, American philosopher, Charles Taylor, in *The Secular Age* (2007), agrees there's been such a decline. He argues that while it was virtually impossible hundreds of years ago to not believe in God, today many find it virtually impossible to believe in God. He claims this is especially prevalent in Western society where "the presumption of unbelief has become dominant" and "achieved hegemony in...academic and intellectual life...whence it can more easily extend itself to others." (p. 12, 13) He concludes that "for the first time in history a purely self-sufficient humanism came to be a widely available option." (p. 18)

In this decline, many consider Christianity's biggest problem is the problem of evil, especially horrendous evils that seem pointless or out of proportion and beyond comprehension. This is both the focus of the book—helping to solve the evidential form of the problem of evil—and my motivation for writing it, with its hope of better identifying God's rational design of life as an intellectually satisfying, Scripturally sound ground upon which today's Christians can stand.

* * *

Since this is a Christian theodicy, my argument also aims for Scriptural support. In that regard, I largely employ an interpretation method advocated by T. Norton Sterrett in his book *How to Understand Your Bible* (1974). Sterrett recommends general principles such as "considering the context" and "grasping the author's intention" and special principles such as interpreting some passages as "figures of speech," or "symbols," or parables and allegories" in addition to understanding some passages literally.

A further maxim is one I borrow loosely from the rules of legal interpretation: when a law or statute is poorly drafted (e.g., inconsistent terms, ambiguous) a court interpreting it should first apply the plain meaning of the words, and then, if that fails, apply a charitable interpretation. A charitable interpretation means an interpretation that renders the law or statute coherent in its whole, and rationally satisfies the objective for which it was aimed.

Clearly, given historical schisms within the church body—i.e. disagreements about how to interpret this passage or that passage— there seems to be both ambiguity, at least within our interpretation of Scripture, and a need for charitable interpretation.

* * *

This is a work in Christian apologetics, meaning a it is a rational response against the objections people bring up about Christianity. Here the objection is that Christianity's God can't exist because of evil in the world. This doesn't mean I'm apologizing for my faith but, rather, affirming the reason for my faith.

Apologetics works rely on logic and logical inference. I understand Scripture as instructing us to speak up in logic to defend our faith. As Peter charges: "Always be prepared to give an answer to everyone who asks you to give the reason for the hope that you have [that Christ is

Lord]." (1 Pe 3:15) This means rational, human logic, as "answer" in Greek means "apology" or speaking in defense from logic.

Theodicies are logical arguments defending God's essence as all-powerful and wholly good, despite the obvious and often horrendous imperfections (evils) of life. Though God's loving grace may be apprehended only by a revelatory experience that resonates spiritually and emotionally (i.e., by being seized by God's love) people who are engaged in theodicy nonetheless believe in the divine value of reason as a path to God's grace.

Theodicy can be a path to grace in that it opens one's heart, through the mind's reason, to the probability of God. Theodicists believe this quest is possible because it assumes our faculty for reason is one of many gifts from God to apprehend God's love and enjoy the same in fellowship. For example, without the power of reason how can we understand (let alone simply read) Scripture?

This theodicy has provided me with renewed confidence that God made no mistakes with creation, and that God truly uses/converts all evil to good. May it enrich your faith and hope in, and ripen your love for, God, as it has for me.

– PART 1 –

THE PROBLEM
OF EVIL

You are free to eat from any tree in the garden, but you
must not eat from the tree of knowledge of good and evil, for
when you eat of it you will surely die.

God (speaking to Adam and Eve), Ge 2:17

Of all the difficulties that hold people back from
religious belief, the question of evil and suffering in
the world is surely the greatest.

John Polkinghorne, *Exploring Reality:*
The Intertwining of Science and Religion

Either God cannot abolish evil, or
he will not; if he cannot then he is not all-powerful;
if he will not then he is not all-good.

St. Augustine, *Confessions*

THE PROBLEM OF evil or the argument from evil, in all its forms, is a philosophical argument used by atheists against God. The argument is used to argue the perfectly powerful and loving God of Christianity doesn't exist, or that it's at least improbable that God exists, given the great abundance, variety and severity of pain and suffering, injustice and others evils within the world.

Being a philosophical argument, the problem of evil is based upon human reason's tool of logic and is debated, primarily, within the disciplines of philosophy and theology. Thus, the arguments are usually delivered in arcane forms and terms unique to academic specialists. Thus, the philosophical arguments raging within philosophy are usually unfamiliar to the lay reader.

However, as Plantinga tells us, lay readers should not be intimidated by philosophical arguments. He says (1977) that "Philosophical reflection is not much different from just thinking hard." (p. 1) Plus, since I am primarily aiming this work for the critically thinking Christian, I will use the following tools to make the philosophical debate about evil accessible to the lay reader: e.g., personal stories, humor, thought experiments, explanations of technical terms in ordinary language.

The problem of evil has been called both Christianity's greatest problem and atheism's foundation from which to launch broadsides against God and those who believe in God.

There are two common forms of the problem: the *logical* form of the problem and the *evidential* form of the problem. Many if not most philosophers seem satisfied the logical problem has been solved with American analytic philosopher Alvin Plantinga's "free will defense." Some disagree, feeling the defense is not as robust and vindicating as a theodicy, and that the free will defense best applies only to moral evils (and not natural evils), plus does not address or solve the more difficult problem posed by the evidential form of the problem of evil.

Regardless, I think it's instructive to understand the logical argument and Plantinga's defense in order to prepare not only for the challenge of the evidential argument but to build and improve upon Plantinga's free will defense (see: Part Two B)

1.1 The Logical Problem of Evil—Epicurus

Atheodicists use the *logical* form of the problem of evil to argue it's not "possible" for a world created by a wholly good and all-powerful God to contain evil.

The logical problem of evil—first credited to Greek philosopher Epicurus (341-270 BC)—is a set of three statements. To examine his statements, and illustrate logical technique, let's refer to them as Set A:

A1. God is omnipotent.

A2. God is wholly good.

A3. Evil exists in the world.

Two inferences rationally arise from statements A1 and A2:

Inference A4 is that, being omnipotent, God could prevent evil in the world; and inference A5 is that, being wholly good, God would want to prevent evil in the world.

With inferences A4 (God could prevent evil) and A5 (God would want to prevent evil) added to Set A, we can reasonably conclude that set Set A is an *inconsistent set*. That is, the statements are not logically compatible. How, for example, can evil exist in the world (A3) if God is as claimed A1 (omnipotent) and A2 (wholly good) given the inferences A4 (God could prevent evil) and A5 (God would want to prevent evil)?

There are various ways to make this a consistent set by changing the statements. One solution is to change A3 (evil exists) to say Evil does not exist in the world. Asserting that evil doesn't exist, makes Set A a consistent set, however almost no one agrees evil does not exist in the world. Thus, changing statement A3 (evil exists) might result in an consistent set of statements but results in an unsound statement because arguing evil doesn't exist is probably not true.

Assuming you don't change A3 (evil exists), but instead change A1 to say that God is not omnipotent or change A2 to say that God is not wholly good then you have a consistent set.

New inference arises from changing A1 to God is not omnipotent and/or A2 to God is not wholly good. Inference A4 becomes: since God is not omnipotent, God could not prevent evil (e.g., God is a lesser or impotent God). Inference A5 becomes: since God is not wholly good, God would not want to prevent evil (e.g., God is a malevolent God).

Set A can easily be made into an argument, let's call it Set B:

B1. God is omnipotent and could prevent evil.

B2. God is wholly good and would want to prevent evil.

B3. Evil exists.

B4. Therefore, either: God does not exist; God exists but is not omnipotent; and/or God exists but is not wholly good.

This argument appears to create both a valid and sound argument.[5]

---

5 In philosophy, a valid argument means that the conclusion logically follows from the premises. A sound argument means the premises are true.

1.2 The Evidential Problem of Evil—Rowe and Martin

There are various versions of the *evidential* problem of evil argument. Perhaps the most famous is credited to William Rowe (1931-2015), professor of philosophy. Let's call his argument Set C:

C1. There exists instances of intense suffering which an omnipotent being could have prevented without thereby losing some greater good or permitting some evil equally bad or worse.

C2. An omniscient, wholly good being would prevent the occurrence of any intense suffering it could, unless it could not do so without thereby losing some greater good or permitting some evil equally bad or worse.

C3. Therefore, there does not exist an omnipotent, omniscient, wholly good being. (1979, p. 336)

Premises C1 and C2 creates a challenge to theodicy to justify occurrences of intense suffering by showing: (a) some greater good that would be lost without the intense suffering, or (b) some equally bad or worse evil that would occur without this occurrence of intense suffering.

This challenge seems almost insurmountable if the occurrences of intense suffering are considered pointless or gratuitous. By definition alone, there can be no good reason for gratuitous evil, because the definition for gratuitous evil is that there's no good reason for its occurrence. God can never be defended by theodicy if pointless evils exist. If God is omnipotent and wholly good, then, ipso facto, there's always a point to evil. Theodicy's task is to point out the point of seemingly pointless evil.

Rowe supported his argument by giving two specific factual situations of gratuitous evil, one is an example of natural evil (Bambi) and the other is an example of moral evil (Sue).

Bambi

In some distant forest lightning strikes a dead tree, resulting in a forest fire. In the fire a fawn is trapped, horribly burned, and lies in terrible agony for several days before death relieves its suffering. (1979, p. 337)

Sue

This is an actual event in which a five-year-old girl in Flint, Michigan was severely beaten, raped and then strangled to death early on New Year's Day on 1986. The case was introduced by Bruce Russell, whose account of it, drawn from a report in the *Detroit Free Press* of January 3, 1986, runs as follows:

The girl's mother was living with her boyfriend, another man who was unemployed, her two children, and her 9-month old infant fathered by the boyfriend. On New Year's Eve all three adults were drinking at a bar near the woman's home. The boyfriend had been taking drugs and drinking heavily. He was asked to leave the bar at 8:00 p.m. After several reappearances he finally stayed away for good at about 9:30 p.m. The woman and the unemployed man remained at the bar until 2 a.m. at which time the woman went home and the man to a party at a neighbor's house. Perhaps out of jealousy, the boyfriend attacked the woman when she walked into the house. Her brother was there and broke up the fight by hitting the boyfriend who was passed out and slumped over a table when the brother left. Later the boyfriend attacked the woman again, and this time she knocked him unconscious. After checking the children, she went to bed. Later the woman's 5-year old girl went downstairs to go to the bathroom. The unemployed man returned from the party at 3:45 a.m. and found the 5-year old dead. She had been raped, severely beaten over most of her body and strangled to death by the boyfriend. (1988, p. 119)

The Bambi example was intended by Rowe as a difficult case of natural evil (evil caused by nature, its properties and processes like an earthquake) while Sue was intended as a difficult case of moral evil

(evil caused by human action/inaction like murder). He saw them as representative of the horrendous evils that occur daily.

He further boiled his argument down to propositions I label Set D:

D1: No good state of affairs we know of is such that an omnipotent, omniscient being's obtaining it would morally justify that being in permitting Sue or Bambi. Therefore,

D2: It is likely that no good state of affairs is such that an omnipotent, omniscient being's obtaining it would morally justify that being in permitting Sue or Bambi.

Given D1, Rowe concludes in D2 that it is likely (probable) that there's no moral justification for the evil visited upon Sue and Bambi.

Here, we might ask what is a "good state of affairs" that we might know of? Rowe says to know a good state of affairs is to conceive of such a state and recognize that such a state of affairs is intrinsically good. Rowe suggests examples of intrinsically good states of affairs include pleasure, happiness, love, and the exercise of virtue. (1988, p. 123)

* * *

Another evidential argument was formulated by American philosopher Michael L. Martin (1932-2015). It sets forth a slightly different challenge than what Rowe argued, which some argue is the best formulation of the evidential argument. Following is Martin's argument (1981), known as Set E:

E1. An omnipotent God could prevent the horrendous evil we experience unless such evil were logically necessary.

E2. A wholly good God would prevent horrendous evil unless he had a sufficient reason to allow it.

E3. Evil exists in great abundance only if either God has a sufficient reason to allow the abundance of evil or the greater abundance of evil is logically necessary.

E4. If one has good reason to suppose that the existence of evil in great abundance is not logically necessary and that there is no sufficient reason for God to allow such evil, then the abundance of evil counts as strong evidence against the existence of God.

E5. One has good reason to believe that the existence of evil in great abundance is not logically necessary and that there is no sufficient reason for God to allow such evil if the theist fails over a long period of time to provide an acceptable explanation for the abundance of evil we experience.

E6. Despite repeated attempts, no one has provided a good reason to believe that God has a sufficient reason to allow horrendous evil to exist or that such evil is logically necessary—that is, no one has been able to provide an acceptable explanation for the horrendous evil we experience.

E7. The abundance of evil we experience counts as strong evidence against God's existence.

E8. There is no (or little) positive evidence with respect to God's existence.

E9. If there exists strong evidence against God's existence and no (or little) evidence that God exists, it is most reasonable to believe that God does not exist.

E10. (Therefore) It is most reasonable to believe that God does not exist. (p.175-84)

Set E seems to be both a consistent set and a valid argument creating today' challenge for theodicy.

[Note: With this evidential form of the problem of evil, there seems to be a concession of the possibility of some evil within a world created by an all-powerful and loving God. Rather, the objection is to horrendous evils for which it seems God could have avoided through allowing lesser evils without thereby negating any higher good desired. Theodicy's task for this evidential form of the argument, therefore, is to identify God's goal/s for creation (God's good reason) and then explain why that good reason necessitates not only evil but, especially, horrendous evil. (Rowe calls this unnecessary evil "intense suffering," while Martin refers to it as both "abundant evil," and "horrendous evil." I will refer to it as horrendous evil).]

In ordinary terms, a lay atheist who admits to some evil but draws the line at horrendous evil might rage that God went overboard, that there's simply too much horrendous evil that seems over-the-top over-kill (to use a bad metaphor). Surely, they argue, God could have achieved whatever divine goals God had in mind with creation, with less horrendous evil, since horrendous evil often creates more doubt than faith, more hate than love, more despair than hope. So how can horrendous evil justify any higher good reason?

Part Two provides a brief tour of responses, defenses and theodicies to the problem of evil. Many of them, especially traditional Christian responses, rely on various techniques that, true or not, and scripturally strong or not, do not seem to meet the test for an intellectually satisfying theodicy.

– PART 2 –

ARGUMENTS
FOR GOD

Cursed is the ground because of you; through
painful toil you will eat of it all the days of your life.
It will produce thorns and thistles for you, and you
will eat the plants of the field. By the sweat of your brow you
will eat your food until you return to the ground,
since from it you were taken; and dust you are
and to dust you will return.

God (evicting Adam and Eve from the Garden of Eden and
into the world—to a place east of the Garden of Eden), Ge 3: 17-24

For my thoughts are not your thoughts, neither are
your ways my ways, declares the Lord. As the heavens are higher
than the earth, so my ways are higher than your ways
and my thoughts higher than your thoughts.

God, Isa 55:8-9

When will our eyes be opened, our minds released,
to see love as God's essence and life's perfection? When will we
really know? We will not come to this truth by argument,
by reasoning from true premises to correct conclusions.
We will come to see the truth of love when we are seized by the
act of love. When we are in fact loved by the love made
visible at the cross of Christ, when we accept this love, we will
know that here is this perfect thing which come to us.

Lewis Smedes, *Love Within Limits*

THERE ARE MANY traditional Christian responses to the problem of evil but insufficient consensus that any of them meet the criteria for a good theodicy.

But first, let's define what a "good theodicy" is, and, second, let's address the elephant in the room: Doesn't the Bible answer the question from evil?

What is a good theodicy? First, of course, a theodicy must provide an answer to the problem of evil. That is, it must provide an argument that justifies God's reality and essence as omnipotent and wholly good despite evil within the world.

For this book, I am answering the *evidential form of the problem of evil*. Specifically, I aim at what Martin charged in Set E, E6: "Despite repeated attempts, no one has provided a *good reason* to believe that God has a sufficient reason to allow horrendous evil to exist or that such evil is logically necessary—that is, no one has been able to provide an acceptable explanation for the horrendous evil we experience." To that challenge, I add Rowe's charge in Set C, C1: "There exists instances of intense suffering which an omnipotent being could have prevented without thereby losing some greater good or permitting some evil equally bad or worse."

Combined, the challenge is to defend God against the charge that horrendous evils occur in the world that are unnecessary because God could have prevented them "without losing some greater good or permitting some evil equally bad or worse."

A good theodicy must do more than just provide an argument for God. It must also meet certain criteria to render it intellectually and Scripturally satisfying.

While there are various lists of criteria for a good theodicy, I like English-American philosopher and theologian John Hick's (1922-2012) criteria—T1, T2, and T3—because it reflects criteria found in other tests. I add a fourth, T4, with those of Hick's:

T1: *Logical Coherence*: Does the theodicy make sense logically. That is, is it internally consistent (or valid)?

T2: *Scriptural Coherence*: Is the theodicy consistent with and supported by the religious tradition upon which it is based? Here, that would be Christian Scripture. (Note: some would insert here *moral coherence* requiring the theodicy must rest upon accepted moral principles. Scripture is my source of moral authority unlike secular morality which seems relative and transitory.)

T3: *Scientific Coherence*: Is the theodicy consistent with and reflective of the world as reflected by scientific inquiry into the "specific facts of moral and natural evil?"

T4: *Common Sense Coherence*: Is the theodicy consistent with one's sense of reality?

[Note: I add this one because modern analytical philosophy often refers to "other possible worlds" with various *possible* states of affairs that can't be verified or falsified, and, thus, are "possible." Often these theoretical possible worlds and scenarios simply defy our common sense understanding of this world. I think it's important for a theodicy to make sense and leaves one's "sense of reality intact."]

Another factor I find worthy of mention, but not necessarily a criteria, is *humility*. A theodicy should recognize its limits. We are dealing with transcendent possibilities, with supernatural or metaphysical phenomena that are beyond the reach of scientific validation or falsification. We cannot prove God exists. We cannot prove God's goal/s for creation or God's sufficient reason for evil in creation. Conversely, no one can disprove these matters.

The most a philosophical argument defending God can show, it seems, is that God's existence and essence as omnipotent and wholly good is probable (or likely to be the case, or plausible/reasonable). Conversely, despite the rigid, absolutist claims of some atheists, including some of our most learned scientists, the most atheism can do is to argue that God probably doesn't exist.

Secondly, there's the obvious issue: *Doesn't Scripture resolve this problem of evil? Doesn't it explain why the fawn burned to death in the forest, or Sues murder?*

The short answer is that it does, but not easily, since Scripture appears ambiguous (perhaps purposely?) on the subject of evil.

The Apostle Paul (AD 5-AD 67), for example, exposed a major

contradiction when he taught us that God is omnipotent, possessing an unfettered will (suggesting divine predestination whereby God can but doesn't abolish evil) and yet desires us to repent and turn to Him in loving faith (suggesting creaturely freedom whereby God chose to allow the possibility of evil).

As another example of Scriptural ambiguity, there are three different passages suggesting three different theories for the source and cause of evil: (a) "I bring prosperity and create disaster; I, the Lord, do all these things." (Isaiah 45:7 NIV); (b) "Where then did the weeds come from?" Jesus answered, "An enemy did this." (Matthew 13:28 NIV); (c) "Or those eighteen who died when the tower in Siloam fell on them—do you think they were more guilty than all the others living in Jerusalem? I tell you, no!" (Luke 13:4,5 NIV)

Isaiah suggests a predetermining, omnipotent God controls evil. Matthew suggests enemies—probably rebellious, free creatures, earthly and heavenly—cause evil. And Luke suggests no one causes evil; it's just woven into the ambiguous, indifferent architecture of nature.

Most theodicies cling to one of these passages to the exclusion of others, as it appears no theodicy embraces all three possibilities.

Of course, there is the plight of Job, an enigmatic perspective on evil (suggesting only God knows why evil exists) that will be more fully discussed later in Part Two.

Another Scriptural glimpse into a solution can be found in St. John's Gospel: "As he went along, he saw a man blind from birth. His disciples asked him 'Rabbi, who sinned, this man or his parents, that he was born blind?'" Jesus replied: "Neither this man nor his parents sinned...but this happened so that the work of God might be displayed in his life." (Jn. 9: 1-3)

Jesus then healed the blind man. The story not only showcases Jesus's power, but reveals that all evil (here blindness) presents an opportunity for charitable love in helping relieve the suffering to the afflicted. In this one sense alone—where evil presents opportunity for morally good action which glorify God—God turns all evil to good.

This particular passage from John and the rational inference drawn from it is part of an existing theodicy that argues evil presents opportunity to show our love for God by engaging in morally good action toward victims of evil. I argue that through the argument of this theodicy and others, Scripture's apparent ambiguity on the question of evil can be rationally understood.

2.1 Traditional Christian Responses

Following is a brief analysis of four traditional Christian responses to evil, viewed in the light of the above criteria for a good theodicy.

2.1.1 Totally Depraved Humans Are to Blame

A classic understanding of God's reason for evil flows from the story of *the Fall* in Genesis (Ge: 3). Traditionally, this passage has been interpreted as evidence humans are to blame for evil. Everything was perfect in paradise until Adam and Eve disobeyed God's command. That act of disobedience angered God. God evicted Adam and Eve from the Garden, from paradise where they were united with God. God evicted them into a harsh place, "east of Eden" where they would suffer.

One classic interpretation of this story is that it proves humans are *totally depraved*, sinful beings who deserve the wrath of God and the punishment meted out. In which case, when we ask: How did evil come into the world? the answer is: We brought it in because we are bad to the bone. This understanding assumes that God, being morally perfect, had no part in humanity's original sin, and, thus, bears no responsibility for evil.

This may be a metaphysically true literal account of how evil came into the world, but that's not the point of this book. The point is— whether literally true or merely allegorical—the story and it's classical interpretation does not solve the problem of evil in terms of being a good theodicy.

Reduced to its basic premises, the Adam and Eve argument that humans are to blame for evil because they are totally depraved, goes as follows:

A&E1: God being omnipotent could have created Adam and Eve to not be totally depraved.

A&E2: God, being wholly good, would have wanted to create Adam and Eve to not be totally depraved.

A&E3: Adam and Eve are totally depraved.

This creates an inconsistent set and logically infers that God does not exist, at least an omnipotent and/or wholly good God.

One way to possibly rescue the set is to add another premise:

A&E4: God had a good reason to create humans who were totally depraved.

With the argument that evil is the blame of totally depraved humans, I am aware of one possible good reason (argued by predestination theologists who believe God knows and controls the future even to the extent of knowing who will be saved or not saved, even before they are born). God's good reason is that having totally depraved humans allows God to showcase His grace, glory and mercy by granting salvation to certain preselected totally depraved humans who do not deserve God's redeeming love.

Anything is possible, but this reason doesn't seem probable because it's nonsensical. Specifically, to whom is God showcasing His grace, mercy and glory given that the game is rigged (so to speak)? It seems to no one since God has predetermined the outcomes and humans, like puppets on a string, are merely playing out parts already scripted by the Almighty. Therefore, it violates my common sense (T4).

Without a rationally plausible good reason, the innately depraved argument also violates T1 (logical coherence) in that it is internally inconsistent.

Also, a literal understanding of The Fall violates T3 (Scientific Coherence) in two respects: there is no historical evidence of Adam and Eve and the Fall as literally reported in Scripture; and it violates the widely accepted theory of evolution in its claim that humans didn't evolve but were suddenly thrust into the world from Paradise.

As this argument treats the Fall literally and not allegorically, it fails to meet almost all the criteria of a good theodicy, except T2 (Scriptural

Coherence). Once again, a literal interpretation of The Fall may be metaphysically true. However, in terms of our scientifically generally accepted facts, and in terms of our logic and common sense, we can rationally conclude that it's not a good theodicy.

[Note: not all of Christianity sees the Fall literally or as a tragic fall downward into sin as did theologian and philosopher St. Augustine (354-430) and, thus, how most of Western Christendom traditionally came to see it. St. Irenaeus, Greek bishop of Lyons (130-200), a foundational pier of Eastern Christianity, did not see the Fall as a tragic fall downward but, rather, as a hopeful fall upwards.

Irenaeus understood the Fall allegorically, signifying God intentionally placing humanity distant from paradise as an opportunity for human growth and maturity unto Christ through a struggle with free choice. Irenaeus saw the Fall much as he would see a mother bird kicking her beloved young out of the nest to end dependency and promote personal growth.]

There are various ways to understand the Fall. The story/parable is ambiguous and in that ambiguity two different streams of theodicy flowed in early Christian thought. As will be shown, understanding The Fall allegorically, as a powerful message revealing God's reason for permitting evil in the world, can satisfy T1, T2, T3 and T4. The Fall can be woven into a good theodicy.

2.1.2 Totally Depraved Nonhumans Are to Blame

Another popular approach is to *blame nonhuman entities*, specifically Satan and other fallen angels who rebelled against God. This is a quick and popular default position for defenders of God when horrendous moral and/or natural evil occurs. It's popularity rests not only upon Scripture's obvious reference to the battle between good and evil, but also exculpates God from any responsibility for evil in the world, especially natural and horrendous evil.

American theologian Gregory Boyd's theodicy *Satan and The Problem of Evil: Constructing a Trinitarian Warfare Theodicy (2001)*, is an example of this approach. Boyd focuses on love as God's good reason for evil, arguing that God is love, and, out of love and for love,

God imbues humans with a libertarian free will. God does so upon Boyd's premise that "love must be freely chosen." (p. 23)

It is a convincing argument given that God is love, a reason that resonates with most of our life experiences as to what is great and beautiful about life. But Boyd's argument seems less compelling for how it justifies horrendous natural evils such as the 2004 Asian tsunami that killed over 250,000 people or horrendous moral evil such as the Holocaust where around 6 million Jews were victims of a genocidal massacre.

For horrendous moral and natural evils Boyd looked to Satan and fallen angels for the answer, arguing they also possess libertarian free will and, thus, have supernatural powers to wreak havoc on earth. "I will argue that there is a class of evils in the world that cannot be explained adequately except by appealing to Satan....While appealing to Satan is not itself sufficient to explain 'natural' evil, I shall argue that no explanation that ignores his activity is adequate." (p. 17, 18)

This is both a current and historical standard response from the pulpit to assuage the congregation that God does not cause, or is in any way to blame for, horrendous acts of evil. It also finds favor among many theodicists to fill explanatory holes in their theodicy. But, true or not, is it a good theodicy?

Let's reduce the Nonhuman argument to its basic parts:

NH1: God being omnipotent could create nonhuman creatures that do not rebel against God's plan for creation, thereby causing evil.

NH2: God being wholly good would want to create nonhuman creatures that do not rebel against God's plan for creation, thereby causing evil.

NH3: Nonhuman creatures exist and rebel against God's plan for creation, causing evil.

Once again, this creates an inconsistent set and infers that God either does not exist or is either not omnipotent or wholly good.

Once again, one way to possibly make the set consistent and overcome the inferences against God is to add another premise:

NH4: God had a good reason to create nonhuman creatures that would rebel against God's plan, thereby causing evil.

What is that good reason? One possible reason for creating not just humans but also heavenly nonhumans is to help God administer creation. If so, one must ask: What sufficient good reason (or GR) arises from creating fallen angels that can visit great pain and suffering on humans? If God is omnipotent, God, logically, doesn't need intermediaries to help manage creation. Why are non-human creatures necessary for God to achieve the divine plan for creation? Also, assuming God needed help in the form of additional eyes and ears watching over creation, why would God create them with a rebellious nature that would be used to despoil God's plan for creation?

God, being omnipotent, is also omnipresent. That is, God can be everywhere and at all times. God, being the creator of the physical world and its laws of physics, is not bound by such a physical world or its natural laws. We cannot be everywhere and at all times because we are humans bound by natural properties and processes. When we anthropomorphize God and think of God as human, it is natural to assume—given the vastness of the universe and complexity of all phenomena—God needed and needs help. However, being God and being omnipresent, God can be with each of us and at every second. We are not so tiny and insignificant within the cosmos that God could not possibly care for us, or that angels are necessary to help out with this task.

One can argue it's possible that nonhumans like Satan exist, for whatever GR, and that God gave them a free will that makes them capable of rebellious actions that create evil within creation—because anything's possible—but is it probable? Does this reason pass the smell test of T4 (common sense coherence)? It doesn't mine.

Another reason blaming Satan and nonhumans seems to be a poor theodicy is that it doesn't satisfy criteria T3 (Scientific Coherence). There is no scientific evidence of nonhumans like Satan but, of course, that doesn't mean they don't possibly exist as supernatural phenomena beyond our observational reach. However, it appears science has traced almost all natural evil to natural causes and properties. And, as concerns moral evil, abundant evidence exists to trace most all of it to human frailty: mental illness, jealousy and rage, addiction, excessive pride in self or one's tribe, anger at and covetousness of others, etc.

Given this stare of affairs, do we really need Satan to explain natural and moral evil? German-American philosopher and theologian Paul Tillich (1886-1965) says no, arguing that our destructive experience of evil in the world is not "caused by some external force. It is not the work of special divine or demonic interferences, but it is the consequence of the structure of estrangement itself," (1971, Vol II, pg. 59-60). And the "structure of estrangement itself" is sin, which Tillich understands as being estranged from God. Our state of sin is both innate (God having removed us from paradise) and any and all actions (such as human pride) that serves to advance separation from God.

It seems more probable than not that almost all the evil we complain of, even horrendous evils such as the Holocaust or the 2004 Asian earthquake/tsunami event, can be understood by natural properties and causes and/or by human frailty in committing morally wrong actions/inactions.

Finally, blaming evil on fallen angels doesn't solve the problem of evil. If the original problem is: How can a perfectly powerful and good God allow evil? Then blaming Satan merely rephrases the problem as: How can a perfectly powerful and good God allow Satan?

2.1.3 Christianity is About Spiritual Revelation and Not Human Logic

A third traditional response is to argue that the Christian experience is *primarily a spiritual encounter* that has *little to do with human logic or reason*, that it's more about love than logic, more relational than informational. American Christian writer and theologian Lewis Smedes (1921-2002) expressed this sentiment powerfully in his book *Love Within Limits (1980)*:

> When will our eyes be opened, our minds released to see love as God's essence and life's perfection? When will we really know? We will not come to this truth by argument, by reasoning from true premises to correct conclusions. We will come to see the truth of love when we are seized by the act of love. When we are in fact loved by the love made visible at the cross of Christ, when we accept this

love, we will know that here is the perfect thing which has come to us. (pp. 124, 125)

This compelling line of thought brings to mind a cartoon, drawn by cartoonist and writer Jules Feiffer, I enjoyed many years ago. In a panel of drawings, Feiffer shows a young man sitting at a bar, alone, thinking about his girlfriend. He progressively says words to the effect: she's beautiful; she's smart; she's popular; she's wealthy, well dressed and poised; my friends and family like her; we enjoy the same things. Then he pauses, ponders and concludes "I guess I love her."

Feiffer's satirical logic illustrates that there is no algorithm for love, supporting Smedes' point that love is not the result of "reasoning from true premises to correct conclusions".

As far as Smedes goes, I agree wholeheartedly. The desired end point of one's Christian walk is to come to God in faith, which is a courageous act of love. From Christ's selfless, sacrificial love displayed on the cross for us, to the greatest commandment, and from the parable of the Good Samaritan to Revelation telling us that the endgames result in God getting his "bride" (Rev. 19:7, 21:2; 21:9; 22:17), it seems clear that love is central to the Gospels.

Perhaps Smedes was firing a missile at Blaise Pascal's argument which argues for coming to God not from love but rather from a cold blooded statistical analysis driven by selfish desires.

Pascal's Wager (1958), for those who are not familiar with it, is this argument by French scientist and philosopher, Blaise Pacal (1623-1662): "Let us weigh the gain and the loss in wagering that God is. Let us estimate these two chances. If you gain, you gain all; if you lose, you lose nothing. Wager, then, without hesitation that He is."

Smedes seems to be making it clear that God's goal with creation is not to forge relationships with a selfish, play-it-smart person merely wisely leveraging their post-death possibilities to their advantage.

Fine. But that doesn't mean that human reason and logic do not play a critical role in arriving at this moment of faithful love. I argue it does. Can a rock, for instance, come to know, appreciate and love God? No. For that, we need a sentient creature who can think and reason, that is: comprehend things, engage in communication, acquire and grow in knowledge, be able to make discriminating decisions.

What does Smedes's message mean to a stone or bucket of water? Can a stone or a bucket of water receive, know, understand and appreciate a bolt of revelation from God, like Paul did on the road to Damascus? If not, what else did Paul need to respond to God and commit his life to the Gospels. Smedes doesn't say, but, obviously, the path to epiphany goes through reason and logic. Paul had to have the sense to realize he was talking to God, to understand language, to comprehend the miracle that was happening to him, and have the rational power to understand his new task and what that entailed.

As a theodicy, the thought that logic has nothing to do with the end goal of Christianity is inadequate because, by it's own terms, it indicates logic and reason have nothing to do with God's plan for us. Plus, it provides no reason for God allowing evil, so it's not an adequate solution to the problem of evil.

The Christian walk toward the Christian maturity of embracing the selfless love displayed by Christ on the cross necessarily involves not only positive or good experiences of life but also negative or evil experiences of life. I argue we can use our reason and logic to understand why this is so, as these ambiguous experiences can (but not necessarily do) lead us to know, appreciate and love God.

We can logically understand God's design of life, even though the final leap is one of faith—of courageous love—and not pure logic. Even the fact that the final leap is a leap of courageous faith and not one of rock solid certainty can also be understood logically.

2.1.4 God's Reasons Are Inscrutable, Beyond Our Ken, Ineffable

There are various lines of thought, all closely related, and called by various names—*inscrutable divine mystery, ineffable, beyond our ken*—that provide a Christian with some comfort, some perspective, in the face of not knowing the *whys?* of God's ways, especially allowing evil in creation. A person could also call this the Job Lesson.

One classic response, usually attributed to French philosopher

Pierre Bayle (1647-1706), is the argument that Christianity is a matter of faith and can not be understood or penetrated by the power of human reason. It is beyond our ken.

American theologian Reinhold Niebuhr (1892-1971) reflected Bayle's view when he argued (1996) that:

> Though the religious faith through which God is apprehended cannot be in contradiction to reason in the sense that the ultimate principle of meaning cannot be in contradiction to the subordinate principle of meaning which is found in rational coherence yet, on the other hand religious faith cannot be simply subordinated to reason or made to stand under its judgment. When this is done the reason which asks the question whether the God of religious faith is plausible has already implied a negative answer in the question because it has made itself God and naturally cannot tolerate another. (vol. 1, pg. 165, 166)

To me, Niebuhr seems to be saying that trying to fully explain the world through human reason is the deification of reason, and the folly of that attempt should be quickly apparent given all the paradoxes and contradictions of reality. Perfect reason lies within transcendence, with God. So we should be humble in our reach, as pride, to Niebuhr, was humanity's greatest sin, and we should accept that God's perfect reason is beyond our ken.

Niebuhr goes on to argue that this insight is the key to the paradox of Job's suffering. God tenders Job to Satan's evil will and ways, saying "Have you considered my servant Job? There is no one on earth like him: he is blameless and upright, a man who fears God and shuns evil." (Job 1:8 NIV) Job proceeds to suffer horrendous evils—horrendous because they seem gratuitous and greatly excessive.

Job, using human notions of fairness that prevailed at the time, eventually complains of the injustice visited upon him by God. Job is baffled. God responds sternly "Who is this that darkens my counsel with words without knowledge?...Where were you when I laid the earth's foundations?" (Job 38: 2, 4 NIV)

God then proceeds to describe God's perspective as Creator, listing God's many wonders, making Job realize the limits of Job's ability to comprehend God's reasons. Job, chastened, humbly replies "Surely I spoke of things I did not understand, things too wonderful for me to know." (Job 42:3 NIV)

Niebuhr (1996) continues his argument: "God's will and wisdom must be able to transcend any human interpretation of its justice and meaning, or it would be less than the centre of that inclusive meaning which alone can comprehend the seeming chaos of existence into a total harmony. This surely is the significance of the message of Job." (vol. 1, pg. 168)

This "beyond our ken" thinking of Bayle and Niehbuhr mirrors a philosophical response to Rowe's evidential argument from evil known as skeptical theism which will be discussed below in the next section: Responses and Defenses.

Closely related is the belief that God is *ineffable*—too wondrous for words.

How can we know, describe or discuss that which is too wondrous for words?

Finally, many simply argue that evil is an *inscrutable divine mystery* and we should not attempt to explain God's reasons for evil in creation.

Stated as an argument for God, it would go like this (let's call it the Job set):

Job1: God being omnipotent could have created a world without evil.

Job2: God being wholly good would have wanted to create a world without evil.

Job3: There is evil in the world.

Job4: We cannot know God's good reason for allowing evil in the world, although we believe God had a good reason since God could have and wanted to prevent evil in the world.

As an answer to the problem of evil, the lesson of Job says there is no answer knowable by humans. Since the goal of theodicy is to provide some answer, this argument, though possibly true, admits to defeat.

All of the above traditional Christian responses, then and now, might be metaphysically true. I especially appreciate the notion (Smedes) that Christianity is primarily about being seized spiritually by Christ's love displayed upon the cross. And I acknowledge the cognitive limits of humans (Job) as to God's ways.

These concepts of human cognitive limits suggest that love is and must be an act of faith and not factual certainty, that God is necessarily distant from us so as to create doubt, thus allowing room for love to be an act of courageous faith. In this sense, we can begin to understand that love must be freely chosen in doubt and anxiety, challenged by the myriad, ambiguous choices available within a radically free world.

As will be shown, these classic Christian insights help fuel the best of our theodicies today and lead to various keys to unlocking the mystery of evil.

Next, I review philosophical arguments—both responses, defenses, and existing theodicies—to illustrate the challenge remaining for theodicy.

2.2 Responses and Defenses

2.2.1 Skeptical Theist Response to Rowe—Wykstra

American philosopher Stephen Wykstra's theory, Conditions of ReasoNable Epistemic Access (CORNEA) (1984), is a response to Rowe's argument, above, in D1 (no good state of affairs justifies God in allowing the pain and suffering of Sue and Bambi). Wykstra argues that just because we don't know of any good or sufficient reason for God allowing Bambi and Sue to happen, doesn't mean God doesn't have a sufficient reason.

From the premise of D1—that we don't know of any sufficient reason for God allowing Sue and Bambi—Rowe concludes in D2 that it's unlikely God had a morally good reason for the horrendous pain and suffering of Sue and Bambi.

Wykstra argues that Rowe assumes we can know or be cognizant of God's sufficient or good reasons that would justify the horrendous pain and suffering of Sue and Bambi. But Wykstra says that assumption is unreasonable: "if we think carefully about the sort of being theism proposes for our belief, it is entirely expectable—given what we know of our cognitive limits—that the goods by virtue of which this Being allows known suffering should very often be beyond our ken." (p. 91)

Wykstra supports this position by posing an analogy between parent and child and God and human. Does a one-month old baby understand, for example, why a parent makes it go to bed, or quit crying, or feeds it when it doesn't feel like eating? And if a baby can't understand why a parent does this, does it naturally follow that a parent doesn't have a good/sufficient reason for doing these things?

Other skeptical theists have provided other analogies. For example, just because a lay person can't understand a scientist's theory of quantum mechanics, doesn't mean the author of the theory doesn't have good reason for the theory.

The skeptical theist response to Rowe is very much like the Christian argument that God's allowance of evil is an inscrutable divine mystery (or beyond our ken) but is stated as a philosophical argument. Like those arguments, this argument doesn't offer a good theodicy because it admits to not knowing God's good reason for allowing evil.

Here's a simple story I tell to more easily illustrate this entire line of thinking from all of the above—Wykstra, Niebuhr, Bayle, Job. I call it the Tanglewood analogy.

It was 1975. I was eating lunch with my good friend Tibor Csizmadia, an architect who fled from Hungary in 1956 when the USSR invaded.

I was talking about my angst caused by not fully understanding God, the concept of Heaven, and of eternity. I could not imagine it under any scenario of understanding. So I asked Tibor about it, since he was always so calm, at peace, gentle and kind. It was Tibor, I thought, who should suffer angst, him being so far from home, having not seen his family for almost 20 years. What was his secret?

Tibor smiled, looked down at the ground, at ants scurrying across the sidewalk with bits of food. And Tibor said: "You lived in Massachusetts. Did you ever go to Tanglewood in the Spring to hear the Boston Pops symphony?"

"Yes," I replied. "It was beautiful."

"Do you think those ants down there have any conception of Tanglewood? Do you think they can easily ever comprehend Tanglewood?"

"No" I replied.

"You are that ant, and your Tanglewood is eternal Heaven. Just because you can't comprehend it, doesn't mean it doesn't exist."

Touché. From that moment on, although I have never stopped trying to comprehend God, I always remember what I am reaching for and the cognitive limits associated with it. As Niebuhr and others argue, it is the height of pride and arrogance to think that the limits of my cognitive ability limit God. They only limit me.

2.2.2 Plantinga's Free Will Defense

In *God, Freedom and Evil (1977)*, Plantinga argued that Set A, as formulated by Epicurus, can be seen as a consistent set.

Plantinga's solution is known as the "free will defense." The defense rests upon the assumption that God granted humans a libertarian free will, with libertarian free will meaning an ability to act or choose not to act independent of any external deterministic force, including God's will.

[Note: This idea that humans have a libertarian free will is contested and controversial both in scientific circles (because of the theory of causation or causality) and in many religious circles (because the idea of God's omnipotence/omniscience necessarily precludes human libertarian free will). The controversy will be discussed in Part Three C1.]

Plantinga further argues that if humans possess a libertarian free will, then God *cannot prevent some moral evil* in all the possible worlds he creates because if God could prevent all moral evil, then we would not possess a libertarian free will. Therefore, it is "possible" some moral evil might exist in a world created by an omnipotent, wholly good God.

For a justification, he argues that giving humans a libertarian free will possibly creates a divine good, which justifies evil in the world. That is, if humans truly have free choices between good and evil options, then humans have moral power and are morally consequential. He claims "A world containing creatures who are significantly free (and freely perform more good than evil actions) is more valuable, all else being equal, than a world containing no free creatures at all." (Plantinga, p. 30)

Plantinga approvingly repeats the observation of St. Augustine of Hippo that (1977):

> Such is the generosity of God's goodness that He has not refrained from creating even that creature which He foreknew would not only sin, but remain in the will to sin. As a runaway horse is better than a stone which does not run away because it lacks self-movement and sense perception, so the creature is more excellent which sins by free will than that which does not sin only because it has no free will. (p. 27)

Plantinga argues that Epicurus's statements A1 (God is omnipotent) and A2 (God is wholly good) do not necessarily infer A4 (that God, although omnipotent could prevent evil in the world). It is possible, given Plantinga's argument, that an omnipotent, wholly good God allows evil in the world because of the over-riding good reason of populating the Earth with significantly free creatures.

His argument has been conceded by many if not most philosophers as proving it is logically "possible" that God, despite being omnipotent and wholly good, designed a world that created some evil. Thus, given this *possibility*, the three statements A1 (God is omnipotent), A2 (God is wholly good) and A3 (evil exists) are not inconsistent if you add another statement: God, despite being omnipotent and wholly good, could not prevent evil in the world because of granting humans a libertarian free will.

Not every philosopher agrees with Plantinga's argument. Australian philosopher J. L. Mackie (1917-1981), for example, argues that if God is truly omnipotent, then God could have created a world with libertarian free will that contained only moral good and no moral evil (Peterson, 2011).

[Note: Plantinga's and Mackie's dueling arguments turn on precise terms and definitions. One *definition* they both share is that God's omnipotence does not mean, as some people believe, the power to do all things, even illogical things. Most philosophers, such as Plantinga and Mackie, argue that even an omnipotent God cannot bring about nonlogical, impossible states of affairs. God cannot, for example, create square circles or married bachelors. God cannot exist and not exist. Nonlogical states of affairs are incoherent. Our great gifts of reason, math and logic seem consistent with the notion that God is rational, and as we advance in our reason we more understand God's reason.]

Another criticism is that Plantinga's defense is not a theodicy, but only a defense. A defense need only meet the burden of proof that its conclusion is *possible* whereas the burden of proof for a theodicy's conclusion is that it is *probable*. A defense is not as robust a justification of God as many theologians would like. By Plantinga's own admission, his defense is not a theodicy.

Further, Plantinga's defense doesn't claim as true that God's motive for evil is free will—or even that we have free will—but only says it's *possible*. Many theologians don't like God sliding in by a mere whisker of "possible" or in merely assuming what God's motive and methods are versus a more positive affirmation.

Plantinga thinks a whisker is sufficient and that it's acceptable to not claim to know Gods reasons or methods (1977): "No doubt the theist would rather know what God's reason is for permitting evil than simply that it's possible the He had a good one. But in the present context (of investigating the consistency of [Epicurus's] Set A), the latter [a free will defense instead of a theodicy] is all that's needed." (p. 28)

Another criticism is that the free will defense at best provides a rationale for moral evil but not as robust one for natural evil (although many have argued that human free will, and/or the free will of non human creatures (e.g., Satan), cause natural evil, like earthquakes). Also, to some it doesn't satisfyingly explain horrendous evils and the evidential problem of evil.

Finally, not everyone agrees the divine good of free will can ever be outweighed by horrendous evil. I am mindful of Ivan's angry reaction to a young child's brutal death in Russian novelist Fyodor Dostoevsky's (1821-1881) novel *The Brother's Karamazov*:

> Listen: if everyone must suffer, in order to buy eternal harmony with their suffering, pray tell me what have children got to do with it? It's quite incomprehensible why they should have to suffer, and why they should buy harmony with their suffering....And if the suffering of children goes to make up the sum of suffering needed to buy truth, then I assert beforehand that the whole of truth is not worth such a price....they have put too high a price on harmony; we can't afford to pay so much for admission. And therefore I hasten to return my ticket....It's not that I don't accept God, Alyosha, I just most respectfully return him the ticket. (p.244, 245)

Ivan doesn't believe the type of evil he has seen in his life—a general having a young boy torn to pieces by his dogs for the crime of throwing rocks at them, or Turkish soldiers bayoneting pregnant Armenian women, ripping their babies from their womb then tossing the babies into the air and catching them on the bayonets—justifies any divine good reason he can imagine.

This weighing of divine goods versus the costs of evil is particularly relevant to the evidential problem of evil. The evidential form of the problem of evil concerns itself not with evil, per se, but rather horrendous evil. It balances God's good reasons for evil versus the sometimes unbelievably high cost of horrendous evil, concluding that it is *improbable* a perfectly powerful and loving God exists.

Plantinga's free will defense does not address the evidential form of the problem. Rather, he claims that it's enough to show that it's *possible* an omnipotent, wholly good God is logically consistent with evil in the world.

Most theologians disagree and argue there's still a need for theodicy to provide a more robust defense of God that both affirmatively states God's reasons for evil and, further, shows it is *probable* an omnipotent, wholly good God exists despite horrendous evil in the world.

The evidential form of the problem of evil seems to be the most problematic today for theodicy.

2.2.3 G.E. Moore Shift

A simple logical rejoinder to Rowe is to take his conclusion that there is no omnipotent and wholly good God and reverse it and make it a premise: to wit: that there is an omnipotent and wholly good God.

Philosophically known as the "G. E. Moore Shift," and named after English philosopher George Edward Moore (1873-1958), the argument goes that:

1. There exists an omnipotent, omniscient, wholly good being;
2. An omniscient, wholly good being would prevent the occurrence of any intense suffering if it could, unless it could not do so without thereby losing some greater good or permitting some evil equally bad or worse.
3. (Therefore) It is not the case that there exists instances of horrendous evil which an omnipotent, omniscient being could have prevented without thereby losing some greater good or permitting some evil equally bad or worse.

The G. E. Moore shift turns Rowe's argument on it head. It doesn't solve Rowe, but merely changes Rowe's conclusion to its opening premise. Rowe starts, as a premise, with the observation there is horrendous evil that a perfectly powerful and good God would and could prevent, and winds up concluding there is no such perfectly powerful and good God. Moore simply starts with a premise Christians should agree with: an omnipotent, omniscient, wholly good God exists. That being the case, the logical conclusion is that there can be no horrendous evil in the world that is unnecessary given that God is omnipotent, omniscient and wholly good.

Which is more convincing? That depends upon your reason and experience as to whether it's more probable or not that such a God exists (Moore's premise), or whether it's more probable or not unnecessary evil exists (Rowe's premise).

In this increasingly secular, scientific and post-Christian world, it would seem that Rowe has more adherents. Today, it seems unassailable to assume the Holocaust, for instance, was an experience of unnecessarily horrendous suffering. That is to say, it was an unimaginable experience of horrific pain and suffering, unfairness, disproportionate, excessive evil for which God's good reason could surely have been achieved equally well with less evil without thereby failing to achieve God's good reason.

For example, wouldn't simply the imprisonment of six million Jews have been sufficient? Did they have to die? And couldn't the young children and women been spared from the gas chambers? It seems the Holocaust experience created more doubt than faith, more hate than love, more despair than hope. Surely, whatever good reason God had for allowing the Holocaust did not advance any obvious goals such as love, faith, and hope? (So the atheodicy argument goes.)

The Jewish experience of the Holocaust caused a sea change in how Jews viewed God. "God died at Auschwitz," declared Holocaust survivor Ellie Wiesel. By that, he might have meant the idea of a personal, caring God that intervened in reality died at Auschwitz and was replaced by the older Jewish concept of a distant, aloof, uncaring God.

Epic, especially heinous, examples of evil, like the Holocaust, make Rowe's argument convincing (at least in terms of our limited cognitive ability to comprehend God's ways). Rowe remains the high hill to climb.

The challenge confronting Moore is to address these especially horrendous and seemingly pointless evils. The challenge seems to be, as stated by English novelist Thomas Hardy (1840-1928) in his poem *In Tenebris II*: "...if way to the Better there be, it exacts a full look at the Worst." Theodicy must account for the Holocaust, epic natural tragedies and seemingly gratuitous evils, large and small. It must *extract a full look at the worst.*

2.3 Existing Theodicies

There are many theodicies, probably too many to expect anyone to read all of them, and definitely too many for me to discuss in any detail. So I turn to a simple categorization based on key features which should help to understand different theodicies.

For those wanting a deeper discussion of various theodicies, there are excellent books as well as excellent discussions online. I'd recommend the following books as both comprehensive and approachable for the lay person.

- Peterson, M. (1992.) *The Problem of Evil*. Notre Dame, University of Notre Dame Press;
- Hasker, W. (2008). *The Triumph of God Over Evil*. Downers Grove, InterVarsity Press;
- Neiman, S. (2002). *Evil in Modern Thought*. Princeton, Princeton University Press;
- Meister, C. and Dew, J. (2013). *God and Evil*. Downers Grove, InterVarsity Press.
- Boyd, G. (2001). *Satan and the Problem of Evil*. Downers Grove, InterVarsity Press.

In this review, I'll discuss a dominant variable dividing and defining most theodicies: the tension between God's sovereign will and humanity's will. Which will controls? Are they necessarily incompatible in that one must yield to the other? If so, which one? Or, can the two wills be seen as compatible?

2.3.1 Incompatibilism: God's Determinism

At one end of the spectrum lies theodicies that favor God's determinism, as in predestination thinking. It is referred to as incompatibilism in that God's will is incompatible with the notion of human free will. One must yield, and it's human will that must yield to God's will under predestination thought.

These theodicies include Calvinistic thought and some Catholic circles such as Thomism. Leaning on God's omnipotence, and traceable to Augustine, the argument goes that God controls all of creation.

Augustine, whose thoughts formed the foundational piers for the Western Christian church, suggested predestination when he argues in *The City of God* that all wills are subject to God's will. Fear not, the argument seems to be, all actions eventually work to God's will and plan for creation. Everything has a purpose for the greater good.

Determinism/predestination theology has two major strengths. It is the logical extension of what one interpretation of "omnipotence" means. That is, if God is truly omnipotent then God must exhaustively control and foreknow all future outcomes. Secondly, predestination thought provides immeasurable peace and comfort to those worried about the future being open, free, contingent and unknown.

Many people prefer to have the future fixed and certain, in God's sure hands, even given the negative implications associated with that notion—the main negative being that humans have no power over the future, even their future actions. The concept of an open, contingent and unknown future creates such anxiety in many people that they seem willing to trade freedom for the notion of God's certainty. There seems to be great peace and comfort in thinking God controls the future, as evidence by common cliches such as: What will be will be; We are in God's hands; God will provide and protect us; God has His reasons; God's ways are not our ways; and Everything has a purpose.

However, these reassuring, comforting cliches largely illustrate predestination's disadvantages. If the future is fixed, even to the point of arguing, as hard determinism does, that God has preselected who will be saved—even before they are born and despite what they do in life—then in what sense are we free? How can we be morally conse-quential if God controls our thoughts and actions? How can we freely choose to love or believe? What's the point of faith, prayer, belief, good deeds, spreading the gospel? In fact, given predestination, what's the point of anything for us? And, what is the point of anything for God if creation contains no surprise, no spontaneity, no unexpected joy, no freely chosen love?

The attractiveness of predestination partly comes down to a value judgement. Is the fear of freedom and the responsibility that comes with personal freedom preferable to having the freedom, and risk, to author your own life?

If you think it is, then that urge is understandable. However, it's reasonable to ask: Why did God send Christ to die and suffer for our sins if our sins were predetermined and not the result of personal effort? Whose sins did Christ suffer and atone for if no one is responsible for sin (since we have no freedom and are merely going through the motions of a predetermined life, not unlike a puppet on a string)?

One predestination answer is so that God can showcase His glory and mercy. But, critics ask, To Whom? Who is there to appreciate this showcasing?

In American theologian Bruce Ware's rebuttal to open theism, *God's Lesser Glory* (2000), he argues that:

> If the problem of evil is solved (in Arminian and openness theologies) by appeal to human freedom, such that God is not responsible for the evil done by free creatures over whose actions he had no control, then one may regard this as the "problem of goodness." That is to say, if God should not take the *blame* for the evil done by human freedom, then correspondingly, he should not get the *credit* for the good done equally freely and fully outside of his control. (p. 226)

Ware goes on to argue "The Scriptures make so very clear that our good is found not in our independent ability, our autonomy, or our self-reliance; rather, our good is found in humble, poor-of-spirit dependence on God" then quotes John 15:5: "he who abides in me and I in him, he bears much fruit, for apart from Me you can do nothing." (p.227)

Of course, this doesn't have to be a zero sum game as Ware suggests. Couldn't God gets the glory and credit for designing a world where love and moral behavior is possible, while at the same time receive some responsibility for a design that necessarily will result in evil? And couldn't humans get some credit for choosing to love God, without in any way diminishing God's glory, while, at the same time, receive responsibility when we choose sin?

True, we can do nothing without God in the sense that we are the creation and not the creator, and, true, without God we can never transcend the limits of our physical existence. But that does not necessarily mean that God's selfless love is such that the joy of glory is limited only to God. Can't we see God's essence as charitable love such that God would desire that we, also, experience the joy of glory when we join with God in love?

Another issue or perspective is to understand the nature and essence of God. If, for example, God knows and controls all future outcomes then, as one critic of predestination thinking, American philosopher Dallas Willard (1935-2013) said, such a predetermining God as "an unblinking cosmic stare." (1998, p. 244) Another critic, German theologian Walter Kasper (1986 , p. 306), described such a God as a "solitary narcissistic being, who suffers from his own completeness."

These are harsh, seemingly blasphemous words indeed to use when speaking of God, but if God controls all future events and outcomes, then God foreknew and predetermined these comments by Willard and Kasper. The men who spoke them had no control over their utterances and, thus, are not culpable for their blasphemy, because it wasn't their blasphemy. Rather it was all part of God's divine blueprint. (So goes the predestination line of thinking.)

Another problem is the logical inference that predestination makes God the author of all evil. For example, God—since he designed and absolutely controls all future outcomes—literally caused the Holocaust. If God authored the Holocaust, and every other evil within creation, then how can one argue God is wholly good? With predestination thinking, you can argue for God's power but not so easily for God's love.

It is this last problem of God's culpability for evil, that led John Wesley's (1703-1791) mother to protest predestination theology. In a 1725 letter to her son (a cleric and theologian who later founded the first Methodist church), she wrote: "The doctrine of predestination, as maintained by the rigid Calvinists, is very shocking and ought utterly to be abhorred, because it charges the most holy God with being the author of sin". (Thuesen, 2009, p. 73)

How are we to go forward and live our lives if we really believe in predestination? This question reminds me of a story that's I've labeled the "Rick Gipson Refutation of Predestination."

My senior year in high school football, I was the right end and Rick the right tackle. Rick was a big, strong fierce football player. But on this one Friday night game against arch rival Unity, he played lackadaisical in the first half, clearly not using his best effort.

During halftime, I asked Rick what was wrong with him. He said he'd learned about predestination at church last Sunday. He said he was sorry but there's absolutely nothing he can do about his play. "It's preordained" he explained. "Not only that" he continued, "but tonight I"m going to get drunk and there's not a damned thing I can do about it."

Was Rick right? Is this how predestination works? Do our efforts really mean nothing? Can we pass off all our sins and flaws upon God so easily?

2.3.2 Compatibilsim: Methodism and Molinism

Methodism (including Arminianism from which it evolved) and Molinism are theological constructs that sought relief from Calvin's harsh predestination thinking and its unsavory inferences (e.g, that faith and works, prayer and contrition, aren't relevant to salvation since God has predestined all things). They try to forge a middle view, a compromise, of the tension between God's will and our will.

These theological schools of thought argue God doesn't control us via a predetermining will. However, God foreknows the future exhaustively. Thus, these theodicies are often referred to as compatibilism arguments because they posit that both human and divine wills have room to operate.

Molinism believes God has various ways of knowing. Through God's "Middle Knowledge," God can foresee every possible choice/ reaction a human might make in every possible world in every possible future situation. God uses this Middle Knowledge to control circumstances (that is, to manipulate a particular future circumstance out of infinite potential circumstances) to maximize the possibility that a person will freely choose to do what God wants.

Most defenders of Molinism argue God doesn't engage in this Middle Knowledge to determine outcomes, merely to influence moral behavior through maximizing the possibility of positive moral outcomes.

Methodism stresses that we are free in every sense of the word even though God foreknows, but doesn't control, our future decisions and actions. This foreknowledge is part of God's omnipotence and exists, metaphysically, beyond our rational comprehension. We experience a sensation of freedom of choice in our living. For all practical purposes, we are free despite God's foreknowledge.

The main advantage of compatibilism theology is its promise of balancing the tension between who controls/determines futures outcomes, especially evil outcomes. God is still all-knowing, though not all-controlling, theoretically allowing wiggle room for human free will to exercise power. Compatibilism theology also creates an argument that humans create/cause evil through this exercise of their free will. Thus, God is exculpated from blame, and, thus, Mrs. Wesley is proud of her son for getting God off the hook.

One criticism of compatibilist thinking is that it's illogical. Critics argue that God foreknowing our future decisions/actions, but not controlling them, seems a distinction without a difference. Specifically, if God foreknows our future actions/decisions then in what way can we overcome that foreknowledge? Logically, if I am free as to some future action, then how can God foreknow my action? And if God foreknows my future action, how am I free? Logically, either humans possess a libertarian free will that is incompatible with God's determinism, or they don't possess such a free will.

If God foreknows all outcomes of human behavior then life seems a play scripted before the performance.

2.3.3 Incompatibilism Human Free Will

Open theism or openness theology is also, like predestination thought, an incompatibilist theology in that it argues God's will and human will are incompatible and one must yield. But, unlike predestination theodicies, open theism argues God's will must yield to human will.

Open theism suggests we have a libertarian free will that is not fully determined by factors external to our internal will power—even by God's sovereign will. Although God might foreknow all of our possible decisions/actions, God does not know which decision/action we will take (at least, our decisions that have moral consequences). Thus, under open theism God does not control nor exhaustively foreknow the future of human action. In this sense, God's omnipotence and omniscience's is self-limited.

There are several advantages of such a theodicy. First, openness theology enables love under the assumption that love must be freely chosen. Second, creation means something—both for humanity and God.

Humans possess moral consequentiality by possessing a self-determining libertarian free will. Humans can freely choose this action or that action. They may be responsible for bad actions, but they also are authors of good, moral action. Having this sort of personal power means life for humans is consequential. One might say, we author our own fate.

Further, creation means something for God under open theism. As Tillich (1971) said:

> ...the world process means something for God. He is not a separated self-sufficient entity who, driven by a whim, creates what he wants and saves whom he wants. Rather, the eternal act of creation is driven by a love which finds fulfillment only through the other one who has the freedom to reject or to accept love. (V. 3, p. 422)

Openness theology means that prayer, faith, courage, love and other moral action all matter and have consequences because, being free, humans are responsible for their actions. Openness theology allows a dynamic relationship to flourish between God and the created. The concept of a caring, personal God has been greatly advanced by this line of thinking.

Openness theology, with its emphasis on human freedom, creates an argument that much of what we consider evil lies within human action/inaction. God is largely exculpated from actual acts of evil although God made evil outcomes possible by granting creatures a freely determining will.

Another advantage is that openness theology provides a logical explanation for evil in the world. By God self-limiting part of his power—limiting the power of omnipotence to control everything and the power of omniscience to know everything, including future things—evil becomes possible through freedom's abuse by humans.

Despite these seemingly positive outcomes, there are several criticisms of free will thinking such as open theism. One is that life is rendered open, free, contingent, and uncertain. This may create *great anxiety* for people to realize, for example, that the fate of their sickly child is not in the hands of the Lord. Freedom sounds wonderful as the word rolls off your tongue, but, fully understood, freedom can be terrifying due to the realization of: one's personal responsibility for action; one's capacity for evil and self destruction; one's awareness of the open, contingent (i.e., unknown) future that freedom begets.

As American psychiatrist Irvin Yalom said in his book *Existential Psychotherapy*, (1980) "Both to constitute (to be responsible for) oneself and one's world and to be aware of one's responsibility is a deeply frightening insight...To experience existence in this manner is a dizzying sensation....groundlessness is a commonly used term for a subjective experience for responsibility awareness." (pg. 221)

Another disadvantage is that in stressing freedom openness theology elevates God's love to the apparent exclusion of God's power. If love must be freely chosen, then God, out of love and for love, foregoes some degree of omnipotence (and omniscience which I assume to be part of omnipotence) so as to allow love. However, I argue that God has the power to not do what God has the power to do; God has the power to voluntarily abstain from exercising a power.

Lewis says, this is a miracle—God foregoing a power so as to actualize love and, in the process, risk loss and disappointment (2001).

> ...it is objected that the ultimate loss of a single soul means the defeat of omnipotence. And so it does. In creating beings with free will, omnipotence from the outset submits to the possibility of such defeat. What you call defeat, I call miracle: for to make

things which are not Itself, and thus to become, in a sense, capable of being resisted by its own handiwork, is the most astonishing and unimaginable of the the the feats we attribute to the Deity. (p. 129-130)

Critics think this concept of God foregoing the power of knowing the future renders God a lesser god, one unworthy of praise and worship. They argue open theism robs God of the glory for the good in the world by transferring power over good and evil from God to humans. (As indicated earlier, an excellent example that uses this line of thinking in criticizing open theism can be found in *God's Lesser Glory* by Bruce Ware.)

Once again, the issue involves a value judgement. Which God is a being than which no greater can be conceived?: The God who is an all-knowing, unchangeable, immovable God of unlimited power, or the most moved, personal, caring God of love? If it's the latter, and if love must be freely chosen, then could the God who, out of love and for love, limits some of his power be considered *a being than which no greater can be conceived*? Or is such a self-surrendering God (who surrendered some power, out of love and for love) a lesser god? Well meaning people disagree on this value judgement, but I side with those who favor a God who foregoes some power to enable love.

Another criticism is that while open theism can logically account for much of evil within creation, it is primarily moral evil it seems to best accounts for. It doesn't account as well for natural evil, nor does it easily explain horrendous evil. For horrendous evils (natural as well as moral) open theism seems to blame non-human creatures like Satan. As Boyd said: "I will argue that there is a class of evils in the world that cannot be explained adequately except by appealing to Satan." (p. 17)

* * *

I would hope many if not most people see and appreciate the great good that flows from the structure of creaturely free will. If love must be freely chosen, then creaturely free will potentiates love. I argue it also potentiates courage, faith, and other moral behaviors. It renders creation meaningful, for both God and humanity. It allows for creativity, spontaneity, surprise and joy. As Augustine conceded, a runaway horse is better than a stone because a stone does not have the will to runaway while the horse does possess such a will. We are not stones if we possess a libertarian free will.

I understand the criticism of sufferers of horrendous evil, like the Holocaust. The evil was so horrendous that whatever divine good was advanced by God granting humans a free will seems clearly overridden by the cost in pain and suffering, despair and loss. Horrendous, often seemingly gratuitous evil, is not only a great challenge for open theism, it's a great challenge for any and all faith construals believing in a perfectly powerful and loving God.

Despite shortcomings, many of our strongest theodicies embrace this notion of creaturely freedom to explain evil. Some excellent examples, besides the works of the aforementioned theologians and philosophers, that are recommended reading include: American philosopher, William Hasker's *The Triumph of God Over Evil* (2008), American theologian Clark Pinnock's (1937-2010) *Most Moved Mover: A Theology of God's Openness* (2001), Gregory Boyd's *Satan and the Problem of Evil: Constructing a Trinitarian Warfare Theodicy* (2001).

2.3.4 Other Theodicies

Not all theodicies fit the framework of whose will controls: God or human. Here are six others. Four of them are stand-alone unique: evil doesn't exist; redemptive suffering; process theology; and das Nighte. The other two—Hick's Christian soul-making and Swinburne's theodicy—form, along with open theism, the bedrock of my theodicy.

* * *

First, there's one argument that solves the problem of evil by arguing *evil doesn't exist*. This argument says God makes no mistake, God is perfect, and that everything God made is good because God is perfect. Just because humans perceive an experience they consider evil, this is a problem—an error of human perception.

The argument's strength is that it easily solves the problem of evil, by arguing there is no evil. Our experience, logic and common sense seem to suggest otherwise. It also seems to defy our definitional understanding of evil.

The dictionary says evil, both as a noun and adjective, defines something profoundly immoral, depraved, malevolent, tending to harm, even demonic. My definition for purposes of this theodicy is that evil is the negative consequence of living in a state of sin. True, my definition is more expansive, including, for example, injustices such as being unfairly passed over for promotion, or having a friend betray you, that may not rise to the level of being depraved or malevolent. However, I would argue that everyone has either personally experienced, or knows someone who has experienced, being the subject of profoundly immoral, harmful behavior.

Therefore, the argument that there's no problem of evil because there's no evil, fails many of our criteria for a good theodicy.

* * *

Redemptive suffering presents a solution to the problem of evil that focuses on the cross of Christ as evidence of God's use of suffering to draw us into a close, loving relationship. Proponents include philosopher and Episcopal priest Marilyn M. Adams (1943-2017).

Adams (Peterson, M. 2011) argues God created humans to enter into freely chosen relationships of self-surrendering love with God and others. That is the ultimate goal of God with the ultimate good being intimacy with God and the worst evil being separation from God. She argues that participating with God through suffering, like Christ on the cross, is a path to loving intimacy with God and others.

Distilled to its essence, Adams' theodicy seems to be saying that exposure to suffering leads us to intimacy (and a deeper love) for others on earth. It also leads us to intimacy with God through understanding the suffering love of Christ's on the cross. Suffering itself is the path to loving God.

Adams criticizes analytic philosophers for focusing on a *logical* solution to the problem of evil arguing that if God is a mystery then why shouldn't evil be a mystery: "For Christians as for others in this life, the fact of evil is a mystery. The answer is a more wonderful mystery—God himself."

She argues that proof of God's existence as a "logical possibility" offers little comfort for the sufferer. The sufferer wants to know that God is "actually" trustworthy. And that sense of actual trustworthiness comes from personal experience and encounter with God's reality and grace, an experience that usually defies explanation.

Adam argues that God's mystery, like evil's mystery, is:

> ...part of God's deliberate design since it is necessary to make possible the relationships He wants with us and for which we were created. For what God wants from us is wholehearted trust and obedience. Yet it is conceptually impossible to trust someone if you know in advance every move that he will make....even if such knowledge were possible, it would be a source of great temptation. For example, if God were known to have a fixed policy of rendering temporal goods for well-doing and temporal evils for wickedness, then the observant might even try to manipulate the equation to use God as a means to their end. (p. 172)

She argues that this insight is one way to view the enigmatic book of Job. Despite Job's excellent and faithful life, he suffered greatly rather than receiving divine goodness. When Job complained of this unfairness to God,

> God answers Job with a theophany: Job is reprimanded for his insolence in presuming to grasp the divine goodness in such a simplistic way; he is allowed to see and experience God's goodness but told he will have to trust God to save him in his own way, without advance billing of his plans. Job had loved God too much for his effects and benefits; now he has seen God and must love him for himself. (p. 172)

Interestingly, Adams does concede that while the problem of evil is a pastoral problem, "it has a philosophical dimension in that it might be partially alleviated by some sort of explanations of how God is being good to created persons, even when he permits and/or causes evils..." (171) Thus, Adams seems to not only concede that a rational explanation (other than "mystery") helps the faithful with the problem of evil, but, also her argument is presented in the analytic (logically precise) philosophical method.

One advantage of Adam's line of thought is that it explains all evils, even horrendous evils. Suffering is suffering, whether understandable and justified or unknown and unjustified (even pointless). And all suffering is medicinal and restorative and has the potential to draw us to others and to God. Thus, it would answer the problem of evil by arguing God's good reason for evil is the experience of redemptive suffering which brings us closer to God's essence as self-surrendering love.

A criticism is that Adams, in relying heavily upon the personal narratives and subjective experiences of the suffering of others—especially Biblical characters like Job, Abraham and Christ on the cross—lacks the philosophical rigor that analytic philosophy demands.

Admirers of this line of thinking argue that pain and suffering of people is not easily reduced to analytic precision, clarity and rigor, but, rather, is deeply felt, personal and subjective and, thus is best understood by personal narrative. Just because subjective narratives of suffering are hard to be expressed with mathematical precision, doesn't mean that it's not the spot to look for the answer to evil. One could argue this was Danish theologian and philosopher, Soren Kierkegaard's (1813-1855) answer to God's reason for evil: that suffering and ultimate despair naturally leads us to the Cross of Christ.

I admire Adam's argument—that God's plan does not involve a cold-blooded, selfish temporal cost-benefit analysis—as a good explanation for the enigmatic suffering of Job. I also share her belief that God's partial hiddenness (his uncertain reality) is part of an intentional design so that we can come to God in loving faith, and not certainty.

* * *

Process theology is, like open theism, based upon creaturely free will, but is different from open theism in several respects. Process theology is a vision of God and the world (including humans) in mutual, interdependent evolution, each having the same beginning, each moving forward, learning and maturing eternally.

God is evolving, learning from the world, and the world is evolving, learning from God. Reality, under this notion, is constructed not so much of physical things (e.g., atoms) but of individual dynamic experiences, each creating memories that impact future experiences, constituting a series of *eternal creative experiences*. God in this schema can only influence humans through persuasion but never controls the future because the future of everything is unknown to God who is evolving.

As such, process thought sees a world in *perpetual dynamic evolution*, always becoming but never being. It is a world that is totally open, contingent and uncertain. Even God does not know where it's eventually heading, what with God perpetually and dynamically evolving, also always becoming but never being.

Admirers of process thinking argue it does a good job of marrying metaphysics with contemporary physics with its "uncertainty principle" found in the strange world of quantum physics. Further, it helps explain not only moral but also natural evil, especially horrendous evil given that everything in creation, even God, is radically free and contingent. It reveals a God intimately engaged with and involved with creation, as opposed to an aloof, disinterested God. In fact, one cannot image a schema with a more involved, entangled God than the God of process thought.

Critics argue process thought cannot explain the origins of life as coming from God, or from anywhere else, as God and the world are in contemporaneous, eternal evolution. That is, there is no object (God) that created subjects (life, otherness, matter) that stands over and against the world. God could not have created the world since God is inseparable from the world. Likewise, there's no end game, no end to finitude, no heaven beyond the physicality of the world, no reason/purpose for creation other than an infinite evolution of experiential building blocks. Further, critics argue that process thought is not ontologically grounded nor is God grounded as to a necessary nature. As Boyd argues (2001), "Process thought requires us to believe that each actual occasion constitutes itself [including God's experiences] as a virtual *ex nihilo*. I submit that this concept is incoherent." (p. 275).

While process thought holds that the future of everything is unknown to God, openness theology thinking says the only things unknown to God are individual human decisions with a moral dimension. Except for that, God exhaustively foreknows and controls creation—from beginning to end, Alpha and Omega.

* * *

In Swiss theologian Karl Barth's (1886-1968) idea of *"das Nichtige"* (the nothingness), he argues that whatever God did not say "yes" to in creation resulted in God saying "no" to everything else. This "no" is the "nothingness" that is the "formless void" chaos of Genesis.

Barth (along with other theologians) see Satan and the demonic array spelled out in Scripture as mythological expressions of the "null and void," the "nothingness" or "no" of what God did not create: das Nichtige.

As Boyd (2001) described Barth's das Nichtige, it is the "perpetually 'menacing' pervasive reality that is menacing precisely because it has no reality of its own. It is non- being perpetually trying to be, as it were, over and against the creation that God has chosen. Hence Barth can appropriately characterize das Nichtige as a realm of falsehood that becomes evil when it encroaches on the realm of creation. Indeed, in Barth's view 'all the personifications of evil in Scripture (that is, the devil, demons, Leviathan) are mythological expressions of this cosmic menacing force.'" (p. 285)

* * *

Hick created a theodicy centered on the good reason of *"soul-making"* whereby humans can mature in Christian love through various mechanisms (or structures of being or life processes). One such life processes is freely struggling against great adversity—specifically including experiencing horrendous evil—within the world.

Hick argued this structure of free will is largely achieved by God keeping an "epistemic distance" from humanity (*veiled*, so to speak). By God being distant, humans are largely left to their own devices (i.e., being forced to cope, learn and grow, and decide moral issues on their own, which is another way of saying free will) Being free, humans, as pointed out, have the capacity to commit evil.

According to Hick (1981), the world must be "religiously ambig-uous, both veiling God and revealing Him—veiling Him to ensure man's freedom and revealing Him to men as they rightly exercise this freedom." (p. 46)

Hick's use of the term *ambiguously* suggests yet another struc-ture of being besides free will to enable love: ambiguity. Both Hick's soul-making theodicy and Boyd's open theism seem to agree that for free will to be meaningful there need to be meaningful alternatives or choices to fuel moral maturity. Both seem to argue that God's reasons require mechanisms (structures of being?) for implementation. Further, Hick seems to agree with not only Kant, but also Boyd's observation that "If God in all his glory, power and splendor were perfectly obvious to us from the start, it is doubtful our choice to love him could have a distinctly moral quality to it." (2001, p. 258)

Here, in these more mature theodicies, we start to see emphasis not only on God's good reason for evil but also the necessary enabling mechanisms that actualize God's good reason.

Hick's theodicy (1978 and 1981) builds upon the theological insights of Irenaeus (c. 130-c.202 AD) who believed God purposely made humans imperfect so they could use their free will to mature in Christ. Irenaeus, who is largely credited as a foundational thinker for the Eastern Orthodox Church (as Augustine is for the Western Church), saw the story of Adam and Eve as a parable of why God evicted Adam and Eve from paradise. It was not because Adam and Eve were totally depraved but, rather, because God wanted them to mature in Christ (Christian soul-making) through being chiseled in love—from selfishness to selflessness—through freely navigating the harsh experiences of adversity (usually felt as evil).

As indicated, Hick's theodicy opens the door to the notion that God's good reason isn't self-enacting. Christian soul-making requires enabling mechanisms to achieve God's good reason—here, not just creaturely free will but God's distancing from the the walk Christians must take through life (what Hick called God's *ambiguity*).

* * *

Providence and the Problem of Evil (1998) by English philosopher, Richard Swinburne, adopts, like Boyd and Hick, the premise that humans possess a libertarian free will. He also argues that "almost all Christian theologians" affirm that humans possess a free will. However, some see that in the compatibilist sense while others in the libertarian sense. Swinburne concludes that "If the only free will humans have is compatibilist free will, there will be no distinction to be made between God allowing some human to do a bad act, and causing him to do it. For then humans will inevitably do the acts they do because of the way they were made. And if there is a God, it is God who made them that way. If they do bad acts, that will be because God causes them to do bad acts." (p. 34)

Like Boyd and Hick, Swinburne sees good necessarily coming from the potential for evil. Swinburne identifies some of God's "good goals" as: beauty; thought and feeling (e.g., beliefs, desires, emotions); action (e.g, the greatness of being of use); worship." In addition, Swinburne stresses the need for knowledge ("deep awareness of God") " and appreciation.

Swinburne stresses that knowledge of evil provides us with empathy for others and opportunities to exercise our morally good muscles to help others in need. Every negative event (e.g., someone's child dies, an earthquake destroys a village) presents opportunities to display Christ's selfless love on the cross.

Swinburne addresses the argument that God could have minimized the amount, depth and breadth of evil in the world, by, say, creating a world "where all pain is 10 per cent of its intensity in this world, people only suffer it for at most eight years…where evil desires are only 10 per cent in frequency and intensity of those in our world, and people only have 10 per cent of the choices and can only make 10 per cent of the differences which they can in this world." (p. 242, 243)

Yes, this would make a difference in the amount, depth and breadth of evil, but, Swinburne argues:

> …as regards the kinds of goods to which I have drawn attention in this book, it would be a toy world. Things would matter…but they would not matter much. It would not matter very much if we made the wrong choices, because not very much would depend upon them.

For most of the starving would get food even if we did nothing; and although some might die, they would not feel much pain....And our children, though valuing our love if they got it, would not mind it too much if they did not get it. (p. 243)

Swinburne then asks: "Is it really so obvious that God would be less than perfectly good if he gave us a world where things matter a lot more than that? Of course not." he answers. (p. 243)

Swinburne stresses how evil actualizes moral action based upon Christian love. Boyd stresses love. Hick stresses Christian soul-building. Perhaps these are all sides of the same coin.

All three—Boyd, Hick and Swinburne—show a need for a "mechanism" that transmutes evil and good experiences into actualizing God's good reasons. Boyd stresses free will as that mechanism. Hick stresses free will and the ambiguity of God. Swinburne stresses those mechanisms plus talks of knowledge and appreciation (to generate a "deep awareness of God") which Swinburne includes as one of *God's good goals*.

I believe that this is the *future of theodicy*: revealing God's architecture (i.e., God's structures of being or life processes) for the lived experience that shapes and channels (but doesn't dictate or determine) human behavior to achieve God's *good goals*. And within that divine design there are necessarily experiences of both good and bad (or evil). As Tillich (1987) argues: "Life is not unambiguously good. Then it would not be life but only the possibility of life. And life is not unambiguously evil. Then nonbeing would have conquered being. But life is ambiguous in all its expressions." (p. 151)

* * *

These and other thoughts on evil are all interesting, often complex, often intellectually and Scripturally satisfying, and contribute to the body of serious, heart-felt, hard-chiseled efforts to vindicate God's justice.

If I have misunderstood or mischaracterized any of the above theodicies, defenses, or thoughts on the problem of evil—or omitted any worthy arguments—I apologize. It was unintentional, due to the complexity of the subject matter and limits of both my cognitive abilities and time to read everything on the subject. Perhaps in the near future, an artificial intelligence program, filled with every thought—spoken or written—throughout recorded history, will spit out a better report in mere seconds.

* * *

Any attempted responses and defenses to defend God against the negative inferences created by the problem of evil, might be true. Some seem stronger than others, and by stronger, I mean in meeting the criteria for a good theodicy (although the responses and defenses are not theodicies).

I especially enjoy Smedes argument and acknowledge Plantinga's break through work in converting free will thinking from the past into the logically demanding framework of modern analytical philosophy. At a minimum, Plantinga's work represents an intellectually strong plank upon which Christians can stand while deflecting charges their faith is incoherent. Of course, I am humbled by the arguments that, like Job, we simply cannot know God's reasoning. However, I believe Christianity needs theodicy and that theodicy is possible; otherwise why did God give us gifts of reason like logic, math, critical thinking, the ability to synthesize?

In terms of what I consider the stronger theodicies, I would include, as indicated, open theism, Swinburne and Hick.

What I believe this theodicy adds to all of the above body of work includes the following:

1. It states not only God's good reason (e.g., enabling relational love with God and others and building Christian character) but also how God designed the experience of being alive to actualize God's goal or good reason.
2. It describes God's architecture of love by stating what shaping and channeling forces/mechanisms (i.e., structures of being or life processes) are needed to create predicate human abilities (i.e., the ability to know; the ability to appreciate or discern and the ability to become morally mature) so as to enable relational love

with God and others, build Christian character, and potentiate moral action.

3. It describes not only how each structure of being necessarily advances God's good reasons, but it also explains how/why each structure either necessarily creates evil or is considered evil per se.

4. As concerns each structures of being, it discusses whether or not that structure actually exists in reality. In that regard, it strives for scientific support and compatibility with widely accepted world views of science (such as the theory of evolution).

5. It provides Scriptural support for all that is said about each structure of being.

6. It synthesizes various strong (usually free will) theodicies to showcase common themes.

7. Using thought experiments, humor and popular insights about about life, it attempts to buttress the common sense bona fides of the argument so it doesn't seem merely theoretical but, rather, resonates personally as the way things actually are.

8. It doesn't need non-human creatures to understand horrendous evil.

* * *

Let's conclude this discussion with a thought experiment about what kind of world you would design if you were God. Say you are the last remaining person on earth, that you are a master computer programmer, and that you desire to create a program that creates relational entities to talk to/correspond with, perhaps even have one or more of them come to know you, perhaps love you. Let's say your sovereign aloneness is inconsistent with your nature of selfless love and, naturally, wanting others to share love with.

Program One is designed with distinct individual sentient units with conscious self-awareness that are precisely programmed to act in a predetermined way. There are no surprises, no unknown. Everything is not only foreknown but controlled and fully determined. Some units evolve to discover you, talk to you, even come to profess their love for you. But you foreknew these outcomes because you designed these precise outcomes into the program.

The program is interesting for a while—something to do—but, Question: What do you eventually get from the program? You cannot be surprised by love from the created units. Nor could you be disappointed by the created units. If your purpose was merely to showcase your power and glory, then to whom and for what purpose? To puppet units?

Or, you could design Program Two: a design where you don't control the dynamic evolution of your created units; however, you fully foreknow how each unit will behave.

Questions: What chance does any unit have to change its destiny given that you already foreknow their future actions? What possibility exists that you will be surprised by future actions and outcomes of the created units if you exhaustively foreknow all future actions and outcomes? Can you be surprised by love? In other words, is there any substantive difference between controlling and foreknowing future outcomes?

With Program Three, you create individual units and give them self-determining power (free will) over their decisions/actions, especially involving moral actions. You want these units to come to know that you are *out there* in a reality outside the computer software matrix, to come to know your attributes and essence, and hopefully come to appreciate and love you.

You design certain life processes that shape, channel and limit their behavior so as to encourage desired outcomes, but not predetermine that behavior. You not only don't control but also don't foreknow how the units will develop over time and experiences, thus, you intentionally self-limit your programming power. The balance is delicate: enough evidence is provided to achieve some success but not enough to avoid loss and disappointment.

Maybe a unit will come to know they have a creator, realize your attributes and essence, maybe come to appreciate you, even come to love you. Maybe not. After all, it didn't ask to be created, nor be given self-consciousness. They might deplore being burdened with a free will—from which there is no escape—and the responsibility, stress, shame and guilt associated therewith.

Regardless, the point is that with Program Three creation means something to you with the possibility of being surprised by love and having freely chosen relationships. True, you might be disappointed and saddened by rejection. Creation also means something for the units, of being something rather than nothing, of potentially having an endless relationship with you, of sharing in the essence of you, the programmer.

There are other possible Programs. But the point is to illustrate that an omnipotent, omniscient, wholly good God may not necessarily design computer program One or Two.

2.4 Divine Goals, or God's Good Reason

As we've seen from the above, a common thread in defending God is to show a divine goal or good reason for God allowing evil within creation. A second, equally critical task, is to show that the amount of suffering (or evil) is necessary to achieve the good, otherwise, the excess suffering (evil) is unnecessary (pointless or excessive).

Before addressing this, we first need to ask *do we need a justification for every evil?* Some atheodicists, like Rowe, argue we do, but Swinburne argues it would suffice if a justification could be found for a "sufficiently impressive range of evils."

The editor of the *Standard Encyclopedia of Philosophy* agrees that "What Swinburne says here is surely very reasonable, and I can see no objection in principle to a defense of this sort." But it then provides this qualifying criticism which lies at the heart of the problem with theodicy today:

> The problem with it [Swinburne's argument] is that no theodicy that has ever been proposed has ever been successful in the relevant way—that is, there in no impressive range of undesirable states of affairs where people initially think that the wrong making properties of allowing such states of affairs to exist greatly outweigh any right making properties of such states of affairs associated with doing so, but where, confronted with some proposed theodicy, people come to believe that it would be morally permissible to allow such states of affairs to exist. Indeed, it is hard to find *any* such cases, let alone an impressive range. (sec. 6.3)

The consensus appears to be that there is no theodicy that logically justifies God allowing the range, type and depth of evils in the world today, if not to each and every evil event then at least to a *sufficiently impressive range* of them.

I agree with Swinburne and argue the theodicy presented herein logically justifies a sufficiently impressive range of evil outcomes.

What then are some good reasons for evil in creation given in defense of God over the years?

* * *

Divine goals (or good reasons) that necessarily result in evil, and that have been advanced by others for God allowing evil in its various forms include the following, some of which have already been discussed:

- Evil is a way of bring us to repentance and salvation;
- Evil presents a test of loyalty to God (Job);
- Evil is punishment for sin (Genesis);
- Evil is a means of bringing us closer to God (of restoration—Adams);
- Evil (or suffering from evil) is a means of revealing something about the inner life of God and other people;
- Evil experiences promotes Christian maturation (John Hick and Irenaeus);
- Evil is a necessary path to love (Boyd and open theism).
- Evil is inevitable from imperfect creatures because Perfection cannot create Itself (Hasker).
- Evil shows how dependent we are on God since we don't know what God wants.
- Evil is the absence of God, the negative forces of that which God did not create—the nothingness left out of the something that God created (Barth).
- Evil allows God to demonstrate his forgiving and merciful ways (Calvin and Reformed Christianity) .
- Evil fulfills a higher divine purpose (Augustine).
- Evil is the result of demonic, nonhuman forces who control matter, in part, and oppose God's will for creation.
- Evil creates the possibility for morally significant choices, in that immoral evil presents opportunity for morally good action. (Swinburne)
- Evil presents the opportunity for the victim or sufferer to show "courage and sympathy in the face of their suffering and that of others" thereby showing others how to become "naturally good people." (Swinburne)

To which I add: evil enables learning, appreciation or discernment, and morally mature behavior which are all predicates for building Christian character, especially belief in and love for God and charitable love for others.

* * *

You will note the good reasons advanced above start with the premise of evil and then gives God's good reason for allowing evil. Thus, it appears that none of these divine good reasons can be achieved without the pain and suffering attendant to evil experiences.

Assuming the evil of suffering obtains God's good reason, this illustrates the positive value of evil. I argue evil does serve a positive role in its negative effect; however, it's not so much evil itself, but evil as both a counterpoint to the good or positive in life, and as a shaping and channeling force that leads us to come to know, appreciate and love God.

The good or positive in life (ultimately God) is only made manifest and illuminated by its depravation. There can be no knowledge of or appreciation of good and evil without both forces of good and evil standing in opposition to each other. God becomes apparent, appreciated and loved only in the midst of evil.

Agreeing with open theism and similar theological schools of thought, I argue the primary good reason for God designing life is love, of others and God. Importantly, I add the good reason of love requires humans to have certain abilities, as selfless Christian love doesn't just arise automatically within us without growth in our Christian walk.

To come to love God means, first, to come to know God, then appreciate God, and finally love God. These are abilities—ability to know, ability to discern or appreciate this over that, and ability to mature in love—that require certain structures of being or life processes that enable their flourishing.

We've talked of how Boyd, Hick and Swinburne recognize this dynamic and address what they see as necessary mechanisms of implementation.

Separating God's good reason/s from the mechanisms necessary to achieve said divine goals greatly advances theodicy because, I argue, it's the mechanisms or structures of being that produce the evil outcomes in the process of achieving God's good reason/s. God's good reason/s for creation are not self-implementing. They need mechanisms (e.g., structures of being or life processes) for implementation.

* * *

I argue that God's architecture of the human experience of life has two dynamic layers. One layer is the life processes/structures of being that shape, channel and limit certain human attributes. The second layer is the human attributes themselves.

Those abilities include the ability to: *Learn (knowledge); to discern (appreciation); and to mature in love and other moral consequential behaviors.* (Discussed fully in Part Three.) These human abilities arise from certain structures of being for their actualization.

The structures of being dynamically drive us, by shaping, channeling and even limiting our behavior: to know what God is and wants from us; to discern the good from the bad in our choices; and, finally, to morally mature in selfless Christian love. These structures of being include not just free will but also: *ambiguity; anxiety; doubt; and self-conscious individuals living within a world.* (Discussed fully in Part Three.)

In summary, I argue these structures of being create the potential for humans to come to know, appreciate and love God.

As will be argued, these structures also either necessarily produce evil or constitute evil (by definition alone), thus justifying God's self-imposed inability to prevent evil in the world, despite being all powerful and loving.

* * *

True, a critic can argue: *But why didn't God design us to arrive at the end point of mature Christian love without having us painfully travel through an imperfect evil world? If evil experiences are necessary for coming to know, appreciate and love God, why not simply program those abilities and those experiences into our DNA?*

In response, I would argue, along with the existentialists, it is *concrete experience*—that is: hard felt, emotionally powerful, painfully deep or ecstatically high, experiences—that shape and channel human behavior. If true, then I argue there's no practical difference between God programming such concrete experiences into our DNA, thus avoiding actual life experiences, and us having to actually live out concrete experiences in real time in reality. Either way, we have to painfully experience evil.

- PART 3 -

A THEODICY OF DESIGN

Where were you when I laid the foundation?
Tell me if you understand. Who marked off the dimensions?
Surely you know! Who stretched a measuring line across it?
On what were its footings set, or who laid its cornerstone—while the
morning stars sang together and all the angels shouted for joy?
The Lord, Job 38: 4-7

Early death, destructive social conditions, feeble-mindedness and
insanity, the undiminished horrors of historical existence—all these
seem to verify belief in fate rather than providence. How
can an almighty God be justified (theos-dike) in view of the
realities in which no meaning whatsoever can be discovered?[6]
Either He has not sufficient love or He has not sufficient power.
As an emotional outburst this question is very understandable.
As a theoretical formulation it is rather poor.[7]
Paul Tillich

Theodicy, in the narrow sense, allows the believer to
maintain faith in God in the face of the world's evils. Theodicy,
in the broad sense, is any way of giving meaning to evil that helps
us face despair. Theodicies place evils within structures that
allow us to go on in the world. Ideally, they should reconcile us to past
evils while providing a direction in preventing future ones.
Susan Neiman, *Evil in Modern Thought*

----

6 Tillich, *Systematic Theodicy*
7 Tillich, *The Unity of Love, Power and Justice*

3.1 Argument In A Nutshell: God's Plan for Creation

MOST SIMPLY PUT, my bold contention is that this imperfect world is perfectly designed. If God is X and God's plan for creation is Y, then creation's design must be Z, wherein necessary evils must occur within the lived experience of creation to achieve Y.

For a Christian, it should be uncontroverted that God, being omnipotent and wholly good, designed creation without mistake. If there are evil imperfections in the world, then this evil must be necessary to achieve God's purpose (Y) such that no lesser evil would work to achieve God's plan for creation. Basically, this is G. E. Moore's proposition.

The persistent problem for theism remains rationally understanding how horrendous evil (often seemingly pointless, or at least incomprehensible) can exist within Z if God is X. Couldn't God, being omnipotent, have designed a world without the quantity, range and intensity of pain and suffering and still achieve Y? Couldn't, for example, God have redirected that tornado's path away from the house where a young child was killed and out into the empty field? Who would have known? The challenge is for someone making a G. E. Moore-like claim is to rise to meet the burden of proof and present intellectually sound arguments that it's probable God X created a world Z.

I argue this theodicy does just that. I argue that God's plan Y can only be achieved through design Z, which necessarily potentiates if not creates all the evil we experience in the world: moral and natural; simple and complex; fair and disproportionate; minor and intense; understandable and incomprehensible.

* * *

As concerns premise Y, God's *plan for creation*, it is revealed in the Bible: God desires a "bride," with bride being a symbol for a church, or a gathering of faithful or, as Taylor phrased it in *A Secular Age*, (2007) "a network of agape."

Scripture indicates that God desires relational love, yet God, being complete unto self has no needs, not even love. In *The Triumph of God Over Evil* (2008), American philosopher William Hasker talks about the paradox of understanding creation if God is sufficient unto self. Specifically, if God is perfection itself, and has no need, then why create anything?

Hasker's concedes the answer is beyond our ken. "The notion of being able to think in the same way the Creator of the universe would think is ludicrous or terrifying or both at once." He says we can "arrive at some very limited understanding, however thin and abstract, of the conceptual structure of a decision to create a world" (p. 92).

I argue that to arrive at "at some very limited understanding" we can turn to God's essence as revealed in Scripture. The answer is love as revealed in the Trinity, in Christ's kenotic love on the cross, and God's grace as a natural outflow of God's love being perfect (charitable, sacrificial, agape).

Hasker argues "It is part of God's greatness and generosity that he both wishes and is able to create other beings who along with him determine the outcome of his creation." (p. 93) He adds

> We may affirm that the life of God is completely rich, fulfilling and satisfying without reference to creation, and therefore God has no need whatever for a created world in order for the divine life to be complete and perfect. Insofar as it makes sense to quantify such matters, we may say that God's life is infinitely satisfying, and the satisfaction cannot be increased by anything that might be added by a created order. Creation, we insist, is a free and gracious act of God. (p. 98)

Hasker concluded his insight into creation by arguing:

> ...that in deciding to create, God brings about the existence of a realm of *imperfection*, whereas without creation there is only the perfection of the divine life itself. And surely it isn't self-evident that 'perfection plus imperfection' is better than perfection all by itself. It's true, of course,

that *for us* perfection is fully appreciated only by contrast with that which is imperfect. (p. 99)

God does not need love as God is love. Being charitable love, as revealed in Scripture, such love is naturally broadcast infinitely and shared in loving grace.

I argue *God's plan Y* requires maturity in Christ or, as Hick called it, Christian *soul-making*. To achieve Y, sentient creatures must have the ability to know, appreciate, mature in and eventually love God. Said abilities are birthed, shaped and channeled by certain innate structures of being that God wove into the warp and woof of lived experience. These shaping and channeling structures of being necessarily create (or outright constitute) the evil found in the world. Logically, it probably cannot be otherwise.

I argue it is God's plan for creation and not our narcissistic desires that drives the logic behind creation's design. The task, then, becomes whether we can rationally understand and appreciate the divine function of life's design (Z) with all its apparent imperfections to achieve God's perfect plan (Y) for creation.

The G. E. Moore Shift merely argues there cannot be gratuitous suffering (or intense suffering) because an omnipotent, omniscient, wholly good God exists. But it doesn't justify *Sue* and *Bambi*; it merely argues Sue and Bambi must, automatically, satisfy some good reason of God that necessarily cannot be otherwise, given God's attributes of power and love. Moore's Shift doesn't specify God's good reason. It doesn't argue why the amount and type of evil is necessary to achieve the good reason without the use of a lesser evil. It doesn't argue that the good reason morally justifies the personal human cost in suffering.

This theodicy aims to provide evidential support for G. E. Moore's Shift, thereby countering Rowe's statement in Set C, C1, that "There exists instances of intense suffering which an omnipotent being could have prevented without thereby losing some greater good or permitting some evil equally bad or worse."

* * *

As concerns my *foundational premises X,* I will not argue it. Rather, I will explain *my understanding* of it.

As concerns X, I assume that *God exists* and that *God's essence or nature is love, life and the creative,* with *God's attributes being omnipotence, omniscience, and being wholly good.*

By "God exists," I mean God is real, real as in the ultimate reality. I will avoid, as largely irrelevant, the issue of whether God is a tangible thing among things—such as an actual father figure, heavenly or otherwise, or an intangible spirit or some sophisticated "ground of all being." My assumption is that there is a there there, that personally interacts with us in some fashion.

I argue that no finite creature can prove or disprove the infinite (e.g., the metaphysical or supernatural—that which transcends the finite). Finite inquiry is limited to that which can be experienced by our five human senses: sight, sound, feel, taste, touch. As Kant argued (1783):

> The very concept of metaphysics ensures that the source of metaphysics can't be empirical. If something could be known through the senses, that would automatically show that it doesn't belong to metaphysics; that's an upshot of the meaning of the word 'metaphysics.' Its basic principles can never be taken from experience, nor can its basic concepts; for it is not by physical but metaphysical knowledge, so it must be beyond experience. (Preamble I, p. 7)

Rather, we believe in supernatural possibilities from personal faith, spiritual revelation, and rational arguments that buttress our faith testimonies. As Paul told the church at Corinth, "We live by faith, not by sight." (2 Co 5:7)

True, there are logical arguments for God. In American novelist and philosopher Rebecca Newberger Goldstein's book, *36 Arguments for the Existence of God (2010),* she lists 36 such arguments. For example, her "Argument From Fine-Tuning of Physical Constraints," is that the various physical properties that allow life to exist on earth (e.g., gravity, magnetism) all exist within such an almost unimaginable narrow band of tolerance, it seems life is a miracle. Just a microscopic change here or there and we either fly off into space or be crushed. (p. 357-358)

All thirty-six arguments, being philosophical arguments about metaphysics, contain unprovable assumptions. At most, they have a high degree of persuasiveness and probability. (On the other hand, arguments denying that God exists are also just that: arguments.)

This theodicy is not primarily an argument that God exists. Rather it is an argument that it's more than just possible—it's likely or probable—that the world, as actually designed, with evil, was designed by a God of perfect love and power. If persuasive, it should buttress the notion that God exists.

* * *

As to God's nature or *essence*—*love*—I mean the highest form we can image—charitable, or selfless—the kind displayed on the cross by Christ. By *life*, I mean something instead of nothing, being instead of non-being. By *creative*, I mean making something out of nothing, as in Creation.

Our love is innate, at first self-centered or narcissistic: a baby crying and thinking the whole world is listening and responding. But it can grow. We have the power to mature in love, toward the selfless, perfect love Christ displayed upon the cross.

Our life is unique, ours to own authentically, this miracle of being something rather than nothing, this ability to make new life and to celebrate the joys, hopes and feelings of being alive.

Plus we have the power of creation: of creating our values and beliefs, creating our responses to existence, self-creating ourself into who we want to be, with one option being lovingly dedicated to an eternal relationship with God.

The seeds are there; the dynamic life processes exist to point the way. How we freely respond to the life processes that shape and channel our behavior is up to each of us. How we use these gifts from God is up to each of us. We are responsible for the outcome of choosing God in love or not choosing God's love.

If we are created in the image of God, I believe this refers to our possessing God's essences of love, of life, and the creative and not physical attributes.

As concerns Gods *attributes*, I assume God is *omnipotent*. By that,

I mean as Swinburne (1998), "An omnipotent being is one who can do anything logically possible, anything, that is, the description of which does not involve a logical contradiction: such a being could not make me exist and not exist at the same instant, but could eliminate the stars or cover the earth with water just like that." (p. 3)

I consider God's *omniscience* to be included in God's omnipotence. However, many theorists separate this attribute from omnipotence and define it as the ability to know everything logically possible for God to know.

Of course God's logic, and what God could possibly know, exceeds ours. God, for example, as creator of the world could reasonably exhaustively foreknow the future as to all things God chose to predetermine. We, on the other hand, can understand the concept of a future but can only dimly peer into the future or predicate it exactly.

And yet we possess the gifts of logic, math, reason and other cognitive tools. Atheists might argue they are simply evolutionary adaptations born of necessity and chance that might have no reality or meaning outside of the neurons in our adaptive brains. But Christians can (and should) see them as gifts from God for various possible reasons: e.g.,to begin to glimpse God's logic and reasons for creation; to comprehend Scripture and the meaning of its powerful stories, parables and lessons; to comprehend the world—its physical laws, construction, mechanisms of life, etc.—that reveal God's majesty, beauty and genius.

As concerns God being *wholly good*, I also mean perfectly good and, also, perfectly loving.

First, I argue God cannot sin, by definition alone, with sin being defined as the condition of being separated from or estranged from God. God being God is in a state of eternal self union.

Second, since evil is, in my understanding, the negative consequence of being in a state of sin, God can commit evil. However, given that God intentionally, and for good reason, created separation from creation, evil became possible within creation. I argue that act of separation (whether via an interpretation of the Fall, or Hick's *epistemic* distancing (or partial veiling) or some other understanding) constitutes neither sin or evil. This assumes that God's good reason for this creative act justifies sin and evil within the world. If God's good reason doesn't justify the kinds of evils experienced within creation—that is, such evils are pointless or unnecessary—then I concede God may not be omnipotent or wholly good or both.

* * *

The Bible seems a fairly straight forward love story between God and creation. It aims for the relational more than the informational, though the informational can rationally lead to the relational. It aims for love more than logic, though God can be revealed through logic. It seeks faith more than facts, though facts can undergird faith. It seeks altruism over algorithms, though the miracle of math points to the genius behind life. In short, the Bible is a love story, not a physics quiz, although physics and math and logic are stepping stones—properly understood as gifts from God—for us to come to know, appreciate and love God.

3.2 Human Abilities Necessary to Achieve God's Plan for Creation

ELATIONAL LOVE IS God's good reason for creation. For creatures to enter into relational love with God and others, they need certain minimum capacities or abilities to mature in Christ. Those capacities include: the ability to *learn* or come to know; the ability to *appreciate* positive experiences over negative experiences; the ability to *mature in love* and be otherwise morally consequential entities.

3.2.1 Ability to Learn (Knowledge)

How can we come to know God?

One might start by asking: How can we know anything? What is the mechanism of knowing? How do we know if our knowledge is true?

This particular philosophical inquiry is known as epistemology. Like all philosophical issues, it is complicated, not subject to mathematical exactness, but rather is a matter of argument and logical persuasion. Following are my assumptions of how we can learn or come to know and the mechanisms (structures of being) that enable knowing. Throughout this discussion of human abilities necessary to achieve God's plan, I'll use examples of things we know: like the color red and the quality of loyalty.

First, obviously, we must be a *thing that can learn and gain knowledge of something.*

French philosopher and mathematician Rene' Descartes (1596-1650) argued we can only know one thing with certainty: "Cogito, ergo sum" (I think, therefore I am). Descartes was searching for the one true thing that we can unambiguously know, and *cogito, ergo sum* is what he came up with.

A stone doesn't think, at least it doesn't appear to think. A stone is an inanimate object, lacking life. To be something that thinks, therefore, requires life—an animate object. Further, the animate object must be sentient, that is, have the capacity to perceive or feel things.

In Descartes dictum, the "I" was perceiving that not only was it an "I" but that it was thinking. Hence, we have a structure of otherness essential to learning: a learner (or subject) and a thing to know (an object), which we'll discuss later.

Humans, of course, perceive things through their five senses: taste, smell, touch, sight and sound. They do this via direct experiences. We also possess a sophisticated brain that can logically infer things from experience, which I call our ability to reason. Thus, we can also learn not just from direct experience but also from hearing of the experiences of others and from drawing logically inferences from those direct and indirect experiences. Besides reason and experience, Christians believe in a third way of knowing: revelation. Revelation is believed to be a supernatural experience of knowing in a spiritual way. Being supernatural, this form of learning is not recognized by science because it's beyond the reach of science's empirical methods.

While inanimate objects like stones do not appear to have sense perception, other animals clearly do while plants might be able to perceive things in their environment.

Secondly, another requirement for learning is the *ability to differentiate* this from that. Educational psychologists argue that for a child to known, say, X, it needs to know what X is not.

Take the color red. If everything our senses perceive is the color red, such that our entire visual field was filled with only one color, being a red of the same hue, saturation and brightness, the color would mean nothing. But, if there was a second color, say blue, then the color red would be one thing and the color blue another thing. To know something about the color red requires knowing that it's not blue. Thus, when shown a blue ball and a red ball, a learner would know the red ball is not the blue ball.

The same analogy applies to our experiences and what they mean to us. Take the quality of sensing someone is loyal. If every experience in our life resulted in everyone else always forgoing their own self-interest for our self-interest, then all we would know is the quality of loyalty. It would have no meaning. Only by also experiencing disloyalty or betrayal from another, can we know the quality of loyalty.

Let' say that one day we ask a friend to help us because we are in desperate need. And let's say that friend has always responded to our pleas and provided the help requested. But then one day our friend says he'll help but, instead, they betray us—say, they don't go call an ambulance for us when they promised they would. For whatever reason of theirs, they lied to us, betrayed us in our hour of need.

That would feel different than all the past episodes where they provided aid and assistance to us in our hour of need. In that difference, we would then know something valuable about loyalty. We would know it's not disloyalty or betrayal. We'd also know the quality of both acts—loyalty and disloyalty—feel different, are different, and means several things, such as no longer being able to automatically rely upon this disloyal friend in the future.

Chinese philosophy refers to the phenomena of one thing having a complimentary opposite thing—say, dark and light, hate and love, despair and hope, whereby each is inextricably intertwined with the other—as yin and yang.

In *The Power of Myth* (1991), writer and literature professor, Joseph Campbell, argues that we can only think in opposites: "The mystery of life is beyond human comprehension. Everything we know is within the terminology of the concepts of being and not being, many and single, true and untrue. We always think in terms of opposites. But God, the ultimate, is beyond the pairs of opposites, that is all there is to it." (p. 57)

This suggests learning could not occur nor grow without the ability to differentiate one thing from its complimentary opposite thing.

Finally, it should be noted that *human knowledge is limited*. Take Descartes dictum of I think therefore I am. We can ask *What is "I?"*

We rationally infer from looking around at other people, and looking in a mirror, that the "I' we sense ourselves to be is a physical, walking, talking person of blood and bone. But, it's theoretically possible we're a brain in a vat, or in a psychotic state, or a zombie, or in a dog's dream. These possibilities certainly don't seem probable; however, the point is that we cannot verify to a scientific, mathematical certainty that we are what we assume.

Descartes understood our cognitive limits and, thus, limited his baseline knowledge merely to noting that he is something that thinks, without further defining the term "I."

Our ability to know things objectively is also limited by the fact knowledge is generated by individuals, with each individual's experience generating a certain qualia (the internal and subjective component of sense perceptions, arising from stimulation of the senses by phenomena). Science tries to objectify experiential evidence. But if personal experiences are subjective (unique to the experiencer), it is doubtful science can ever objectively know the qualia of a person's experiences.

[Note: This is not to say science cannot know the truth of phenomena discernible by one or more of our five senses. It can and to such a high degree as to generally be considered objectively true. But science cannot observe metaphysical/supernatural phenomena (such as God) and, I suggest, the exact qualia of my felt experiences.]

As often argued, we can study the bat and learn everything we can about bats except what it feels like to be a bat (because that knowledge resides within and is unique to each bat).

Therefore, the structures of being necessary for and related to our ability to learn or know are: a self-conscious sentient entity (this is one part of the structure of a subject observing an object); ambiguity (which allows for differentiation); and doubt (which reflects our cognitive limitations of knowing).

3.2.2 Ability to Discern (Appreciation)

Just knowing something, does not mean you treasure or appreciate it. As indicated, to know loyalty requires experiencing disloyalty. The first experience of both loyalty and disloyalty imparts knowledge and starts the process of discernment, of appreciating this over that. *Repeated ambiguous experiences create the ability to discern*, say, the good from the bad, the positive from the negative, the desirable from the undesirable.

Over time and repeated experiences of both prongs of the loyalty-disloyalty polarity, our knowledge accumulates. As it accumulates, we draw firmer ideas and convictions about what these two polar opposite human behaviors mean to us.

I argue that as concerns our own life, and the lives of our families and those we love, the quality of loyalty in others is increasingly prized as something very valuable. Life is hard and there are many times we need to be able to count on the loyalty of others. Conversely, disloyalty is held in disdain. If we cannot believe the promises or good faith of another to act in our best interests, possibly even to betray us to our detriment, then we increasingly avoid such people. They are not reliable, cannot be trusted, and possibly are dangerous.

We only come to these more mature conclusions about other people, what we like and dislike about them, and how we choose to lead our own lives, from the repeated ambiguous experiences of polar opposite behaviors, such as loyalty and disloyalty.

In the yin and yang of Zen, loyalty and disloyalty would be two sides of the same coin, each inextricable intertwined with the other, and only understood by reference to the other. In yin and yang philosophy, these two sides of the same coin would be content neutral, that is, neither is good or bad. Rather, each is simply the opposite of the other.

However, in Christian thought there is usually a difference between good and bad (or good and evil, or positive and negative). The good leads to God while evil points to what is not God.

Over time, and repeated experiences involving the variable of, say, loyalty versus disloyalty, we mature in our Christian walk. That is, we increasingly come to know and appreciate God's perfect loyalty. We begin to more fully understand and appreciate what Paul meant when he said "Love...always protects, always trusts, always hopes, always perseveres. Love never fails." (1 Co 13:7-8) Not only do we come to know and appreciate God, but we should also come to a realization of of what God desires of us as a Christian.

As with most moral/ethical issues, the matter can become complex. For example, in times of war, deception/betrayal/disloyalty can be seen as morally justified as a necessary higher good for one's cause. The Japanese engaged in deception and betrayal of the U.S. in WWII with its attack on Pearl Harbor. The Japanese undoubtedly rationalized their deceit as justified by the higher good of defeating an enemy in combat. U.S. citizens and leaders saw the deception and attack as evil, justifying retribution. Thus, among humans, the loyalty/disloyalty moral justifications are subjective and depend upon a person's particular allegiance, motive and rationalizations.

It is only with God's perfect loyal love that each of us can be assured loyalty exists for those whose allegiance resides with God.

Therefore, our ability to appreciate God through the increased ability to discern occurs when free creatures have ambiguous experiences of oppositional qualities, say, loyalty and disloyalty. Necessary structures of being for discernment in learning needs not only self-conscious sentient creatures, but free will that allows for choice of this over that, and ambiguity (which is the fundamental structure of polar opposite choices).

3.2.3 Ability to Love and Engage in Other Morally Consequential Behaviors (Maturity)

Armed with knowledge of a positive value (loyalty, for example), and appreciating this positive value (loyalty) over its opposite negative value (disloyalty), paves the way for Christian maturity in terms of love, courage, faith and other morally consequential behaviors.

If we come to know and appreciate, say, loyalty over disloyalty, and realize we are both free and responsible for our behavior—that is, to choose to be loyal or disloyal ourselves—then we have become morally mature consequential people capable of selfless love.

The love we are on the brink of is a more mature Christian love, moving from a self-love to a selfless love. This happens because we increasingly appreciate, for example, the charitable loyalty being displayed to us. It's but a small leap to realize that what is treasured by us when receiving loyalty from another is probably treasured by others when received from us. Thus, when we (hopefully) emerge from our youthful narcissism, and begin to think and care about another person, we should want to give them a treasured gift: loyalty, especially a selfless loyalty that advances their self-interest, possibly even at the expense of our own self-interest.

For example, let's assume your business partner lies seriously injured in the woods, far from civilization, and looks to you as the only person nearby, to help/save them by running for help.

Armed with both the knowledge and appreciation of loyalty over disloyalty, and being fully aware of how betrayal of our business partner lying injured in the woods, could lead to self advantage, you are faced with a moral choice. You could do nothing and let your partner die and be materially enriched thereby (let's say you get the entire ownership of the business and/or the business life insurance proceeds), or you could save your partner and lose this chance at material enrichment. Perhaps by saving him you even risk personal loss (let's say you know that your business partner is in the process of severing the relationship and forcing you out of the business, plus having an affair with your wife). By saving him and putting his interests ahead of and to the detriment of your own interests approaches Christ's perfect love displayed on the cross. Smedes framed it well when he said (1978):

> Any person who feels a pull toward another, an urge to care simply because the other is there, is in touch with eternity. The wife who cannot stop caring for a husband, even after he has long bruised her life and ignored her needs, after eros is dead, is in tune with the essence of God. The parent whose heart expands in loving affirmation of a rebellious child, grown now into an estranged adult who gives no affection in return, is sharing divine perfection. The business partner who is able to see through the conflicts of competition to a hurting soul within a competitor is living on the fringe of heaven. (p. 124)

To sacrifice one's personal gain or self-interest for the personal gain or self-interest of another in need is a morally rich action. To betray another is also a morally rich action. The former is a morally good action (commonly simply called "moral"), at least within Christianity and most moral codes, while the latter is generally considered a morally bad action (commonly simply called "immoral").

This calculus of self versus others applies to all decisions and actions such as love, courage and faith and other morally consequential decisions/ actions. Each requires a decision that contains risk and sacrifice, on the one hand, or perceived selfish gain, on the other hand.

To act courageously is to risk personal safety or self interest for the self interest of another person. All morally consequential actions involve risk to self and sacrificing self to another, be it another person in need, God, or some higher ethic beyond self interest.

Faith is an act of courageous love. Without the possibility of loss or harm to self, the acts of courage and love and faith would be meaningless. If we know with certainty, for example, that God exists and wants us to engage in Christian selfless loyalty to others, then self-sacrificing acts of loyalty would be an easy choice what with the risk or cost minimized if not erased by the certainty of God. But if we are not certain God exists, or what God wants us to do in a situation, then abandoning self-interest for the well-being of a stranger presents a difficult decision. There is risk. It is both the cost or risk to self, combined with our love of self versus love other others, combined with uncertainty, that makes our responses in life to others in need a difficult decision.

There is always risk in every decision of self versus others and for various reasons. The first reason is that we are free in deciding what to do. We are free because (a premise) love and other morally consequential actions must be freely chosen. No thing, person or outside force predetermines our decisions. We are the authors of and own our decisions.

Second, for a decision to be truly free a person must have a menu of choices. In our previous examples of how to respond to the needs of another, there is (1) an example of self-sacrificing love in promoting the interests of another or (2) an example of selfish love of oneself. These are two choices. There may be shades of each action, but the point is there are always choices. Without different options or choices, free will would be meaningless.

Third, to be truly free, the choice to be made is not clear. That is to say, there is no objective guideposts in life that scream out *this is the right way or this is the wrong way. Every decision is contingent, uncertain, filled with doubt.* If we knew with absolute certainty which choice to make, then how free (and courageous) would it be to pick that obvious choice?

Fourth, facing important free decisions, that present with choices that are contingent, uncertain and filled with doubt, creates decision-making *anxiety.* They create anxiety because we don't know with certainty that our choice will be the right choice. They create anxiety because we know or at least should know that we are responsible for our decisions in life.

Yalom said of free will that "Both to constitute (to be responsible for) oneself and one's world and to be aware of one's responsibility is a deeply frightening insight." (p. 221) Thus, it is should be no surprise that our many psychological defense mechanisms—e.g., denial, projection/displacement, repression, rationalization, intellectualization—are maladaptive techniques to avoid the "deeply frightening insight" of the power and responsibility attendant to our free will.

Decisions clearly carry risk, thus faith, courage and love are always in play.

Here's how Hasker (citing Roderick Chisholm) described courage (2008):

> Courage is certainly a good thing, but one cannot be courageous unless there is something that one fears, and fear is something that is bad. So we can say that when a person is courageous the badness of the fear he or she experiences is *defeated* by the goodness of his or her courage. We cannot coherently say, in such a case, 'I am glad she showed courage but I wish she had the courage without the fear.' The goodness of a person's courage depends precisely on the fear he or she had to overcome; it even seems to be true that the greater the fear that is overcome, the greater and better is the courage that is shown. (p. 216)

God wants the human response to the needs of others to be both freely chosen and, thus, difficult. God doesn't want immature Christians untested by fire. God has built into every person, at birth, a self love that naturally puts self above others. Through experience, we come to know and appreciate the difference between, say, loyalty and disloyalty. At first, in our Christian walk, we might manipulate others through false loyalty to gain a personal advantage. We might, for example, say we are their friend only for the purpose of getting material benefits from them. But, over time, if we grow in Christian love—away from self love or narcissism and toward selfless love or agape—we should come to not only tell another we're their friend, but also to want to enrich their life, be there for them in times of need, to be that loyal support in their darkest, despairing moment—as God is with us.

Therefore, growth in Christian maturity requires, once again: self-conscious, sentient creatures that have a free will that enables love, courage and other morally consequential behavior; ambiguity; and doubt. We also need the structure of anxiety, which is the necessary outcome of self-conscious creatures freely choosing among ambiguous choices that are cloaked in doubt.

* * *

These outcomes of knowledge, appreciation, and morally consequential behaviors, especially the capacity for love, are necessary to achieve God's goal or good reason for creation. They potentiate relational love of God and others. However, these human attributes of learning, discernment and Christian maturity do not self-actuate. Certain necessary structures of being are needed to complete a process of lived experiences that matures into sentient beings capable of knowing, appreciating and loving God.

Following are five structures of being: their definition; argument as to how they are necessary to promote God's good reason for creation; argument for why they necessarily create evil; a discussion of whether or not they exist in reality; and their support in Scripture. One structure—free will—has already been discussed in some detail while another—ambiguity—has been briefly noted. Here, they, along with three other structures of being, are discussed in more detail.

3.3 Structures of Being Necessary to Achieve God's Plan for Creation

3.3.1 FREE WILL

If God desires a bride made up of people who genuinely love him...
he must create people who have the capacity to reject him....[because]
love must be freely chosen....no one can force another person to actually
love them....this...explains why God created a world in which evil was
possible....If love is the goal, it could not be otherwise.

Gregory A. Boyd, *Satan and the Problem of Evil*

...the world process means something to God. He is not a separated
self-sufficient entity who, driven by a whim, creates what he wants
and saves whom he wants. Rather, the eternal act of creation
is driven by a love which finds fulfillment only through the other one
who has the freedom to reject and accept love.

Paul Tillich, *Systematic Theology*

Free will is what has made evil possible.
Why, then, did God give [creatures] free will? Because free will,
though it makes evil possible, is also the only thing that makes
possible any love or goodness or joy worth having.

C. S. Lewis, *Mere Christianity*

Overview

If love is God's reason for creation, then free will is the method that enables it, and evil is the necessary cost of the method. Creaturely free will means creation is meaningful for both creatures and their Creator because love, and all other meaningful moral actions, such as courage and faith, require creatures to have free will.

If humans are not free, then what does God get out of his creation? What do humans get out of creation? If not free, why should humans try? Why pray? Why hope? Why dream? Why believe? I argue creation only makes sense if humans are free, because, only then, is love and moral action possible.

Admittedly, there are powerful arguments—in both science and religion—that humans are not free. However, there is evidence—in both science and religion—that we possess free will.

Premises

P1: Love and all other morally consequential decisions/actions must be freely chosen.
P2: Humans possess a free will.
P3: Humans, possessing a free will, have the capacity to create not only good but also evil.

Definition

By *free will*, I mean, as Boyd (2007): "Free actions are not deterministically caused by the sum total of antecedent conditions, for they are free and not determined. Neither are they uncaused, for they are free and not capricious. Rather, insofar as they are free, they are caused by the *agent* who initiates them." (p. 77)

A closely related definition is from Plantinga (1974): a person is free with respect to a given action if he "is free to perform that action and free to refrain from performing it; no antecedent conditions and/

or causal laws determine that he will perform the action, or that he won't." (p. 29) Plantinga goes on to say this definition specifically applies to decisions/actions with a significant moral dimension.

And by *will* I mean the faculty by which a person decides on and initiates action, or decides not to act despite one's natural impulse to act.

By *determinism* or deterministically caused, I mean the theories that our behavior is governed by forces—e.g., antecedent causes, causal laws, external forces such as God's will—over which we have no control. Free will is not making decisions based upon God's will, economic determinism, psychological determinism, biological determinism, or causal determinism.

Within theodicy the definition is further parsed into free will and libertarian free will. The difference between the two terms has to do with whether our free will can be seen as compatible, in some way, with God's determinism or is incompatible.

As previously discussed in Part Two, there are two general schools of thought on this question; compatibalism and incompatibalism.

Compatibalist schools of thought (e.g., Methodism, Arminianism and Molinism) argue that God's will can coexist with human's free will . Critics argue this is illogical, insisting that only one will, God's or ours, can control.

Incompatibalist schools of thought argues human free will is inconsistent with God's will. Incompatibalism theory offers two diametrically opposed solutions: God's will determines human action (e.g., Calvinism, Reformed theology) or and human will determines human action (e.g., Open theism, Process theology).

Open theism, process theology and related schools of thought are incompatibilist schools of thought of the latter variety. They believe humans have free will such that God does not control or even foreknow our future decisions. They differentiate themselves from the ordinary free will definition by referring to a "libertarian free will."

Free will theodicists like Hick, Boyd and Swinburne, are libertarian free will theodicists, but, once again, they often simply use the term "free will." Free will theodicists understand free will to mean we possess the ability to overcome our biology, with its instincts, drives and genetic predispositions, and all other deterministic forces impinging upon our behavior, even God's sovereign determinism.

For this discussion, I am assuming we possess the capacity for a libertarian free will. Sometimes, for brevity, I will simply say "free will." When and if I do, that term means libertarian free will.

This understanding is critical in moral/ethical situations which usually occur when we are challenged to act or not act for the benefit of another even though there's no benefit to self—in fact, often a cost or risk to self.

Let me elaborate. The normal biological urge of evolution, based upon evolutionary theory, is to survive either for oneself or one's species. Thus, to risk personal loss for the benefit of a stranger not of one's species is not rational. The rational, expected behavioral response under evolutionary theory is to only help oneself or one's group (e.g., tribe, species, family).

Altruism—a selfless concern for others even not of one's family/species/group—is not a rational evolutionary response. While evolutionary theory can explain altruism within a family/species/group, it cannot adequately explain altruistic behavior to outsiders. It cannot explain why, for example, the Good Samaritan stopped on the road to Damascus to help a sick Jewish person who was passed by and ignored by his own tribe of people. Yet a Samaritan, a well known adversary of Jews, stopped to help this Jew, according to Scripture. (See: Lk 10:25-37, "The Parable of the Good Samaritan".)

Jesus told the story of the Good Samaritan as an example of the duty every human owes to every other human: selfless love requires we care more about the interests of another in need than of our own self interest.

It was and is a radical call to action that runs counter to the survival imperative of evolutionary theory. German philosopher Friedrich Nietzsche (1844-1900), disagreed with Jesus's call to selflessness and to help the weak. He argued in *Thus Spoke Zarathustra* (2012) that Christ's message runs counter to what nature tells us loud and clear: that only the strong survive—the weak should and will perish; that our personal job is to survive; that our goal in life is to conquer nature and otherness so humans can become *Ubermensche* or superman.

I am, admittedly, getting a little far afield in my definition of free will, but I believe it is key to associate free will with morally consequential decisions and actions. Being free in a libertarian sense is critical for moral behavior, for Christianity, for the foundation of all laws, for almost everything consequential in terms of human behavior, and for solving the problem of evil.

Good Reason for Structure of Free Will

Benefits of the structure of free will include *enabling creatures to engage in love, courage, faith and other morally consequential actions.*

Upon the assumption that love must be freely chosen, then for humans to love they must be free in that decision, free in the libertarian sense. For God to achieve God's plan for creation, there must be sentient, self-conscious individuals who possess a libertarian free will. Otherwise, how can reciprocal love relationships be possible?

Can God, for example, receive love from a stone? Or does God need the possibility of a free creature, say a horse that can run away and possibly reject love?

If love is not freely chosen—say it's forced at the barrel of a shotgun, or, as in some cultures, your mate is chosen for you—is that love? I suggest that whatever else it is it's not love.

True, some argue God could have simply designed us to love him from the start such that we don't have to go through actual pain and suffering experiences to mature in Christian love. It would only seem like we suffered.

But if God did that, then we'd have no voice, no say, no decision in the matter because not one of us authored our personal growth in Christian maturity; it was all programmed.

Perhaps God could have implanted in our brains a memory or impression of freely choosing God through experiences of suffering. We wouldn't know any different. But God would know that we had no free choice in the matter.

If love must be freely chosen, then that applies to all parties in the relationship. And for us to love God, we have to freely choose to love God. For us to freely choose love, the choice must arise from our own concrete (real) experiences that shape and channel our Christian maturity. Programmed/determined love is not love.

What, for example, if your spouse had no choice in choosing you? How would that feel? Is that what you'd want? Would you want someone who was brainwashed into loving you? Would you want a programmed robot or mannequin with no free choice as your life partner? Or would you prefer that someone freely picked you out from thousands of possibilities they had to be their life partner?

Think of it? Think of how special that would make you feel if someone is free to pick anyone in the whole wide world to be with and they pick you. Doesn't that make it special? Doesn't that impart meaning to the act of love?

Love of another person is only consequential—that is, it has heft, value and significance—if there are other viable choices from which the lover is free to pick.

God desires our love because God's essence is love. Which means God wants our freely chosen love. And that requires that we possess a libertarian free will; otherwise, there would be no capacity for love.

Besides love, there are other acts of the will that arise from within a person that defines them and establishes their moral worth. They include, for example, morally good acts of courage, faith, and loyalty.

In fact, this is what some theodicists (e.g., Swinburne) argue is a key function of evil within the world: presenting opportunities and potential for us to flex our moral muscle and do good. Without evil possibilities, there would be no moral choice to be made. In other words, moral behavior needs something to operate against, to define it, give it heft, meaning and power. Good moral behavior needs an option of bad moral behavior against which to operate. Otherwise, how we would ever know that someone's action is morally good?

Once again, when talking of *morally good action* I am inferring there are morally bad actions. Take the situation where we can either choose to (a) promote our own self-interests over the needs of another in distress (let's say they are broke, desperate for money, and we take advantage of them by buying their car or house at a price below market value), or (b) sacrifice our own self-interest to advance the needs of another in distress (let's say that we loan them money to get through their crisis, knowing it might never get repaid). The world has to offer up bad moral choices to render good moral choices consequential.

A *courageous act* is not courageous unless there's risk of loss to one's self-interest: loss of money, loss of life; loss of reputation, etc.. There cannot be risk to oneself if your action is predetermined because there is no risk to the moral choices presented since there is no choice. But, if you are free in all your thoughts, decisions and actions or inactions then you always have a choice. Free will means you have a choice to act or not act, or to act in a certain way, and you, alone, are responsible for your actions. Thus, your free will always puts your self-interest, be it moral self-interest, economic self-interest, etc., at risk.

Perhaps you dive into a lake after a burning car has plunged into the lake. Let's say someone stole a car after a violent car-jacking incident that seriously injured the car's owner, and in speeding away the thief drives off the road and into a lake. This act of evil presents an opportunity for you to be courageous by diving into the lake and trying to extricate the person or people trapped inside. You don't have to dive into the lake. You can walk away, or wait for someone else, or simply call emergency personnel to come take care of it. And if you do dive into the lake and attempt rescue, you might drown and die, or at least be injured. You have a choice. Everyone always has a choice.

There is risk in this action. The outcome is uncertain. But you must decide. You are not only free to decide, you are forced to decide (under the premise that any and all responses are decisions). Even if you freeze, pretending the situation in front of you is not happening, and decide not to respond, that is a consequential decision of how you responded to the situation. Indecision/inaction in the face of someone's suffering is a response for which you are responsible. As Sartre would say, there is no escape from one's freedom.

Courage is the act of assuming personal risk/danger to selflessly help another. It is an exercise of moral strength in the face of danger to oneself. You could never act courageously if you were not free to choose your action. Free will enables courageous behavior. Likewise, free will potentiates faith commitments and other morally consequential actions, such as charity, kindness and forgiveness. In addition, the structure of free will impregnates life with meaning and value—not just for humans but also for God.

Likewise, the act of *faith* is a courageous commitment in love. Faith necessarily contains a germ of doubt and uncertainty because no matter how rock solid one's personal (i.e., subjective) belief, the object of that belief (e.g., God, Communist doctrine, atheism) can never be objectively proven as an objective fact. Therefore, acts of faith always carry the badge of courageous love because of our innate limits in objectively proving faith. In the words of Decartes, all we can absolutely know is that we are something thinking.

If we're not free entities, then we're just puppets dancing on a string pulled by deterministic forces operating in the world. We may have the illusion of freedom, but, like stones, we're not actually meaningful entities.

Some may argue we may not be free but can still, somehow, be meaningful to God who either controls and/or foreknows our every thought/decision/action. But why? What does God get out of that scenario? Hard determinists argue God gets to showcase His glory. But to whom? Stones? And for what?

It makes more sense that God gets something out of God's creative acts through the pleasure of our freely choosing to love God.

As Tillich's argues (1971): "the eternal act of creation is driven by a love which finds fulfillment only through the other one who has the freedom to reject and accept love." (v. 3, p. 422)

There are good reasons for God creating the structure of free will, the most import being that it enables love, morality and also renders life as meaningful—not just for us but also God.

Necessary Cost of Evil for
Structure of Free Will

Costs of the structures of free will include *morally bad actions, and negative emotions such as anxiety and doubt* that are felt as evil.

Since, under this theory, God doesn't determine human behavior, and since humans possess the power to behave other than God would desire they behave (both premises), then (as Plantinga argues) humans possess the *power to misbehave*. Thus, the gift of *human free will creates the possibility of evil*. Evil is the price of freedom, it is the risk, to God, that, like Augustine's runaway horse, we might reject God's love.

Free will also necessarily creates *contingency* (that is, future outcomes cannot be predicted because they are predicated upon unknown variables such as the free will choices of other people, thus they are subject to chance). But if God, or some other deterministic force, determines our behavior then our outcomes in life are not contingent; they are predictable and necessary and cannot be otherwise.

Being freely able to choose this action or that action, humans render future events contingent. For example, tomorrow I may wake up, dress and drive to work without incident. However, it could also be that another person may be texting while driving and runs a red light, crashing into and killing me. My death in the latter situation was a contingent outcome, one that didn't have to happen, as it all depended at the time upon how all the dynamic variables in play unfold?

If the future is open (indeterminate, subject to contingencies), and not closed (determined and necessary), then *bad things can happen* without apparent reason or by mere chance, even with nature. This creates anxiety, doubt and fear—some might say, the disquieting sense of being out of control, or at least in a chaotic world devoid of control.

For example, the path of a tornado may veer and hit my house and not my neighbors for no reason other than the vagaries of temperature, wind, and other dynamic weather variables. A micro burst downdraft from a sudden weather pattern that suddenly materializes over the runway just as a large passenger jet is near touchdown, might create a tragedy so unpredictable that many would say it's a "act of God" (i.e., no human is to blame).

Even though natural phenomena like weather reacts to physical laws and processes, they are often unpredictable and sudden. Nature's unfolding, although fairly predictable, often interacts tragically with the free actions of humans (say, in a person's attempt to outrun a tornado in one direction rather than another), presenting itself as yet one more contingent variable in a seemingly open process of life.

Such a contingent future is one of the negative effects of living in sin. We are estranged from God, cast into an open and free future, destined to learn and grow and come to appreciate and love God through the ambiguous experience of positive and negative outcomes.

Our free will creates evil in several ways, one being our power to do evil, another is the unknowability of a contingent (open and free) future which creates anxiety, fear, doubt and other negative emotions that, in themselves, are often felt as evil.

Discussion

The critical question remains, are we free in the libertarian sense?

Arrayed against this thesis that we possess a libertarian free will are many arguments and worldviews. Most of them can be loosely organized under the term *determinism.*

Theories of determinism occur in worldviews of both science and religious faith. Many (most?) of them deny humans possess a libertarian free will, arguing that personal behavior is determined by factors external to and beyond the control of our will (e.g., God's will, antecedent causal inputs, or some grand sweep of destiny). Determinists deny that a person's will can be an originator of a causal input. They deny a person the capacity to overcome their fate through personal agency.

Free will, on the contrary, means no one's fate is determined against their will. It means we can change, overcome our genes, our learning, our experiences, our imprinting, our instinctual brain patterns.

If a person has the capacity to overcome their fate through using their will so as to be the originator of a causal input, then the future is open, undetermined. It is contingent upon many unknown facts, specifically including the future decisions and actions of free creatures.

If, for example, I'm free to decide tomorrow to fly an airplane into a building, that will change the future in many unknown ways. Just look how the 2001 World Trade Center disaster changed the United States, even the whole world.

Were those 2001 World Trade Center actions determined? If so, how and by what forces: theological (e.g., God or other supernatural forces) or secular (e.g., Marxism, Hegelianism, causation theory)?

* * *

In terms of religious faith worldviews, we've previously talked of determinism, compatibilism and incompatibilistic freedom, but will briefly review them again.

An excellent discussion of *theistic determinism* (God determines our behavior) can be found in the religious doctrine of *predestination*, which American professor of religious studies, Peter J. Thuesen has thoroughly discussed in his book *Predestination (2009)*. Briefly, the-istic determinism stands for the proposition that God, being sovereign, both knows and controls everything including future human actions. In other words, God *foreordains all things for his purpose*.

As discussed in Part Two, a Christian worldview that holds to this view in its most expansive understanding— hard or strong determin-ism—is Calvinism or Reformed Theology which believes God controls all future events. By logical inference, this means human behavior is wholly determined by external factors (here, God's will) such that we are not free in the libertarian sense. Hard determinists argue human free will is incompatible with God's sovereign will, that God's sovereign will controls, and humans do not possess a freely determining will.

Standing as sort of middle ground or compromise between deter-minism and incompatibilisit freedom is compatibalism, also sometimes called soft determinism.

In theological terms, soft determinism or compatibilism means that while God foreknows our future actions, God doesn't control them. This view argues determinism and incompatibility freedom are compatible and can be understood to coexist.

One view is that God doesn't control human behavior; however, God foreknows future human behavior. It is believed that this, somehow, allows human free will. True, as previously indicated, there are sophisticated arguments (e.g., Molinism) which argue that while God knows every possible future human action of ours, and tries to arrange contingent events to maximize the chance we'll make morally good decisions, nonetheless the final decision is ours.

Soft determinism thinking is an attempt to avoid the logical paradox of how human free will can coexist with God's will, plus exculpate God from responsibility for evil. However, as argued, free will theists argue compatibilism is incoherent insofar as it suggests we can defy God's wishes and foreknowledge.

Incompatibilist free will (e.g., open theism, process theology) believes human freedom is incompatible with any form of determinism—God's will or secular factors. Open theism believes that although God is omnipotent, nonetheless, out of love, and for love, God forsook the ability of predetermining human actions of a moral nature such that we possess a libertarian free will. At least for moral matters, each of us possess a determining will that is independent of God's preordaining will.

Open theism (or openness theology) and process theology are examples of belief systems that embrace libertarian free will. Since the concept of libertarian free will seems incompatible with God's omnipotence, they solve that problem by arguing the definition of omnipotence is but a human value judgement. They argue that a God who willingly forgoes some power (here omniscience), out of love, for love, is *than that which nothing greater can be thought.*

Lewis said this possibility—that we might freely reject God—was a miracle (2001).

Finally, it is objected that the ultimate loss of a single soul means the defeat of omnipotence. And so it does. In creating beings with free will, omnipotence from the outset submits to the possibility of...defeat. What you call defeat, I call miracle: for to make things which are not Itself and thus to become, in a sense, capable of being resisted by its own handiwork, is the most astonishing and unimaginable of all the feats we attribute to the Deity. (p. 129, 130)

Question: Which God do you think is greater: a God who creates the possibility of love through foregoing a power; or a God who doesn't potentiate love because that would diminish some divine power? This is the value judgement a person must make.

* * *

Turning now to *non-theistic worldviews of science, philosophy and secular thought,* we find many theories, but not all, advocating determinism and denying/doubting libertarian free will for humans. They include:

1. theory of causation;
2. biology (genetics, evolutionary behavior, and sociobiology);
3. physics and mathematics;
4. historical determinism (Hegelian dialectic, Marx's dialectic materialism);
5. depth psychology and the unconscious driver (Freud)
6. modern neuroscience;

Theories of determinism seem to predominate in the many academic domains while compatibilistic theories remain popular. From my readings, it seems the minority position within the worlds of science, philosophy and secular thought is that humans possess a libertarian free will.

The deterministic theories seem to defy common sense notions of free will. I say *common sense* because I assume that most people feel, like me, that they do exercise some power over their thoughts and actions. If they thought otherwise, they probably could not believe in punishments and rewards, such as punishing criminals for their illegal behavior, or rewarding people for hard work and/or ethical behavior.

Scientists often deconstruct common sense notions by their reductionist method of reducing every phenomenon to its smallest, most basic constituent part. For example, with personal behavior, neuroscientist break down brain activity to neurons of which our brain has approximately 100 billion. Their theories of determinism are logically powerful and need discussion. Below are brief discussions of six non-theistic views. I say *brief* because any one of these factors are by themselves the subject of many books.

* * *

The *theory of causation, or cause and effect or causality* is the theory that every effect has a prior cause, and that prior cause likewise had a prior cause, etc., ad infinitum.

Advocates of causality argue that if, for example, they knew every antecedent causal input in your life (genetic and environmental) they could predict to 100% accuracy whether, given the choice, you'd choose vanilla or strawberry ice cream. They've never proved this. Of course, their argument being that they can never get enough data.

One implication of causation theory is that we're nothing but a robot or computer responding to a program of causal inputs over which we have no control. Any notion that we are exerting a free will over our behavior is an illusion. We are not personally responsible for our behavior, at least not personally responsible in the traditional sense that each of us is responsible for the behavior at issue through having our free will initiate the cause. This, in turn, logically means criminals should be let free, sinners should not feel guilty or be blamed, anymore than we should hold computers and machines morally and legally responsible for their actions and malfunctions. It also means no one should be praised for bravery nor rewarded for sacrificial good deeds, loyalty or faith.

Machines are programmed to behave a certain way. If they hurt someone by malfunctioning—say, a car's brakes fail, or a hot water heater explodes—are they morally responsible? Since they didn't design themselves, and can only perform as programmed, how can they be culpable for their performance?

One criticism of causality thinking is that it renders humans as nothing more than preprogrammed machines that are not responsible for their behavior. This would seem to insult our common sense, since all of us have witnessed people being the authors of their fate, or so it seems. Also, social control could unravel if our systems of rewards and punishments (such as with our criminal laws and incarceration of dangerous people) were held to be unfair and meaningless given that none of us deserve rewards and/or punishment for behaviors over which we have no control.

Another problem for causation theory—a metaphysical one—is where and how did this chain of causality begin? If everything is caused, then there couldn't be a first uncaused cause: causality has to be infinite.

An amusing anecdote on this very issue is one told about a talk on the cosmos given by Bertrand Russell (some say William James) dealing with gravity and the revolution of the planets around the sun. During the talk, an elderly woman in the audience interjected to say it's all nonsense, that everyone knows the the earth stands upon the back of an elephant who, in turn, stands upon a huge turtle. Russell then asks what the turtle stands on. She replies that it stands upon yet another, bigger turtle. Russell then starts to ask another question when she replies, something to the effect of: "It's no use going on and on. It's simply turtles all the way down."

And that's the answer to the problem of the *first cause* as presented by the theory of causation: it's simply turtles all the way down.

Christians speak of an original uncaused God as the *first cause*, a God outside of, or at least not bound by, space and time, matter and energy, and the laws of physics. God, not being a thing among things but, rather, the originator of all things, is not bound by laws of physics or the limits of human reason. God is uncaused, the original cause, the original fact, creator of all effects.

Over and against this argument, the voice of unbelief typically asks "But who caused God?" Cause and effect advocates can't conceive of an uncaused cause, while people of belief can't conceive of an infinite regress of causes without a beginning. Each finds the others' possibility absurd.

However, neither side can prove their argument or disprove the other. Questions such as: Why is there something rather than nothing? Who caused the world? are metaphysical questions beyond the reach of scientific methodology. We're all left with our personal knowledge and power of reason. Is the answer God (the uncaused cause or Prime Mover), or is it *turtles all the way down*?

The important point to be made with this *theory of causality* is that worldviews of unbelief, like worldviews of belief, are *faith-based*. Both rely upon unprovable predicate assumptions. Therefore, worldviews of belief, like secular worldviews of science are, at their core, faith-based or metaphysical in nature.

Becker understood this. In *The Denial of Death*. (1997) he argues:

> In the mysterious way in which life is given to us in evolution on this planet, it pushes in the direction of its own expansion. We don't understand it simply because we don't know the purpose of creation....There is a driving force behind a mystery that we cannot understand, and it includes more than reason alone. The urge to cosmic heroism, then, is sacred and mysterious and not to be neatly ordered and rationalized by science and secularism. Science, after all, is a credo that has attempted to absorb into itself and to deny the fear of life and death; and it is only one more competitor in the spectrum of roles for cosmic heroics.
>
> ...We can conclude that a project as grand as the scientific-mythical construction of victory over human limitations is not something that can be programmed by science. (p. 284, 285)

Advocates of free will argue that just because all outcomes might be *caused* does not necessarily negate human free will. In his theodicy, Boyd (2001) argues our free decisions are not uncaused but are caused, but not necessarily by forces external to our will. He argues:

> Free actions are not deterministically caused by the sum total of antecedent conditions, for they are free and not determined. Neither are they uncaused, for they are free and not capricious. Rather, insofar as they are free, they are caused by the agent who initiates them. The agent (together with all attending conditions) could be the sufficient reason for either B or -B, and, if the choice between B and -B is truly free, the agent alone ultimately decides the matter. (p. 77)

Boyd also argues that the agent (each one of us) is the "volitional center of causation, an originating agent, an enduring, creative 'I' who can deliberate between options and choose one of them, setting in motion a chain of causality *that it is not itself an effect of.*" (p. 77) Thus our free will is caused. It is caused by our internal will.

Boyd buttresses his argument by pointing both to quantum mechanics and to God. As concerns God, Boyd argues that God's decision to create the world was neither capricious (but, rather, something God wanted to do) nor determined by forces external to God's will. God was not forced to create the world by causal impingements external to God. In other words, God's decision to create the world was born of God's sheer grace, with this decision being a self-determining (i.e., free) act. God, therefore, is the uncaused cause of the world—the original cause.

Boyd then argues that if this traditional Christian theory of God's self-determining free will in creating the world can be understood coherently, then why can't human free will? "Indeed, if humans lack a logically consistent concept of self-determining freedom, what provides the analogical ground by which we can talk about God's gracious self-determining freedom? A concept devoid of all experiential content is vacuous....In short, unless we were free in a self-determining sense, we could never meaningfully say that God is [also free in a self-determining sense]." (p. 70)

I agree with Boyd. Each of us can be the original cause of an effect that would not have occurred but for our free action. Quoting Richard Taylor, Boyd concludes that "some...causal chains...have beginnings, and they begin with the agents themselves." (p. 77)

* * *

Another domain of thought that weighs in on this issue of free will is *biology*, within which I include related domains (e.g., *genetics, evolutionary behavior and/or sociobiology*). They all seem to point to our notion of free will as being illusory.

Evolutionary theory and sociobiology teaches that all behaviors are understandable as outcomes forged within the brutal, bloody maw of survival—of chance and necessity.

Writing in *Harper's* magazine (2014), naturalist/evolutionary biologist/sociobiologist, Edward O. Wilson (1929-2021), argued that free will is a "very fortunate Darwinian" illusion:

> ...the self—celebrated star player in the scenarios of consciousness—can go on passionately believing in its independence and free will. And this is a very fortunate Darwinian circumstance. Confidence in free will is biologically adaptive. Without it, the conscious mind, at best a fragile, dark window on the real world, would be cursed by fatalism. Like a prisoner serving a life sentence in solitary confinement, deprived of any freedom to explore and starving for surprise, it would deteriorate.

> So, does free will exist? Yes, if not in ultimate reality, then at least in the operational sense necessary for sanity and thereby for the perpetuation of the human species. (p. 52)

Wilson's argument is based upon the premise that all behavior is adapted for survival. If a behavior exists, it probably exists because it had features or attributes that advanced chances at survival. Since no animal intentionally chooses adaptive features—rather they are simply selected for having certain features that, for the moment at least, advance survival—free will doesn't seem to have much room to exist. We are selected. We don't select.

And yet, I argue that modern humans have changed the evolutionary paradigm. Our brains have developed to such an extent that we possess self consciousness. We can contemplate desired future behavioral changes (say, to stand up and oppose bullying) and work to burn new neural pathways into our brain's neural structure such as to change our behavior.

Today, we can even change our biologically determined sex and are close to altering the genetic make-up of babies. Soon it is predicted that the combination of artificial intelligence with robotics will create human replicants. These changes were not *selected* by chance or necessity. They are the intentional outcomes of human desires.

Questions: Is evolution still at work in that all of these emergent changes were determined? Or, is the dynamic, contingent, creative effects of free will at work? The debate rages and turns upon concepts of deterministic necessity and chance (evolution) and human free will.

The argument from *genetics* is that we are largely, if not totally, defined by the genetic coding carried in our DNA. From many perspectives, this is understandable. Traditionally, if I was born, say, a woman with an IQ of 89 and unable to hear, that would compel many outcomes over which I have no free will. Admittedly, modern technology and medicine are challenging all of these genetic outcomes such that we can freely choose to change our gender or have hearing implants, but, for many people their choices are limited by genetic inheritance such that our will cannot overcome the limits.

But if we understand genetics as historical experiential data passed down to us from our ancestors, to aid us with our own experiences, and we understand that the experiential data arose from their experiences, then DNA is dynamic, an ever evolving mechanism molded from experiences. This suggests DNA changes, that our own experiences alter the code. If we can be a causal input, then we can exert an influence (change?) to our DNA. That is what I argue: we can override natural urges and instincts that arise from DNA through our will.

I concede that much of who we are is biological in nature, specifically our DNA carrying genetics. We are largely products of billions of historical experiences gifted to us at birth by genes. Also, I agree some of our behavior is subconscious and/or preconscious, that is, we instinctually react before we consciously realize we have chosen to react.

But, despite DNA, experiential conditioning and preconscious action, the fact is that, at a minimum, we can reflect upon our actions after we've acted. In that reflection we can commit to change our reaction in the future. Our commitment to change can rework our neural network as research also shows our brains are malleable, displaying surprising plasticity.

There is an unattributed saying wrongfully attributed to Lao Tzu's (Laozi) (601 BC-531 BC) that I repeat here because I think it accurately expresses the path toward becoming the author of your values. It also suggests how one's will can, by dedicated forward planning, be a causal factor in changing behavior: "Watch your thoughts, they become your words; watch your words, they become your actions; watch your actions, they become your habits; watch your habits, they become your character; watch your character, it becomes your destiny."

Let me give an example from my life of how this wise saying works. When in high school, I saw a person bullied and beat up and I did nothing, just stood there. Whether that was a preconscious reaction, a programmed or determined reaction, I could not tell.

What I can say is that my behavior made me later feel shame. It was not right. I could have intervened, stood up for the weaker person. I had an empathetic connection with the victim, based upon my own experiences, and realized how much I would have appreciated someone's intervention if I had been bullied.

My shame worked on me. I dedicated myself to a mental thought exercise where I reimagined the bullying episode, only in this exercise I moved to intervene on behalf of the victim of bullying. I went over the scenario again and again much like a golfer imagines his swing and the flight of the golf ball right before actually executing the shot. Experts say this helps form a positive mental image and maximizes the chance of perfect execution.

When a similar situation happened many years later, I did react to help the victim, although not as forcefully as in my thought experiments. I was still concerned by the risk in getting involved, realizing that I could get hit, injured or worse. But I at least did some action, yelling at the other to quit, and moving forward as if willing to engage.

Later, upon reflection, I was both pleased I had done better but still a little ashamed I had not done more. So I kept on working on this scenario. Today, I can say there have been occasions that presented risk to me when helping another and I've risen to the occasion much better than in the past.

Are these new reactions merely preconscious reactions? Were they determined by prior causal inputs (e.g., my religious training)? I don't think so. I believe I'm the one who burned the particular response pattern into my neural network.

This may be a small window to crawl through, but it is a real window—of moral action through free will.

I am not a stone. Although I may largely be a puppet on strings pulled by external forces, including my own genetics, I believe free will is there for the grasping, of actually creating and owning your life's moral decisions and actions, of forging new neural pathways.

* * *

In the world of *physics and mathematics*, we also find two possibilities: determinism and indeterminism. Determinism spins around the laws of physics and our ability to predict physical outcomes to a very high degree of probability based upon observation and testing. It carries the mantel of reliability such that great confidence is placed upon it by humans who want to understand existence in a reliable, reassuring fashion.

However, within physics and mathematics, there has arisen over time evidence of inherent uncertainty and fundamental limitations that suggest indeterminism, which undermines the theories of causality. At the micro subatomic level of reality—*quantum physics* or mechanics—we continue humanity's long search to find an indivisible base unit of reality from which all other substances arise. Historically, it was first thought to be the molecule, then the atom, then the parts of the atom—the nucleus of protons and neutrons, together with electrons spinning around the nucleus like the earth around the sun, and then the "purely theoretical" subatomic electronic charges that go by names such as quarks and charms that constitute the most fundamental parts (at least as far as we currently know) of the atom.

When we view the world at this smallest, subatomic level, we find these purely theoretical subatomic particles seemingly blinking in and out of reality. They seem to defy the conventional laws of physics. Their entry and departure points seem random and cannot be precisely predicted. There is an inherent uncertainty about them which German physicist Werner Heisenberg (1901-1976) labeled the "uncertainty principle." Even more complicating is the fact that the positioning of subatomic particles is skewed by our observation of them.

Thus, at the micro level of reality much seems relatively determined and yet ultimately random or indeterminate. We can argue this quantum reality allows some wiggle room for human free will to enter into physical reality, if, that is, human free will needs a physical entry point other than the human will. Maybe it doesn't. But if it does, the indeterminate weirdness of subatomic reality seems to offer such a portal.

As concerns the subatomic world of quantum mechanics, Boyd (2001) notes that scientists can only gauge the range of possible behaviors of a quantum particle, given a "certain set of causal conditions" to a fairly predictable, but not "exhaustively predictable" level of detail. In other words:

> Unless one wishes to maintain that quantum physicists perpetually talk nonsense, this observation must be taken as demonstrating that an intelligible understanding of the relationship between cause and effect [at the quantum level] need not include a deterministic understanding of cause and effect. It also demonstrates that a behavior need not be futuristically predictable to be retroactively intelligible. At a quantum level it simply is not the case that an exhaustive knowledge of the causal conditions would produce the ability to predict the future perfectly. Causal conditions render their particular effects *intelligible* but not *necessary*. (p. 71-72)

It would seem, with this understanding, scientists could never prove which ice cream we'd choose to eat—strawberry or vanilla—even if they knew all previous causal inputs, but, rather, only estimate the probability. In other words, given the reality of quantum mechanics, the indeterminism of behavioral outcomes that free will creates seems possible.

There is one other phenomenon in physics that has serious implications for not only human free will but also ambiguity and self-consciousness, two other structures of being to be discussed later. That phenomenon is known as *quantum entanglement* which has been described as "spooky action at a distance" by George Musser (2015).

With quantum entanglement, if one particle, say a photon, is separated into two particles and then sent off into different directions, their actions (such as spinning up or spinning down) will always mirror each other perfectly, thus apparently *entangled* in some way. Since experiments have repeatedly shown that this mirror-image entanglement occurs instantaneously between these two photons no matter how far apart they become separated, even to far parts of our solar system, the obvious question is How can this happen? It all seems so...so *spooky*.

The argument is that the separated parts seem to be affecting each instantaneously, no matter how far apart. At great distances, this phenomenon appears to exceed the speed of light, a supposed impossibility.

The implication, for physics (and human consciousness and free will) is that science's traditional reductionist method of examining discrete physical entities (that is, reducing each entity down to its smallest constituent part—say, a single neuron for brain function) simple can't account for this phenomenon. Yet the two particles are obviously interrelated (or entangled) through some sort of mechanism/s unknown to science.

One emergent understanding of this phenomenon is that "reality is not made up of discrete objects. It is a variable flux" whereby every physical systems is "always a description of the information a system has about another system."

This new understanding and the above quotes are attributed to quantum physicist Carlo Rovelli's. In his book *Reality is Not What it Seems* (2016), he argues:

> In fact, the entire structure of quantum mechanics can be read and understood in terms of information, as follows: A physical system manifests itself only in interacting with another. The description of a physical system, then, is always given in relation to another physical system, the one with which it interacts. Any description of a system is therefore always a description of the *information* a system has about another system, that is to say, the *correlation* between two systems.... (p. 245, 246)

> What we know is something concerning the relationship between the system and ourselves. Knowledge is intrinsically relational; it depends just as much on its object as upon its subject. The notion of the "state of a system" refers, explicitly or implicitly, to another system....(p. 253)

Rovelli concludes that "in order to understand reality, we have to keep in mind that reality is this network of relations, of reciprocal information, that weaves the world. We slice up the reality surrounding us into 'objects.' But reality is not made up of discrete objects. It is a variable flux." (p. 254)

Known as "integrated information theory," Rovelli's thoughts are currently the "hottest theory" in consciousness studies. Interestingly, Rovelli recently said that his conceptual breakthrough to understand the strangeness of quantum mechanics came from reading a 2,000 year old work from an ancient Buddhist philosopher, Nagarjuna.

Rovelli (2023) said Nagarjuna argued that "the only way to understand something is though its relation with something else—nothing by itself has an independent reality....every thing taken, taken by itself, is 'empty,' including emptiness itself."

Quantum entanglement and its implications have profound implications not only for the structure of consciousness but also of human free will (to be further discussed under the topic of neuroscience) and ambiguity.

* * *

Looking to *mathematics*, the main methodological tool of physics, we find Austrian logician and mathematician Kurt Godel's (1906-1978) famous "incompleteness theorem" he presented in 1931 at age 25. Godel (2008) argued that for any sufficiently precise (i.e., formal) system of axioms and rules of procedure that contained sufficient arithmetical propositions, "are neither provable nor disprovable by the means allowed within the system. The truth of such statements is thus 'undecidable' by the approved procedures." (p. 370) Godel's argument appears to prove mathematically that there are inherent limits—unknowns—to mathematical logic.

This shocked the scientific community of materialism which believed there were no unknowns or unknowables in the physical world, especially in mathematics, and was met with criticism.

Godel's argument is provided not necessarily to prove determinism or indeterminism but, rather, to show that even with our most objective scientific tool—mathematics—there are limits to human knowledge. Perhaps the cold, brute physical world doesn't care about our reason, our intellect, our math? At least that's what one prominent scientist suggests.

Writing in *The Oxford Book of Modern Science Writing (2008)*, American theoretical physicist, Lee Smolin waxed enthusiastically about the beauty of physics and math before conceding that science is also faith based:

> This mysticism of the mathematical, the belief that at its deepest level reality may be captured by an equation or a geometrical construction, is the private religion of the theoretical physicist. Like other true mysticisms, it is something that cannot be communicated in words, but must be experienced....
>
> One feels at these moments [comprehending a mathematical truth] a sense of joy and also—it must be said—of power to have comprehended simultaneously a logical structure, constructed by the imagination, and an aspect of reality. (p. 364, 365)
>
> Of course, what is both wonderful and terrifying is that there is absolutely no reason that nature at its deepest level must have anything to do with mathematics. Like mathematics itself, the faith in this shared mysticism of the mathematical scientist is an invention of the human being....The possibility that the tremendous beauty of the living world might be, in the end, just a matter of randomness, statistics and frozen accident stands as a genuine threat to the mystical conceit that reality can be captured in a single, beautiful equation. This is why it took me years to become comfortable with the possibility that the explanation for at least part of the laws of physics might be found in the same logic of randomness and frozen accident. (p. 366)

"Randomness" and "frozen accident" suggest an admission that reality—at least as grasped by the human mind—is beyond determinism.

* * *

In terms of *historical determinism,* there are various theories that suggest certain forces are at work in the world that deterministically drive the world and/or human behavior in a predictable fashion.

One such theory is the *Hegelian dialectic*, advanced by German philosopher Georg Wilhelm Friedrich Hegel (1770-1831) of a dynamic, ever-evolving three stage dialectic. Hegel argues everything begins with a thesis, then generates its own antithesis, which, in turn, evolves into a synthesis. This synthesis becomes a new thesis, which generates an antithesis, and so on.

According to Hegel we are always cycling upwards toward an ultimate perfect synthesis. It is the necessary cycle of human behavior, a dialectic, an arrow shooting upwards, going somewhere, suggesting we are always progressing.

Kierkegaard disagreed with Hegel and thought we were not progressing upwards toward perfection, and by "we" Kierkegaard was referring to individuals and not society. Society may be changing over time, but individuals come and go, each destined to repeat the innate process of being compelled to freely respond to life based upon their subjective experiences within an ambiguous world filled with doubt and anxiety.

Here's how Scots-Irish writer and academic Paul Strathern described Kierkegaard's view of human progress in Kierkegaard *in 90 Minutes* (1997):

> We know more and more about the world, in almost every field (except perhaps philosophy). But on the level of individual experience—in the way Kierkegaard spoke about it—we remain the same. Where subjective being is concerned, there appears to be no such thing as progress. We all suffer (or enjoy) the same situation: the human condition. And have done so since time immemorial. (p. 12)

Are we cycling ever upward to a more perfect society? If so, in what way? Or are we, as Kierkegaard suggests, repeating successive waves of individual experience, always in the same way as we have since humans could first reason from conscious thought? In this way, one person grows through subjective experiences, then dies, replaced by another to repeat the process of experiencing ambiguous life subjectively.

Another historical deterministic worldview involves Friedrich Engles and Karl Marx's *dialectical materialism* (a theory which, put into practice, is communism) which argues history will inevitable cycle into economic perfection (classless equality) by the sheer driving force of people demanding economic, materialistic equality. Marx (1818-1883) and Engles (1820-1895) argued that dialectical materialism is a reality independent of the human mind. Their theory owes much to Hegel's thinking, as both project a world process toward perfection.

Since Engle and Marx's revolutionary thoughts, the world has experienced many attempts at implementation of his utopian vision of economic equality. These include the Russian revolution, the Chinese revolution, the Khmer Rouge's attempts in Cambodia at creating a proliteriat paradise, and similar state experiments with communism (e.g., Cuba and various countries in South America).

Whatever else one thinks of the results of those communist revolutions, one thing is certain: utopia has never been achieved and has caused great misery in its forced implementation. History seems to show that many, if not most, communist experiments involved great misery and bloodshed. During the Khmer Rouge's forced agrarian reforms, it is estimated that over two million Cambodians were killed. It is estimated that over 65 million people died during Mao's communist revolution in China, plus untold millions were imprisoned or forcibly "reeducated." Stalin is reputed to have killed over 20 million people in his repressive rule over communist the Soviet Union. All told, some estimates put the death from forced implementation of communism at around one hundred million.

At most, dialectic materialism identifies an urge of many people, but not everyone. At worst, the implementation of this theory in the form of communism seems to require forced indoctrination and behavior, with little if any tolerance for free thought and disagreement. This urge for economic equality among many people has not been shown to determine future behavior (although the communist revolutionary spirit still seems to be at work in the world)—of nations or individuals. It seems to be just one more force, among many, impinging upon human behavior and the social order.

* * *

In the world of *depth psychology and the unconscious driver,* the father of psychoanalysis, Sigmund Freud (1856-1939), upset many believers in free will with his theory that all human behavior is driven by *unconscious processes* generating urges that can only be understood and possibly overcome by lengthy analysis. The negative implications for free will theorists is obvious and troubling by suggesting we each possess deterministic forces deep within our unconscious minds but beyond the reach of our conscious will.

However, Freud recommended psychotherapy under the assumption a person can change, can overcome their unconscious urges. The very use and recommendation of psychotherapy suggests our behavior is not necessarily determined. It suggests that through hard work and painful introspection, we can forge another future. Is this free will or merely redesigning a new determinism?

While some (many if not most?) psychologists don't believe humans possess a libertarian free will, there are at least two general theories within psychology suggesting the possibility of free will. These theories, not surprisingly, fall into the one of the two previously discussed camps: incompatible free will and compatibilism.

The incompatible free will camp believes freedom is both possible and necessary for human growth and self-actualization. (see: Maslow (1943), Rogers (1951) and Fromm (1941))

The other view seems to reflect a view akin to soft determinism or compatibalism. That is, the view that it is irrelevant whether or not free will is an illusion. The argument is that if we think we are free, and we act like we are free, then that has the exact same quality as being free: e.g., we are more responsible and try harder, upon the assumption effort matters.

In terms of depth psychology, this might be sufficient. That is, it is enough that we sense we are free and act accordingly. Of course, driving the discussion within depth psychology is understanding and agreeing on exactly what free will means.

A good example of compatibilist thinking is expressed by Daniel Dennett, a philosopher and not a psychologist, but his compatibilist viewpoint seems reflective of psychologists. Dennett doesn't believe in incompatible free will. He believes our behavior is determined. But he doesn't consider himself a determinist.

He argues the solution is in understanding what we mean by free will. Dennett argues that as a practical matter, humans behave as if they have free will, and fully believe in rewards and punishments in terms of behavior. The assumption is so strong that, for all intents and purposes, Dennett argues we are authors of and responsible for our behavior. (One might call Dennett's understanding/definition of free will as practical free will.)

Dennett disagrees with both determinism and the indeterminism suggested by incompatibilist free will. As concerns his argument against incompatibilism, he says (2014):

> Incompatibilists [free will] thus tend to pin their hopes on indeterminism, and hence were much cheered by the emergence of quantum indeterminism in 20th century physics. Perhaps the brain can avail itself of undetermined quantum swerves at the sub-atomic level, and thus escape the shackles of physical law! Or perhaps there is some other way our choices could be truly undetermined. Some have gone so far as to posit an otherwise unknown (and almost entirely unanalyzable phenomenon called agent causation, in which free choices are caused somehow by an agent, but not by any event in the agent's history.

As concerns determinism theories, Dennett argues:

> All of this [Sam Harris's argument for determinism] is laudable and right, and vividly presented, and Harris does a particularly good job getting readers to introspect on their own decision-making and notice that it just does not conform to the fantasies of this all too traditional understanding of how we think and act. But some of us have long recognized these points and gone on to adopt more reasonable, more empirically sound, models of decision and thought, and we think we can articulate and defend a more sophisticated model of free will that is not only consistent with neuroscience and introspection but also grounds a (modified, toned-down, non-Absolute) variety of responsibility that justifies both praise and blame, reward and punishment. We don't think this variety of free will is

an illusion at all, but rather a robust feature of our psychology and a reliable part of the foundations of morality, law and society. Harris, we think, is throwing out the baby with the bathwater.

Here, it seems the theories spin around a person's definition of free will. Plus, being a philosophical question that science is trying to remove from theory to fact, the question remains: is our ability to be freely self-determined in the libertarian sense unprovable? Will it remain a philosophical mystery?

* * *

For *neuroscientists,* all behavior (overt action, planning and other cognitive, mental processes) lies within physical brain stuff, because, *the whole function of the brain is to drive behavior.*

It would appear neuroscience does not agree with Descartes' notion of "dualism"—that mind and brain are two separate things, one ethereal and untethered to the physical body, the other a physical thing: brain matter. Nor do they believe in a soul or spirit or other immaterial substance not tethered to the physical brain, or any part of the body. Rather, they believe that free will, even assuming it exists, is considered by much of modern neuroscience to emanate totally from the neural workings of our physical brain.

Behavior, being brain stuff, means neuroscientists have looked to the brain to find the agent of free will, if any. With the advent and use of Magnetic Resonance Imaging (MRI) and other investigative brain technologies such as electroencephalogram (EMG) and Computer of Average Transcients (CAT), neuroscience at first argued there is no such thing as free will. Today, they are not as sure, saying the argument against free will has possibly been challenged.

The anti-free will theory is that the brain is a physical system, just like our heart, and we no more will our brain to think than will our heart to beat. This prong largely relies on the original work of Benjamin Libet from the1980's, plus follow up experiments, showing that there's electric activity in the brain *before* we act.

Libet showed that this build up of electrical activity occurs before the person consciously makes a decision to act (but only by a matter of

500 milliseconds). This suggests our conscious experience of deciding to act is an illusion, an *add-on, a post hoc reconstruction of events* that occurs after the brain has already set the act in motion.

Later there was additional research into the timing between thought and action which suggested thought actually occurs simultaneously to action and not before as Libet argued. The difference between the two views (free will or unconscious determinism) was merely a matter of milliseconds, with the difference turning on the accuracies of measurement.

Today, neuroscience seems divided on the issue. Some (most?) argue we react unconsciously before we consciously decided to act, while others disagree.

Representing the lack of free will school of thought is a recent book by biologist and neuroscientist, Robert Sapolsky, *Determined: a Science of Life Without Free Will (2023)*. In the book Sapolsky argues vehemently that the world is deterministic and that "There's no free will, and thus holding people morally responsible for their actions is wrong," (p. 11)

He admits he's a hard determinist who disagrees with compatibalists—"roughly 90% of philosophers and legal scholars"—that believe that while human behavior is, in fact, determined, we still have free will. Of course, he also disagrees with those who advocate that humans possess a libertarian free will.

Definitions, as always, matter and here, Sapolsky defines free will as finding a neuron in the brain that started a chain of mental activity leading to action that itself was not the product of or determined by the past. He posed the challenge to the free willer as follows:

> Find me the neuron that started this process in this man's brain, the neuron that had an action potential for no reason, where no neuron spoke to it just before. Then show me that this neuron's actions were not influenced by whether the man was tired, hungry, stressed, or in pain at the time. That nothing about this neuron's function was altered by the sights, sounds, smells, and so on, experienced by the man in the previous minutes, nor by the levels of any hormones marinating his brain in the previous hours to days, nor whether

he had a life-changing event in recent months or years. And show me that this neuron's...wasn't affected by the man's genes, or by the lifelong changes in regulation of those genes caused by experience during his childhood. Nor by levels of hormones he was exposed to as a fetus, when that brain was being constructed. Nor by the centuries of history and ecology that shaped the invention of the culture in which he was raised. Show me a neuron being a causeless cause in this total sense. (p. 14, 15)

The author then spends much of the book arguing that studies show there is no such causeless neuron. He thus concludes we "need to accept the absurdity of hating any person for anything they've done" even criminals for they are not responsible agents for their behavior in the legal/moral sense that they could have acted other than the action dictated by their biology and causal inputs. (p. 403)

Sapolsky's urging that we change our behavior to be more understanding of criminal behavior is based upon the theory that we can see a wrong (say blaming criminals when they're not culpable for their behavior) and influence others to change, like Sapolsky is doing to his readers. Probably unwittingly, Sapolsky is advancing Boyd's thesis that we can be our own change agent.

Dennett (2014) noted this same argument in Sam Harris's book on free will—that each of us can be an influencer, or causal agent, to change others but can't, evidently, influence ourselves—and countered with the obvious logical reply:

And what is Harris saying about whether we can change ourselves? He says we can't change ourselves 'precisely' but we can influence (and hence change) others, and they can change us. But then why can't we change ourselves by getting help from others to change us? Why, for that matter, can't we do to ourselves what we do to others, reminding ourselves, admonishing ourselves, reasoning with others? It does work, not always but enough to make it worth trying.

Dennett's questions are excellent, revealing the flaw in Sapolsky (and Harris's logic) that we can influence others to change for the better or worse but not ourselves. First, where did this urge to influence others come from if we're not free? But, if we're free enough in our behavior to attempt to influence others to change, why can't we influence ourselves? Why indeed!

Critics also say Sapolsky's definition of free will created an impossible task for proving free will (i.e., finding that one little neuron). Plus, not all neuroscientists agree with hard determinism. Arguing that humans possess free will in *The Will and Its Brain: An Appraisal of Reasoned Free Will* (2012) are authors Hans Helmut Kornhuber and Luder Deecke, both German neuroscientists. In the preface to their book, they emphatically state:

> In the end, he or she may agree with the authors in saying that it is extremely necessary to counteract the dogma of total determinism i. e. that we are totally determined in all our actions and doings. This would have the consequence that we are not responsible for what we are doing. Such an all too easy exculpation ("te absolvo"), some call it "self-corruption" is what people and the media may like to hear. However, it is not so. We do have freedom, inner freedom. Thus, we have responsibility for our deeds, and we can put a veto to bad intentions, e.g. when pursuing unethical goals. (preface)

In 1964–1965, the authors achieved a scientific breakthrough with the discovery of the Bereitschaftspotential (BP), or readiness potential. Their research showed that brain action was composed of more than one area of the cortex. They argued that pre-action thought is generated in the frontal lobe (more precisely, in the prefrontal cortex) before the willed action is executed by that part of the brain dealing with acting on thought (the primary, precentral motor cortex) all of which runs through a so-called "motor loop" via the basal ganglia.

The authors argue that the initial thought in the prefrontal cortex creates recordable brain activity known as BP1. The recordable brain activity that deals with action is known as BP2. The problem in past studies, suggest the authors, is that the imaging methods (e.g., MRI) fail to notice the leading role of the frontal cortex because their time resolution is too low.

They also argue that will is based upon a "distributed systems of functions," involving many parts of the brain (such as ones dealing with memory, others with learning, others with executive function, others with planning, etc.).

In discussing these and other brain processing systems, the authors concluded that while, indeed, there is preconscious action, there is also brain capacity for volitional movement. The human will is "a complex function, with all sorts of activities—e.g., consideration, planning, decision-making—that involve both conscious and unconscious routines, acting back and forth, often with corrections authored by conscious control until the behavioral task is achieved.

In other words, Kornhuber and Deecke paint a complex and nuanced brain world of different functions operating in parallel, involving both conscious and unconscious routines, that doesn't seem easily susceptible to study by scientific reductionist methods that tend to focus on the smallest aspect of just one function—say, finding Sapolsky's one neuron.

As concerns free will, they agree that while we have preconscious responses, we also have "degrees of freedom, and can increase our degrees of freedom through self-improvement, but can also lose freedom through mismanagement."

Another work advancing the idea that humans possess free will is Peter Tse, professor of psychological and brain sciences. In his book *The Neural Basis of Free Will: Critical Causation* (2013), Tse argues—as in my previous illustration of trying to rewire my brain to do better in helping another when they're being bullied— that while we might not have free will in the immediate *now* responses, we can exercise free will about future *now* responses. We can use our will to rewire our brain, so to speak, reordering weights and values and priorities of neural synapses, for example.

The work of Tse and Kornhuber and Deecke seem to support the breakthrough work tied in physics to entangled particles. As Rovelli suggests, "in order to understand reality, we have to keep in mind that reality is this network of relations, of reciprocal information, that weaves the world. We slice up the reality surrounding us into 'objects.' But reality is not made up of discrete objects. It is a variable flux." (p. 254)

Sapolsky challenges free will advocates to find that one brain neuron that is the causal agent free of past causal influences. The phenomenon of entangled particles with its rational inferences suggests it's folly to look for one neuron. Brain activity seems much more complex and, yes "spooky," than scientist's reductionist methodology can adequately caputre.

Thus, as suggested before, it appears there is evidence that we possess the ability to alter our brain's neural wiring such as to gain some responsibility or authorship of our decisions/actions. But it takes hard work and conscious effort to grow and mature into a largely self-determining self. I say *conscious effort*, because it appears there is a dance involved in brain activity between conscious and unconscious functions. Meekly surrendering to unconscious functions without willfully exerting some command and control over unconscious functions robs us of our potential for true authorship of our lives as authentic, free actors in life.

Most importantly, there is now some research that solves the paradox of causal determinism by suggesting the human will can be an originating causal agent. Our conscious efforts can mediate unconscious functions such that future actions are not uncaused (hence, random and capricious) nor caused (determined) by forces external to our will.

The solution is what Boyd suggests: that humans, through the exercise of will, can be the causal instigator of an action. Our actions can be determined not by forces eternal to our will, but, rather, by our will, which can reside within our physical body.

Thus, as Kornhuber, Deecke and Tse all suggest, the mere fact that human behavior has a physical basis does not disprove free will. Conscious functions and unconscious functions in the brain always cooperate, thus creating opportunity for a conscious decision to be an original causal agent. This seems doubly true given the spooky world of entangled particles with their "variable flux" suggesting they are not so much discrete objects but, rather, integrated information flows.

While the question of free will seems still unresolved within neuroscience, there appears to be some scientific support for the proposition that we have some control over our actions, our destiny, but it requires hard work and conscious effort. Even accepting, for sake of argument, as true the argument that we unconsciously react in everyday situations, based upon the brain's wiring, that doesn't preclude the rewiring of neural pathways through hard work and intentional effort—through our will power.

Scriptural Support

We can logically infer, even without Scriptural reference, that God, being omnipotent, predetermines the future, including future outcomes. This statement is based upon a reasonable interpretation of omnipotence wherein God foreknows everything. If God didn't exhaustively foreknow everything, then God is not omnipotent, goes the argument. And the Bible is, admittedly, replete with imagery, symbols and passages to the clear effect that God knows and controls the future (theistic determinism). Examples include the following passages:

• "God did not reject his people whom he foreknew." (Ro 11:2)

• "I am God....I make known the end from the beginning, from ancient times, what is still to come. I say: My purpose will stand, and I will do all that I please." (Is 46:9-10)

• "For he chose us in him before the creation of the world to be holy and blameless in his sight. In love he predestined us to be adopted as his sons." (Eph 1:4-6)

• "In him we were also chosen, having been predestined according to the plan of him who works out everything in conformity with the purpose of his will..." (Eph 1:11)

• "For those God foreknew he also predestined to be conformed to the likeness of his Son, that he might be the firstborn among many he also called; those he called, he also justified; those he justified, he also glorified." (Ro 8:29, 30)

• "Does not the potter have the right to make out of the same lump of clay some pottery for noble purposes and some for common use?" (Ro 9:21)

• "What if God, choosing to show his wrath and make his power known, bore with great patience the objects of his wrath—prepared for destruction? What if he did this to make the riches of his glory known to the objects of his mercy, whom he prepared in advance for glory..." (Ro 9:22,23)

• "In his heart a man plans his course, but the LORD determines his steps." (Pv 16:9)

It should be noted that many of these passages come from the Apostle Paul. Peter Thuesen in *Predestination*, (2009) noted that Paul's own conversion experience made him prone to predestination thinking (p. 18). "As he [Paul] neared Damascus on his journey, suddenly a light from heaven flashed around him. He fell to the ground and heard a voice say to him, 'Saul, Saul, why do you persecute me.' 'Who are you Lord?' Saul asked. 'I am Jesus, whom you are persecuting,' he replied. 'Now get up and go into the city, and you will be told what to do." (Ac 9:3-6)

Paul believed he was called out for "special use." He preached that "God, who set me apart from birth and called me by his grace, was pleased to reveal his Son, in me so that I might preach him among the Gentiles..." (Gal 1:15)

However, Paul fully understood the problem with the notion of God's determinism: "But is God unjust?" (Ro 9:14). This is a natural question for those saying it seems unfair that some are saved before they've performed the requisite actions of loving faith and/or Christian deeds, while other are condemned although they adopted loving faith and performed Christian deeds.

Paul later seems to contradict his own predestination language when he says we can speak to a God amenable to acceptance of those who freely come to Him. "Everyone who calls on the name of the Lord will be saved." (Ro 10:13) (Also see: Joel 2:32; Ac 2:21)

This possibility of a person gaining salvation without regard to predestination permeates the New Testament in Christ's message: "Ask and it will be given to you; seek and you will find; knock and the door will be opened to you. For everyone who asks receives; he who seeks finds; and to him who knocks, the door will be open." (Mt 7:7; Lk 11:9; Rev. 3:20)

Many other passages in the Bible suggest God allows creaturely free will. For example, as Gregory Boyd (2001) argues, "The Lord is frequently grieved, sometimes even amazed, at how 'stiff-necked' people are in resisting him (e.g., Ex 33:3, 5; 34:9; Deut 9:6, 13; 10:16: 31:27; Judg 2:19; 2 Kings 17:14; 2 Chron 30:8; 36:13; Neh 9:16; Is 46:12; 48:4; Jer 7:26; Hos 4:16)." (p. 54) Question: How can the Lord be grieved if the Lord determines and foreknows all our behavior? Does that make sense?

And, importantly, what can we make of Christ's painful sacrifice on the cross for our redemption if we have not been offered the opportunity to freely choose to repent, accept Christ as our Savior and be saved, if it has already been decided? Why did Christ say "knock and you shall enter" and "seek and you shall find" when advising the world that his payment in full for our sins can be redeemed by us for the mere asking in loving, repentant faith?

What do we make of God's call that Abraham sacrifice his son? (Ge 22; Heb 11:17-19; Jas 2:21-24) When Abraham displays his faith in God by proceeding to kill Isaac, an angel of the Lord calls out from heaven to cancel the sacrifice: "Do not lay a hand on the boy...Now I know that you fear God, because you have not withheld from me your son, your only son." (Ge 22:12)

Doesn't this sound like a genuine test of Abraham's free will? If the Lord foreknew or controlled Abraham's actions, would God need this test of Abraham? Wouldn't God have already known (and predetermined) Abraham's faith? And if Abraham was not free in the libertarian sense, but was determined by forces outside his will, where was the demonstration of courage, of faith, in his actions? I argue Abraham's actions were meaningless if not free. I argue the story or parable is incoherent if Abraham's actions were determined by forces other than his own will.

There are many other examples that make little sense if, in fact, the people are not free in their actions/inactions. Therefore, given the evidence of both God's determinism and human free will, the Bible seems ambiguous on the subject of creaturely free will.

The Apostle Paul reveals this ambiguity when he teaches us that God is omnipotent, possessing an unfettered will (suggesting divine predestination whereby God can but doesn't abolish evil) and yet desires us to repent and turn to Him in loving faith (suggesting creaturely freedom whereby God can't abolish evil).

Augustine, too, was vexed by this contradiction. Based upon his own conversion experience, on reading Paul's epistle to the Romans, and influenced by his understanding of God's omnipotence, Augustine was convinced of predestination. But Augustine also believed in human free will, conceding that, to God, a runaway horse is preferable to a stone which lacked the free will to runaway.

What to do? In *Confessions*, Augustine argued he really worked for the free choice of human will, but the sovereignty of God won out.

Thuesen (2009) argued that Augustine's decision in favor of predestination (determinism) came down to his logical analysis:

> all humans are born terminally ill with sin and thus deserve damnation. Birth defects prove the point. If babies suffer defects through no fault of their own, then we are forced to abandon all faith in divine justice. Surely, then, some infants are born disfigured or crippled as punishment for their own inbred sin. The fact that God preserves other equally sinful infants from harm—and elects only certain persons to ultimate salvation—merely reveals grace for what it is: something completely unmerited. 'In giving to some what they did not deserve, clearly [God] willed that his grace be gratuitous and thus truly grace.' (p. 21,22)

To this day, many theodicists see Augustine as the father of predestination theology that guided the early Western church. Clearly, he felt evil came into the world when Adam and Eve disobeyed God's command. Augustine argued this original sin reflected humanity's depraved nature (through privation of a divine good) which extends to and infects all of humanity. God, Augustine argued, would convert all evil into good based upon what Boyd called a "Divine Blueprint" (thus, justifying predestination).

This issue is admittedly complex—and Augustine wrestled with the twin prongs of the paradox as best he could—which is natural given that it is a paradox.

One thing is clear: this paradox created an age old debate within Christian theology. The Western church—the church significantly influenced by the thinking of Augustine—went the road of predestination and bloomed in the later thinking of John Calvin, Martin Luther and Thomas Aquinas. The Augustinian argument is that God, being God, must foreknow all future outcomes in the world. (Whether or not Augustine deserves credit for Calvin's hard determinism is a matter of debate.)

But the Eastern church—largely influenced by the thinking of its own foundational theologian: Irenaeus—did not see the Fall of Adam and Eve as a tragic fall downward that displayed humanity's innate sinfulness and total depravity. It did not see Adam and Eve's disobedience as forever staining future humankind, or as revealing humanity's innate depravity. Quite the contrary: Irenaeus saw the story of the Fall as allegorical, illustrating Adam and Eve's fall as upward, toward a Christian maturity forged in the harsh conditions of the world. In this understanding of Scripture, Irenaeus also came down on the side of human free will, arguing that our free efforts could effect a salvation that has not been preordained.

Advocates of Irenaeus argue the paradox of God and evil is solved in a coherent fashion with this understanding: God is responsible for ushering evil into the world; but God is justified in ushering evil into the world for divine good reasons that surpass the cost of evil.

The natural questions arising from this split in worldview about interpreting the Fall are many. Does God's will absolutely precludes any human effort for salvation? Can our free will move God to forgive us and accept us such that it's not preordained? What does omnipotence mean? If we are free, does God not know future outcomes? If so, is God not omniscient? These issues alone have been worthy of many books and commentaries, and explains one of the many schisms within the body of Christianity. Having framed the issue, how do I resolve the apparent contradiction, given that Scripture supports both views? The answer is that I come down on the side of God's determinism for major outcomes such as creation, Christ's birth, life, death and resurrection, but come down on the side of human free will for individual moral behavior.

Finally, there are other arguments for understanding God and evil: e.g., that it's a spiritual encounter of the heart and not a logical analysis of the mind; that suffering itself works its way on the human spirit so as to bring us closer to others and to God; that God is ineffable and/or God's reason exceeds our reason. All of these other understandings also seem to stand upon the premise that we are free to accept God in love. Without that premise, the various explanations point to a prewritten script of no drama, no surprise, no spontaneity, no creativity, no love, no courage, no faith.

The notion of a libertarian free will is, I believe, consistent with Scripture. There exists supporting passages as well as clear logic—not to mention some science—to support this position. It would seem the most charitable resolution to Scripture's apparent ambiguity on this issue is to acknowledge God's exhaustive determination of creation, of life, and major foundational events, but not individual moral behavior. For that, we need to acknowledge God's selfless love in gifting to us the power of free will so that we might come to know love and grow in Christian maturity.

3.3.2 AMBIGUITY

The mystery of life is beyond all human conception. Everything we know is within the terminology of the concepts of being and not being, many and single, true and untrue. We always think in opposites... Everything in the field of time and space is dual.

Joseph Campbell, *The Power of Myth*

It is my conviction that the character of the human condition, like the character of all life, is "ambiguity": the inseparable mixture of good and evil, of true and false, of creative and destructive forces—both individual and social....The awareness of the ambiguity of one's own highest achievements (as well as one's own deepest failures) is a definite symptom of maturity.

Paul Tillich, "The Ambiguity of Perfection," *Time* magazine article

...in deciding to create, God brings about the existence of a realm of imperfection, *whereas without creation there is only perfection of the divine life itself. And surely it isn't self-evident that 'perfection' plus imperfection' is better than perfection all by itself. It's true, of course,that for us perfection is fully appreciated only by way of contrast with that which is imperfect.*

William Hasker, *The Triumph of God Over Evil*

Overview

I agree, with Tillich, that life and everything in it is ambiguous, comprised of both positive and negative elements—the good and the bad (evil). This structure of ambiguity enables critical cognitive functions: learning, differentiation, and maturity. Further, it creates a world rich for free will to flourish, allowing humans to experience (receive and give) love, to exercise faith and courage and otherwise be morally consequential.

We think in opposites and cannot think otherwise. From a theological perspective this presents no conflict with modern science as the structure of ambiguity can be understood as selected both by evolution—for its ability to promote life temporal—and selected by God—for its ability to promote life eternal.

Premises

Stated as premises, the following apply to ambiguity:

P4: Life and everything in it is ambiguous.

P5: Humans acquire knowledge through ambiguous experience, that is, through the experience of opposites which, in the tension of their interplay, provide distinctions between the two oppositional possibilities, such as what something is and what something is not.

P6: Humans acquire the discriminating ability of appreciation of one possibility over another possibility only through a maturity gained by the accumulated knowledge of ambiguous experiences.

P7: The structure of ambiguity provides a sufficient source of alternative choices through which free will can be fully actualized, since free will requires choices to be fully actualized.

P8: A person cannot come to know, appreciate and love God without the life process of ambiguity.

P9: Ambiguity, by definition, necessarily creates negative (or evil) outcomes in its functioning.

Definition

For the purposes of this theodicy, I embrace Tillich's understanding of *ambiguity* (1971): "Every life process has the ambiguity that the positive and negative elements are mixed in such a way that a definite separation of the negative from the positive is impossible: life at every moment is ambiguous. (1971, V. 111, pg. 32) Tillich also says (1963) ambiguity, or ambiguous, means the "inseparable mixture of good and evil, of true and false, of creative and destructive forces—both individual and social." (p. 69)

I argue this binary structure of ambiguity creates a tension between positive and negative experiences of being—between the good and the bad (or evil) of life: e.g., love and hate; life and death; joy and sorrow; pleasure and pain; loyal and disloyal. This tension is what creates the space necessary for human free will to flourish, for learning and maturity to occur, for appreciation of good over bad to be acquired—all leading to moral acts of love, courage and faith to emerge.

In the Chinese philosophy of yin and yang, ambiguity is seen as two sides of the same coin, each so inextricably intertwined with the other as to be meaningless without the other. Examples include: darkness and light; moon and sun; night and day; winter and summer; earth and heaven; soft and hard; interior and exterior; unconscious and conscious.

Darkness (yin), for example, is the opposite of light (yang). We can only know the qualities of darkness by also knowing the qualities of light, and vice versa. If everything were only dark, we would have no idea what dark was like. We can only know dark by reference to what it's not.

However, the structure of ambiguity that I'm proposing is not simply a yin and yang binary structure of two sides of the same coin. It is more complex than that. Unlike yin and yang, it is not content neutral; one of the polarities is often preferable to the other polarity in terms of morality. Being loyal, for example, is preferable to being disloyal for most moral codes. Likewise, being kind and generous is usually ethically preferable to being cruel and stingy.

In terms of being more complex than a simple binary structure, ambiguity's structure can be thought of as an axis in tension, vibrating between the two oppositional poles that represent the maximum possible values—or its expression—of the thing being experienced. Between these two poles—stretched tight by a dynamic, connecting axis—lie a wide array of values within the two polar extremes.

Here is an example of a common human experience of how we feel about someone in terms of how much one person (R) really likes another person (S). That experience will always present as ambiguous, between two extreme possibilities: love or hate. The common experience is that our feelings usually lie somewhere between these two extremes: R might really like S but with some reservations because, for example, of how S treated R rudely last week at the school dance. So R's current feeling on the love-hate axis might be closer to love than hate, but possibly trending away from love based on recent incidents. It was closer to love before the school dance. And it might plummet swiftly toward hate if S doesn't apologize.

This simple example illustrates the axis is always in dynamic tension because every experience is subject to immediate change, sliding from one end to other, based upon many contingent variables (e.g., current experience, the mood you're in, etc.).

Here's another situation, involving whether or not to trust someone. At one end of the spectrum is absolute trust (*I'd trust my life with them*) and at the other is absolute distrust (*I would never trust them with even a penny of my money*). These form the outer or maximal limits of possible choices for this issue of trust and distrust. When a person needs the help of another, the desired (positive) value sought from another is trust. Of course, in most cases, the degree of trust is nuanced, laying somewhere between the two poles, dependent upon various contingent variables.

The key point in both examples is that every decision/response involves—consciously or not—an analysis of the polar opposite variables at hand for the issue at hand (e.g., trust or distrust, love or hate) and all the values in between.

And so it goes, each analysis, each reaction, each decision limited by the choices that dynamically present themselves somewhere along the axis that connects the two maximal possibilities of the phenomena being evaluated.

To complicate matters, an analysis of one variable (say, trustworthiness) often requires a similar, often simultaneous analysis of other related variables.

For example, in evaluating someone's trustworthiness as your friend in a dangerous situation, you might have to consider:

• how well you know them (the issue of certainty of knowledge: certain or uncertain? That is, do you really know them well enough to place trust in them?);

• whether to believe or not believe what someone else (J) told you about the other person's (M) trustworthiness (credibility of another opinion: true or untrue? or trustworthy or untrustworthy? That is, is J credible when J told me that M is trustworthy?);

• the danger of your situation. If someone is charging at you with a knife, perhaps your calculation of your friend's (M) trustworthiness changes. Perhaps your first reaction is to opt for the maximal pole of trustworthiness, but that requires an analysis of the danger/safety profiles of the situation. Maybe you have no choice but to trust in M because someone is charging at you with a knife drawn. Or maybe you realize that your usually reliable friend M does not do well in emergencies, especially physical confrontations.

Of course, in real time, this analysis of multiple, tension-laden polarities is usually instantaneous. In fact, modern studies of behavior suggest much of our immediate responses are preconscious and happen so fast that we only think we are engaged in conscious decisions/actions.

Even if true, even at lightning speed, I argue our preconscious analysis (from sensory awareness of the situation, to analyzing the data received, to formulating a response, to acting) still utilizes the axis of the ambiguity structure described above. Our preconscious hard wiring didn't just arise from thin air; it arose from millions of years of ancestral ambiguous experiences, the accumulated wisdom of which has been passed on down to us. I suggest this ancestral knowledge arose from the same method of oppositional thinking described above.

This is admittedly a long definition. But I think it is critical to understand the structure of ambiguity and the role it plays in unfolding God's plan for the world.

Good Reason for Structure of Ambiguity

The structure of ambiguity is necessary to achieve God's sufficient reason of love through enabling knowledge, maturity, appreciation, and the ability to engage in morally consequential acts such as love.

Without the structure of ambiguity, humans could never come to know God, to appreciate God's essence and nature, and grow to love God and understand and appreciate God's love for us.

Ambiguity's function is to promote knowledge of something by showing both what it is and what it is not. This is a necessary requirement for knowing (or learning).

This is how we come to know God: by experiencing what God is and what God is not. For example, through the ambiguous experience of various degrees of loyalty and disloyalty and betrayal, we come to know the positive qualities of loyalty and the negative qualities of disloyalty, with positive qualities being those we like. Maybe someone's loyalty to us advances our self interest. Perhaps it matches our ethical values. Possibly it fulfills our need for security, for knowing that this other person will always be steadfast and true in their love and support.

The Bible tells us God's love "never fails," (1 Co 13:8) "always perseveres". (1 Co 13:7). Through ambiguous experiences of loyalty and disloyalty, alone, we can come to know what God's loyalty means and what God's essence and nature entails. Through the ambiguous experience of loyalty and disloyalty, we can come to know and appreciate the difference between good and evil.

In the same fashion, we can mature or gain in knowledge, coming to increasingly appreciate this (say, loyalty) over that (say, betrayal). The increased appreciation of loyalty can mature into love, being P5.

As concerns premise P7, the answer is that free will requires choices for that will to be exercised. If there's only one option, there's no choice. What good is the ability to freely choose when there's only one choice? Ambiguity is the structure that always provides choices for every action/decision. It fuels freedom.

If love must be freely chosen, then one choice is to choose God's love and another is to reject God's love.

Necessary Cost of Evil for Structure of Ambiguity

Ambiguity means that life and everything in it contains the *inseparable mixture of good and evil*. Thus, by definition, ambiguity contains evil outcomes.

Ambiguity's cost in terms of evil is significantly different than the cost of the structure of free will. The structure of free will merely creates the possibility of evil. We don't have to choose evil. With ambiguity, evil is part of the structure itself. Ambiguity necessarily presents with evil within the structure of being.

How could it be otherwise? If free will creates the potential for evil, that must mean there are evil choices in the world for our free will to select. Those evil choices reside side-by-side with the good choices, because life and everything in it is ambiguous: comprised of inseparable polar opposite qualities of good and bad, positive and negative, true and false, creative and destructive.

To expand Boyd's equation: If love is the reason and free will and ambiguity are the methods, then evil is the price.

Discussion

There are two key questions: Is life and everything in it ambiguous; and, since the structure of ambiguity presents with evil, does life need to be ambiguous?

First, is the world and everything in it ambiguous? I don't know and can't see how anyone can know, especially if it's true we only think in opposites. Let's assume the world is not ambiguous but is, instead, non ambiguous—a singularity or monolithic nothingness.

If that's the case, then how do we comprehend or understand the world? Understand ourselves? Know what to do? As Yogi once said, how would you know things are good if you didn't know bad things?

Research seems to indicate humans have a strong, innate need to find pattern and meaning in life, even if it's not there. The Canadian philosopher Paul Churchland tells us (1998): "the perceptual world is largely an unintelligible confusion to a newborn infant, but his mind/brain sets about immediately to formulate a conceptual framework with which to apprehend, to explain, and to anticipate that world." (p. 80)

Churchland adds that the baby's mind/brain finds itself "as confusing and unintelligible as it finds the external world." It has to go through the same conceptual framework that it does with the world—two parallel paths—to apprehend itself. Even as a newborn infant, we begin the task of constructing worldviews within which to apprehend the world.

Yalom tells us (from decades of empirical research) that (1980):

...we have established that our perceptual neuropsychological organization is such that...we organize molecular stimuli as well as molar behavioral and psychological data into gestalten, into configurations or patterns. Thus, when presented with random dots on wallpaper, one organizes them into figure and ground; when confronted with a broken circle, one automatically perceives it as complete; when presented with diverse behavioral data...one makes 'sense' out of it by fitting it into a familiar explanatory framework. (p. 462)

What happens, one might ask, when things don't make sense, don't go well? Yalom (1980) says:

When any of these stimuli or situations do not lend themselves to patterning, one feels tense, annoyed, and dissatisfied....We experience dysphoria in the face of an indifferent, unpatterned world and search for patterns, explanations, and meaning of existence. (p. 463)

It appears, therefore, that we are adaptive, optimistic, pattern-find-

ing, meaning-hungry beings. And for good reason: patterns and meaning mitigate the anxiety of meaninglessness inherent in random, purposeless, patternless chaos. Having the cognitive ability to organize chaotic phenomenon into ambiguous structure helps to not only understand and comprehend the phenomenon of existence but also reduce anxiety. It also helps us survive as a species. Humans seem to have an adaptive need to make sense of the world, a task we largely accomplish through creating complex worldviews based upon knowledge gained from experiencing phenomena ambiguously.

Thus, I'm not sure if life and everything in it is actually ambiguous. Life might be a monolithic nothingness, simply an "is." Could it be that we only think in opposites and can't think otherwise, as Campbell claims (see headnote) and cannot comprehend reality in any other way? Is this ambiguous frame an evolutionary adaptation for survival, something not real *out there* in the world but merely a mental construct developed by necessity and chance? Or could it be a gift from God for learning and appreciation?

There is no scientific study I can find to confirm Campbell's claim that we can only think in opposites. Because, if we do think in opposites, it would seem that for all intents and purposes, the world is ambiguous.

Question: How could one prove or disprove this structure of ambiguity since to "prove or disprove" something is itself a binary frame?

We find some affirmation of Campbell's claim in examples throughout the scientific world: *education research* (on learning and instruction); *human nervous system research*; *computers and the digital revolution*; *evolutionary theory*; and *non-ambiguous singularities*.

* * *

In *education research* (for learning and instructing), there is *Theory of Instructions: Principles and Instruction* by American Professors of education, Dr. Douglas Carnine and Dr. Siegfried Englemann (1991). Specifically, their empirical work, known as Direct Instruction, found that the foundation for all *instruction* is to first introduce an unambiguous fact to a learner and tell them what it is. Then, as a second necessary step, the instructor must tell them what it is not. In this way, the learner gains knowledge: A is A and not B. This simple foundation can cascade into more abundant learning, resulting in cognitive abilities such as discrimination, appreciation, valuing, ethical/moral awareness, problem solving, critical thinking.

Turning from instructing (the function of transferring information) to *learning* (the function of receiving and processing information) we find the same need for this binary structure.

In Engelmann and Steely's (2003) *Inferred Functions of Performance and Learning*, the authors argue that the conscious learner—machine or human as both can receive sensory inputs and respond—needs to process the stimulus so as to categorize it in terms of positives or negatives. Speaking of consciousness, they argue:

> ...consciousness is a function of the nervous system....All [agents] know how to plan strategies to avoid or escape from specific conditions that induce negative sensations and how to seek or approach specific conditions that lead to positive sensations. (p. 471-472)

Positive sensations and *negative sensations* form a binary polarity that drives behavior response with negative being dangerous, bad, or unwanted, and positive being safe, good, or desired.

Engelmann and Steely break down a "binary performance" framework into five function-steps: reception, screening, planning, directive and response. Within the final two steps, where the mind directs the body to respond, we encounter the human nervous system's design and function.

* * *

Not surprisingly, the *human nervous system* is also binary: neurons either firing or not firing. Called *action potential*, a neuron fires by discharging an electrical current when it receives a stimulus sufficient to depolarize the delicate electrical balance between the chemically charged ions inside the nerve cell and those outside of it. Positively charged ions and negatively charged ions create a delicate dance of opposites—like clicking a light switch on and off—that enable execution of the response chosen by the agent based upon a binary assessment of positive and negative inputs and outcomes.

Even our physical system of receiving information—the nervous system, including the brain—is not unitary, it is binary. Perhaps there is a biological reason humans think in opposites.

Sociobiology might argue that the brain's binary structure promotes survival because brains that have this binary structure can learn, mature and come to appreciate safety from danger.

A philosopher might argue that the brain's binary structure is an adaptive, learning machine that has evolved to reflect the basic structure of reality: ambiguity.

A theologists might argue that the brain's structure is divine: crafted to enable creatures to eventually come to know, appreciate and love God.

There are many theories of why the brain functions as it does. My point is that my theological perspective can be seen as consistent with scientific construals.

* * *

Today's greatest transformational engine—*the computer (including quantum) and the digital revolution*—is startling in its simplicity. Complex mathematical algorithms are converted into the binary code for computer manipulation. The computers store information in the form of bits in one of two states, 1 or 0. The 1 and 0 can be sequenced in various configurations to express the algorithm. The configurations can encode complex information: from pictures; a trajectory for a rocket's trip around the moon; and sequencing of the human DNA. All of this can occur by simply how we arrange two numerals, 0 and 1.

Vast transformations sweeping the world are thanks to digital technology which, in turn, depends upon what is and what is not; that is, 0 is not 1 and 1 is not 0. They are opposites, both numbers, which by themselves are relatively powerless. Yet when combined in a infinite array of combinations they can express complex problem-solving algorithms. These algorithms advance knowledge, the accumulation of which creates heretofore unthought human progress and potential, enabling humans to better comprehend and manipulate the physical world.

Neal Stephenson (2015) expressed this profound, startling insight in his science fiction thriller novel *Seveneves*. After the Earth has been destroyed, those few who escaped earth's destruction lived in outer space for years. They had taken with them DNA samples of all plant and animal life. Then they digitized it, that is, they converted the DNA sequences to various combinations of 0 and 1.

Thousands of years later, Earth was once again habitable. Descendants of the original survivors planned their return home, able to repopulate the earth as it existed before the "Hard Rain" caused by the moon's explosion. All of life, digitized before the destruction of earth, was stored in a single thumb drive (admittedly of enormous storage capacity) which allowed for the reconstitution of life on earth: "Africa, whose outlines were still vaguely recognizable, though heavily reshaped by the Hard Rain, would have giraffes and lions sequenced from the ones and zeroes dating all the way back to the thumb drive around Eve Moria's neck. Likewise with other battered and reforged continents." (p. 597).

In Stephenson's novel, nothing more is required, nothing less works, for creation of abundant life: just 1 and 0. Together, their creative possibility within the natural world is limitless. This is the power of ambiguous structure.

Quantum computers (which, as I write, aren't fully up and running) have vastly more computational power than our current computers. They use quantum bits, called quibits which can be a 1 or a 0 or something in between—so called superpositions, which are indissoluble mixtures of 1 and 0. Here, we are back to my definition of ambiguity as not simply two binary opposites, but an axis of possibilities that lie within the oppositional poles of 0 and 1.

To repeat, Rovelli concludes (2016) that "in order to understand reality, we have to keep in mind that reality is this network of relations, of reciprocal information, that weaves the world. We slice up the reality surrounding us into 'objects.' But reality is not made up of discrete objects. It is a variable flux." (p. 254)

Thus, Rovelli suggests knowledge of A requires knowledge of B, as Carnine and Englemann argue in their theory of educational instruction. It all suggests that there is no stand-alone, non-ambiguous factor we can comprehend within reality. To be comprehensible, one thing must be understood in relation to another thing, if not things. I suggest the two things have to be complementary, oppositional polarities. Every A needs a B, and every B needs an A, at least for human comprehension of A and of B.

* * *

Englemann and Steely's argument (2004) that conscious learners need to categorize experience in terms of positives and negatives, supports the notion that the structure of ambiguity is invaluable for survival under *evolutionary theory*.

An example of how the structure of ambiguity would have or may have been applied to our earliest ancestors, is also from Neal Stephenson's science fiction thriller, *Seveneves*.

> Kath Two was startled awake by patches of orange-pink light cavorting across the taut fabric above her. A very old instinct, born on the savannahs of Old Earth, read it as danger: the flitting shadows, perhaps of predators circling her tent....She thought of reaching under her pillow for the weapon....By then it had become obvious that the moving light on the tent had nothing to do with large predators. It was too dappled and volatile. Not even birds could move so. Its twinkling and swirling were mysterious, but its hue told her it was the first light of the day. (emphasis added) (p. 569, 570)

In Stephenson's novel, he depicts a human in the far future (Kath Two) acting like we all do, every day: experiencing some sensation perceived through one or more of our senses. At first, we receive the sensate data and process or analyze it for possible responses. The analysis is subject to cognitive tools (e.g., logic and emotions) that contain currently acquired data as well as historical data embedded in our DNA.

The goal/function of the analysis is to determine whether the sensation received is positive or negative, such as safe or dangerous. We plan a response, mentally directing the body to respond appropriately. The physical body then responds physically as mentally directed.

This is what Kath Two did. She, and we, don't consciously break an experience down into its constituent parts that Engelmann and Steely describe in their work. We just react. It happens so quickly and smoothly that a person is not aware of the constituent functions at work in a single incident such as this one created by Stephenson. In fact, there is evidence that much of our response is preconscious with our conscious awareness of the outcome arising from our preconscious calculations arising so quickly as to be impossible for us to realize the preconscious activity.

Scientific construals of human behavior (e.g., *evolutionary theory*; sociobiology) understand this process of receiving sensate data, processing it and then responding in its functional terms as being related to survival. Stephenson's Kath Two is simply reflecting upon and expressing millions of years of sensate data with its accumulated knowledge in order to aid her in forming an optimum (positive) response.

In evolutionary thought, it seems agreed that species that can differentiate positives from negatives (or rewards from punishments) have a better chance of survival. For example, if species A, like Kath Two, has an encounter with some external phenomenon that it knows, from accumulated experiences, is dangerous to A's safety or life, A can and should plan and execute a response to avoid or at least mitigate the danger.

Let's say it is a dangerous predator outside Kath Two's tent. She can: flee; hide and remain quiet, reach for her weapon (which was the action she chose and was close to executing), or generate some other defense/mitigation technique. But if species A lacks this ability to differentiate bad from good, the positive from the negative, life versus death, then it will probably die at the hand of the predator on the day that the shadow on the tent is, in fact, a predator.

Being able to frame sensory data into a binary grid of polar oppositional qualities, such as positive versus negative, good versus bad, reward versus punishment, life versus death, safety versus danger, friend versus foe, etc., creates evolutionary advantage in that it promotes survival. Since staying alive is the only reason driving evolutionary behavior, being able to discriminate among various sensory inputs as positive or negative is a precious cognitive ability for sentient life's survival on earth.

* * *

One could argue that apparently *non-ambiguous singularities*, like the Big Bang or like God, seem to exist without counterpart. Standing alone, they cannot be comprehended. Yet, when we frame them ambiguously—e.g., God and no God, or Big Bang and no Big Bang—we can know something about them. We can, for example, know something of God by being exposed to the idea or experience that there is no God.

In his book, *Church Dogmatics*, Theologian Karl Barth (1886-1968) understood evil as the nothingness ("das Nichtige") that stood over and opposed to God. God is something, the something that allows for the receipt and processing of sensate data, of reason and thought and feelings. God is life, to be understood and valued over its polar oppositional phenomenon: death (or nothingness).

Let's also consider mental states of no ambiguity or at least minimal ambiguity. One such state results from the practice of transcendental meditation where one concentrates upon a singularity, such as one word, or one sound, or one image. A person is not told to think of two oppositional things, like love and hate. In fact, the recommendation is for just one sound—such as ooooommmm—something that has no meaning and, thus, lacks the tension inherent in ambiguous structure.

One goal of this and other meditation methods is that it removes you from the stress of life's experiences. You create a state of near nothingness, of calm, of awareness without distraction. In other words, you are not learning, having tuned out anything else, in a condition of mental nothingness.

With practice, you will learn about the value of meditation and stress reduction. However, even this knowledge is acquired at the altar of ambiguity: meditative calm is at one end of the polar axis, high stress at the other end. In between these polar oppositional absolutes resides the tension of everyday existence. What meditation does is let you temporarily experience the opposite of stress which is calm, just as orgasm during sex lets you temporarily experience the opposite of aloneness, which is union.

I am reminded of a joke I saw from the *Dilbert* comic strip series.

It shows a person leaning back in a chair, wearing a pair of what seems to be virtual reality goggles. His tongue is hanging out. He seems in a euphoric trance. Dilbert is pointing to the picture with a pointer and tells his co-workers: "We found the 'bliss point' for immersive 3-D headgear. The product is so good that 87% of our customers starved to death while using it.." Another character replies: "We never get the customer retention part right."

It is funny but, also, profound. If we were to be lost in a state of pure ecstasy, and nothing else—no awareness of any other need or craving or emotion or thought, even of time and space, even of being hungry—we would never leave that state because we'd not be driven by any other thought, urge, drive, or desire to leave it.

This is the state of pure passion as in the moment of sexual orgasm which, I argue, acquires its power and allure precisely because we temporarily lose ourselves within that immersive moment. We are living but for a moment within the white hot polar purity of belonging, of union (versus alienation and a sense of anxious aloneness and not belonging). We are temporarily rid of the tension of ambiguity. But we cannot live long in such a place. Like Dilbert's person lost in a state of euphoria, we would soon starve to death.

A unitary experience is meaningless without a counter reference point against which to gauge it, evaluate it, gain knowledge about it. Mathematics, for example, would be meaningless without a binary (and, hence, ambiguous) structure.

One could argue, for example, that the equation 1 equals 1 constitutes unambiguous knowledge. I argue it doesn't. The number 1, to have any meaning, requires the possibility of other numbers. If all we knew was 1, without the knowledge of other numbers, 1 would be meaningless. Likewise, the term "equals" has meaning only in contrast to the concept of "not equal." If we had no awareness of the concept of "not equal," we could not comprehend any meaning to the term "equal."

Consciousness, also, is binary if one thinks of the basic structure of consciousness as being intentional—needing both an *object* to observe and an observer (or *subject observing*). A person and the world is a classic ambiguous structure. They exist in tension and are always defined by the other. People define themselves by the world they find themselves enmeshed within, and the world acquires meaning (as we understand meaning) only through our conscious apprehension of it by people.

To a stone, an ambiguous world is of no concern or consequence. Only conscious creatures can apprehend God and others. Consciousness—the seat of all human values—is an ambiguous structure composed of a self, with the *self* as subject (being the center of the theatre of thoughts and emotions, where all sensory inputs flow and reason feverishly work to make sense of what it is experiencing) and the *other* as object (being the thing experienced of which the brain is furiously trying to make sense of). As indicated previously, self and world creates a basic universal polarity.

This same analysis applies to the physical world wherein everything is also ambiguous. Fire gives warmth and comfort but also kills and destroys. The same dual nature applies to every physical feature in the world: e.g., the sun, gravity, magnetism. All are necessary for life, but can be fatal to life if increased or decreased beyond normal limits.

The acquisition of knowledge, maturity, appreciation and moral behavior, it would seem, requires a binary structure from the macro to the micro, from the largest structure of design to the smallest, from a vast universe to be observed to a single existent to observe it.

* * *

Second, but *does life and everything in it have to be ambiguous*? Couldn't God have designed the lived experience without the doubt and anxiety and evil an ambiguous structure creates?

One short answer, as argued, is that without the structure of ambiguity, our free will would have no options among which to choose. If love must be freely chosen, and there is no choice of hate, then how can love be freely chosen?

Plus, as Tillich writes (1987), "Life is not unambiguously good. Then it would not be life but only the possibility of life. And life is not unambiguously evil. Then nonbeing would have conquered being. But life is ambiguous in all its expressions." (p. 151)

The structure of ambiguity imbues life with choices which not only enables love but creates a milieu rich for morally consequential human behavior.

You might also reasonably ask, "what's the matter with a world of only unambiguous good, of only positive experiences?" Think back to the two thought experiments examining the claim that an unambiguous world of only positive experiences is the best of all possible worlds. I repeat them here.

In *Perfect Life—A modern television parable, i*n a 1960 *Twilight Zone* television episode entitled "A Nice Place to Visit", a small-town hoodlum is granted his wish for having his every desire granted.

At first the hoodlum is thrilled, but then, after a short time, he gets bored with everything working out perfectly. He misses risk, the unknown, excitement, spontaneity, joy, of beating the odds. He summons the genie who granted his wish to complain that heaven is overrated, to which Cabot replied: "Who said you were in heaven?"

In Perfect Golf, I talked of a golfer getting a hole-in-one on every hole, and every day of golf he played. It is the dream of all golfers.

At first, it might be euphoric. You never lose. If your partners have the same power, they never lose either. Everyone always shoots 18. Every day. Forever. But soon the game would get boring and lose meaning, joy, adventure and spontaneity. It ceases being fun and you quit the game. You realize golf's great treasure is in the challenge, in marshalling one's talent and effort against all the obstacles confronting you: the weather—rain and wind, cold and dreary; the stress of the shot or the pressure of competition; the tired muscles that don't always move as you want them to; the depression over a missed shot and the need to mentally rebound and get it together; the unfairness of a bad bounce, the arbitrariness of a lipped-out putt because the ball hit a spike mark caused by some a golfer dragging their feet across the green.

These and other imperfections are the result of the tension of ambiguous structures inherent in golf: e.g., being calm versus nervous, strong versus weak, coordination versus incoordination, wise versus foolish. These are the tensions a golfer struggles against. Without them, there would be no joy in hitting a pure shot, of improving your game, of overcoming adversity through hard work, effort, confidence, discipline, sacrifice and force of will.

We can easily see in these two stories that a perfect world, defined as constant wish fulfillment and narcissistic happiness, is sterile, bereft of meaning, value and heft against which to measure and treasure the great joys of positive experiences. Living in a utopian world of perfection where only one force, one unambiguous experience, is at work, can never produce knowledge, maturity, moral consequentiality, or the capacity for love. Such a world would be shallow, bereft of great texture and depth. It would not be dynamic, creative, life-enhancing.

Tillich describes such a vacuous world as an *infant's paradise* when he argues (1987) in favor of an ambiguous life of both good and bad experiences:

> If God had produced a world in which physical and moral evil were impossible, the creatures would not have had the independence of God which is presupposed in the experience of reuniting love. The world would have become a paradise of dreaming innocence, an infant's paradise, but neither love nor power nor justice would have become real. Actualization of one's potentialities includes, unavoidably, estrangement; estrangement from one's essential being, so that we may find it again in maturity. Only a God who is like a foolish mother, who is so afraid about the well-being of her child that she keeps him in a state of enforced innocence and enforced participation in her own life, could have kept the creatures in the prison of a dreaming paradise. And, as in the case of the mother, this would have been hidden hostility and not love. And it would not have been power either.(p. 149)

Tillich argues an ambiguous world of both positive and negative experiences creates a rich and diverse milieu, capable of generating knowledge, morality and appreciation of one experience over another. *It is a necessary milieu for the development of creatures, for their maturity in Christ—from narcissistic, self-loving creatures who believe the world spins around them to selfless, loving and charitable humans who realize nothing spins around them but the love of God.*

With these simple examples and Tillich's insight, we see the possibility of conceptualizing a notion that evil can logically exist in a world created by a God that is omnipotent, omniscient, and wholly good. And we see that Yogi Berra's simple observation, though thought of humorously as a head-scratching contradiction, is, in fact, deeply intuitive: "If the world were perfect, it wouldn't be."

Scriptural Support

In terms of understanding ambiguity as something unclear and open to more than one interpretation, consider this commentary found in NIV's *Quest Study Bible* concerning God's creation of the world in six days. Under the heading "Are these literal 24-hour days?" the book says:

> Many understand the six days of creation as representing long periods of time because the sun, which marks a 24-hour day, wasn't created until the fourth day. And the word *day* is used in chapters 1-2 [of Genesis] in three distinct ways: (1) as approximately 12 hours of daylight (Ge. 1-5); as 24 hours (1:14); and (3) as a period of time involving, at the very minimum, the whole creative activity from day one to day seven (see 2:4, where the word is translated *when* is the same word that is elsewhere translated day). The *light* (1:3) could not have come from the earth's sun, if the sun was not created until the fourth day.

Thus, even something as simple as the start of Genesis is ambiguous, justifying both the theory of creationism and the theory that God chose evolution as the mechanism of how humans came to be.

In terms of understanding ambiguity as oppositional framing, we find that the *Bible is replete with dualism imagery*: heaven and hell; life and death; good and evil. The Book of Genesis begins with oppositional framing: form and void; darkness and light; day and night; water and firmament or dry land; heaven and earth; two great lights—the sun and the moon; God and man; man and woman.

The greatest story of ambiguity in history concerns how evil came into the world through the Fall of Adam and Eve. They were told not to eat of the fruit of the tree of the knowledge of "good and evil for when you eat of it you surely die.". (Ge 2:16-17)

This passage is critical. Ask yourself: Doesn't common sense tell you that the prohibition should have been only against eating the fruit of the *knowledge of evil*? Why would eating of the fruit of the knowledge of *good* be a sinful thing?

Tillich's answer to this obvious question (1987) is that the Fall is a powerful parable of our condition of being in the world today. If we only know "good" then we have no ability for knowledge, appreciation, maturity, or love. There is no frame of reference against which to measure things, to know things, to appreciate and come to love things. Tillich called this pre-Fall state of being an "a paradise of dreaming innocence, an infant's paradise." Therefore, Tillich understands the Fall as representing our death from a non-ambiguous innocence (potential) and birth into a life of ambiguous good and evil experiences (actuality). (p. 149)

In Romans, we find a contrast of opposites between Adam and Christ. Adam is credited with bringing sin and condemnation into the world; Christ is credited with bringing righteousness and life into the world. "For if, by the trespass of one man [Adam], death reigned through that one man, how much more will those who receive God's abundant provision of grace and of the gift of righteousness reign in life through the one man, Jesus Christ." (Ro 5:17)

Closely related is the tension of trespass and condemnation versus righteousness and justification: "Consequently, just as the result of one trespass was condemnation for all men, so also the result of one act of righteousness was justification that brings life for all men." (Ro 5:18)

Both passages reveal the classic Christian tension of humanity in the world: at one polarity lies the negative consequences of sin (of being estranged from God) which includes condemnation, trespass and death; and at the the opposite polarity lies the positive consequences of union with God through a loving faith.

Also, there's a revealed tension between flesh and spirit (or body and soul) as in "The first man Adam became a living being, the last Adam, a life-giving spirit." (1 Co 15:47) In this passage, the "first man Adam" refers to the Adam of Genesis with the "last Adam" referring to Christ.

Just a few verses later, we find the great tension between earth and heaven: "The first man was of the dust of the earth, the second man from heaven." (1 Co 15:47)

Take water. It, too, is ambiguous. In the world, water is both good and bad, creative and destructive. In terms of being good, consider that water is essential for life: our bodies are composed primarily of water (approximately 65%); we must replenish ourselves constantly (without water, it estimated we can only live 3-10 days); and its use is necessary for the production of food. Yet water kills; it can be a negative element of life. The 2004 Asian tsunami resulted in the death of approximately 250,000 people.

In Scripture, water is often a holy symbol of life, of salvation through baptism, even in symbolic reference to Christ as the water of life. Also in Scripture, we find water kills, as in the great flood that almost destroyed all life. (Ge 7:1-24)

Water is both creative and destructive. Like all elements of life—being both the physical world and the individual—it's ambiguous in its experience.

Scripture seems to confirm that we can only think in opposites. And it opens a door to understanding the divine reason for God creating an ambiguous world (and, hence, one containing evil): its transformational power for maturity in Christ—maturing from our innate narcissism (the base level of love) to and toward agape (the highest, ideal form of love, God's essence).

Actualization of God, therefore requires an ambiguous frame, which necessarily contains/produces negative elements. Insofar as negative elements of being are considered bad or evil, then we are deep into understanding evil's ambiguity. Evil is, of course, bad, negative, undesired; yet, it's also good in the sense it potentiates and illuminates the positive, investing it with meaning and value. It is good because it is necessary to fulfill God's plan for creation.

Evil is necessary for learning, serving as the negative counterweight over and against which we come to know and highly treasure the positive. The binary structure of learning, therefore, is to evolution in terms of physically thriving and mentally growing as it is to theology in terms of spiritually thriving and growing in Christian maturity.

There's a difference between evolutionary theory and Christianity in how each understand the role of ambiguity. Evolution selects for survival in the world and argues that how well a species utilizes its ability to think in opposites largely determines its survival.

I argue that in Christian thought God selects for salvation, for life eternal, and uses the structure of ambiguity to promote salvation through awareness, appreciation and love of God. Further differentiating the two worldviews, I believe evolutionary theory argues a species' selection arises from chance and necessity, whereas Christianity argues a person's selection arises from one's free will choice (and, of course, God's omnipresent grace to accept that free will choice).

Evolution uses ambiguity to select for temporal survival; God selects ambiguity for eternal salvation.

3.3.3 DOUBT

For we were saved in this hope, but hope that is seen is not hope;
for why does one still hope for what he sees? But if we hope for what we
do not see, we eagerly wait for it with perseverance.
The Apostle Paul, Romans 8: 24

...in our postmodern times, we are increasingly aware
of the limitations of our human knowledge. We are aware perhaps as
never before of the gap between what we subjectively "know"
and what is objectively true. For people like us, boxed in little bodies
with narrow portals of physical senses that are interpreted by
fallible, limited (yet amazing!) little brains, absolute certainty is a gift
we have not been given. We can only aspire to relative
certainty, which involves relative uncertainty...which leaves room
for—no, more, which actually requires—faith.
Brian McLaren, *A Search for What Makes Sense: Finding Faith*

McLaren...has written or coauthored about a dozen books,
and his utter contempt for certainty....the poison of this perspective is
being increasingly injected into the evangelical church body....
As always, a war is being waged against the truth....Postmodernism
suggests that if objective truth exists, it cannot be known objectively
or with any degree of certainty. That is because (according to
postmodernists), the subjectivity of the human mind makes knowledge
of objective truth impossible....Postmodernism therefore has
no positive agenda to assert anything as true or good....
If we can't really know anything for certain, how can we judge
anything evil?...Postmodernism has resulted in a widespread
rejection of truth and the enshrinement of skepticism.
John MacArthur, *The Truth War:*
Fighting for Certainty in an Age of Deception

Overview

Doubt relates to the limits of human knowledge. Doubt is the uncertainty that necessarily arises not just from the structures of consciousness, free will, and ambiguity, but also other structures of reality such as subjectivity and contingency.

I argue that doubt is a necessary structure of being to accomplish God's plan for creation. It is the structure that limits our behavior, creating both positive experiences of life and negative experiences of life.

Premises

P10: The human ability to know the truth or falsity of the transcendent (beyond the physical world and laws of nature) objects of their faith is inherently limited by doubt.

P11: Doubt arises from free decisions being made by conscious individuals in an ambiguous world.

P12: Doubt is a necessary element of love, courage, faith and other moral actions because objective certainty leaves no room for moral action.

Definition

By **doubt** I don't mean a *subjective belief or faith in transcendent phenomena* that resides within any person's conscious apprehension of the world. Rather, I mean the impossibility of a person trying to prove to others that the object of their belief or faith in metaphysical phenomena is objectively true. By objectively true I mean a truth that is (a) not dependent upon the human mind for existence, or (b) at least is consistent with the current scientific method of verification or falsification.

Doubt as I use it here is of the latter type: objective doubt. I argue the *design of being includes objective doubt*.

Kant argued basically the same thing in his *Critique of Pure Reason*

(1999). Kant argued we cannot know about the "noumenon"—the metaphysical realm—as opposed to the phenomenal—things perceptible by the senses or through immediate experience. Thus, there are inherent limits to knowledge.

This is not to say that we cannot subjectively believe something is objectively true and have no doubt about that belief. And it's not to say that our subjective belief in the object of our belief is not objectively true. It may be. It is merely to say that *no one can objectively prove to another that the object of their belief (or faith) in a transcendent possibility is objectively true.*

Good Reason for Structure of Doubt

The divine reason for the structure of doubt is to enable love, since love must be freely chosen. To be *freely chosen means* there must not only be ambiguous choices, but also *uncertainty (doubt)* as to the correct choice. If there is no uncertainty or doubt in a choice, then it's not free. Rather, it's largely, if not totally, determined by the certainty of, say, chosing A over choices B and C.

Decisions that are driven by certainty lack the courage associated with uncertainty. When there is doubt or uncertainty, there is risk—risk that one is wrong in their decision, risk in the negative consequences that flow from a wrong decision, etc..

Let's assume you see a live grenade land on the ground in a school yard crowded with young children. Let's further assume you know, absolutely and without doubt: (a) the grenade was activated five seconds ago when the pin was pulled; (b) you have thirty seconds left to dispose of the grenade before it explodes; (c) it takes only 10 ten seconds to walk over to a concrete vault and throw the grenade into it; (d) that when the grenade explodes inside the concrete vault, no one will be injured; (e) that there is no risk in you handling the grenade and taking it over to the concrete vault for safe storage; and (f) that all of this is absolutely assured.

Was there any bravery in your actions if you pick up the grenade and take it over to that concrete vault? I argue there was none because there was no risk. The only morally consequential action possible in this situation would be to walk away and let the grenade explode, killing scores of children. If you knew this tragedy was a certainty—let's say you knew no one else would act, knew they would die if you did not act, and you still refused to save the children—then this is a morally bad act. Failing to help someone in dire need, especially when there is no risk involved in action, is repugnant.

Thus, certainty about future events obviates the possibility of morally good action but it still allows for morally bad action.

Also, doubt promotes humility and retards human pride and hubris. If sin is estrangement from God, then sin is the hubristic notion that humans don't need God. Pride, Niebuhr argued, is our greatest sin (1996):

> Man is an individual but he is not self-sufficing. The law of his nature is love, a harmonious relation of life to life in obedience to the divine center and source of his life. This law is violated when man seeks to make himself the centre and source of his own life. His sin is therefore spiritual and not carnal....Man, in other words, is a sinner not because he is one limited individual within a whole but rather because he is betrayed by his very ability to survey the whole to imagine himself the whole. (v. 1, p. 16, 17)

We have pride when we think we know, or can know, things perfectly and can accomplish all things perfectly. Niebuhr suggests that there is a desire to know things perfectly, and this desire arises from the risk and uncertainty inherent in our freedom. This desire for certainty is a flight from the anxiety of our limits of knowing things perfectly. This anxiety arises from not trusting in the Lord. As Paul told the church at Philippi, "Do not be anxious about anything, but in everything, by prayer and petition, with thanksgiving, present your requests to God. And the peace of God, which transcends all understanding, will guard your hearts and your minds in Christ." (Php 4:6-7)

We can never objectively prove to others our subjective truth of metaphysical phenomena, like God's reality. Confronting this limit of knowing, this reality of doubt, can and should promote a state of mind open to God (as opposed to human thought and action, or the physical world) as the only objective ground upon which to stand. That state of mind includes humility, helplessness, need and dependency. Our limits of knowing lead us to God.

Necessary Cost of Evil for Structure of Doubt

I argue that the structure of doubt, by itself, is considered by almost everyone as a negative element of being. We want to know things about the world and ourselves, and we want to know it certainly and without doubt. We don't like risk and not knowing what existence means.

We ask: "Why am I here?" "Is there a God?" "Why doesn't God reveal himself to me in certainty?" "Why let me anguish in doubt and uncertainty?" "What happens when I die?" "What am I to do with my life?" The lack of absolute certainty and objective guideposts to guide us in answering these questions of ultimate concern creates great anxiety and stress among many (most?) people. Anxiety, worry and stress (arising from doubt) are negative states of being, considered by many as evil elements in an imperfect world.

Discussion

A good way to understand the innate nature of human doubt is to understand the structure of **consciousness.** Consciousness is intentional, that is, it is outward directed toward something your consciousness is apprehending. Consciousness requires a conscious subject to be contemplating an object.

Thus, there are two factors involved in consciousness. One is the subject observing an object, and the other is the object being observed. This creates two possible truths, one subjective and one objective.

The subjective truth is the subject's personal assessment of the object. I may say that I have read, thought and observed everything I could about God, and that I find that God exists. To me (the subject), God's (the object) reality is a true fact.

The objective truth concerns the object itself. How do we verify to others the objective truth of our experience of the object? As concerns transcendental or metaphysical phenomena, like God's reality, we can't. And even as concerns the objective verification of physical objects within the world, I argue there are problems.

For example, let's assume I'm observing a red chair and am certain it's a red chair that exists in the world independent of my observing it. What, for example, if the object being observed isn't being observed correctly? Plato's (429/427 BC - 348/347 BC) well known *Allegory of the Cave* is a perfect illustration of this principle.

Plato described people living in a cave who saw shadows on the wall cast by objects walking outside the cave opening. The cave dwellers thought they were seeing the actual objects as they objectively existed. But they weren't. They were merely seeing the shadows. The objects being observed were different than what was believed by their subjective observation. How can we know that our subjective belief is objectively true? How do we know we're not seeing shadows?

What if I'm color blind? What if I'm hallucinating? Or dreaming? Or a zombie? Or a brain in a vat or some software matrix? We're back to Decartes' maxim of the limits of what we can know certainly, only here it's what we can prove certainly. If all we can know with certainty is that, *because I think, therefore, I am*, then we can never verify, independent from our mind, that our perception of reality is really reality.

This is the structure of faith—subject and object, me thinking about God—and it admittedly causes some confusion. Let me unpack it a bit more. First, I can be absolutely sure, without doubt or uncertainty, that God exists. This is subjective faith, that is, a belief I hold within my mind, heart and soul. Every bone in my body might scream it out. I might be willing to die for my faith, it is so strong.

And yet, I cannot prove objectively the object of my faith. I cannot objectively prove that God exists. How can I? How can a finite human prove an infinite thing? I can't. Conversely, no finite human can disprove an infinite thing. No atheist can disprove the reality of God just as theists cannot objectively prove God.

My subjective belief may, in fact, reflect objective reality. That is not an impossibility. However, in metaphysical matters I can never objectively prove my subjective faith. Which was what Paul might have been thinking when he said "We live by faith, not by sight." (2 Co 5:7)

Tillich (1967) goes even further by not limiting doubt to only metaphysical phenomena: "Every encounter with reality, whether with situations or groups, or individuals, is burdened with practical and theoretical uncertainty. This uncertainty is caused not only by the finitude of the individual but also by the ambiguity of that which a person encounters. Life is marked by ambiguity." (v. 2, p. 132)

Tillich continues: "Subjective reason is the rational structure of the mind, while objective reason is the rational structure of reality" (v. 1, p. 77); and adds that this creates a basic polarity, in tension, between relativism and absolutism—that is, between (a) thinking that the truth varies from person to person based upon their subjective perceptions (relativism), and (b) the truth of reality (absolutism) doesn't vary from person to person. (v. 1, p. 86).

This is the tension of faith: our subjective faith and the truth of God.

* * *

Human consciousness necessarily involves the structure of *subjectivity*. Subjectivity as used here refers to the fact that all knowledge of the world is gained at the level of and by each individual. There is no objective, collective, or central bank where knowledge is deposited. All the knowledge in the world is acquired, stored and used in each creature's brain. If there were no creatures in the world, there would be no knowledge gained from learning because there would be no individual consciousness. The brain is designed for learning. Stones do not learn.

Whether or not the world cares about our brains or about human leaning is another matter. Our consciousness, and, hence, our subjective knowledge, may have evolutionary value and function, but the cold and brute universe might not care one whit about human consciousness or learning. I concede that possibility. The point for now is that each of our brains learns about the world. And what my brains learns or feels or thinks or concludes about the world is probably different than yours in terms of what we think is *true*.

Subjectivity is a term I use to describe this inherent disconnect between my brain and everyone else's brain. We have different experiences, different assessments or understanding of the same observed phenomena, different worldviews, different feelings and opinions and prejudices, different DNA. True, there is intersubjectivity—the network of shared knowledge between creatures—whereby we can share our subjectivity feelings. That provides us some approximation of the general consensus as to the truthfulness or falseness of our subjective beliefs, providing comfortable conformation (but not objective certainty).

This is annoyingly obvious upon watching the news presented by different media outlets. Let's say a person is shot by a policeman. According to different commentators, this is evidence of...of what? Is it further evidence of police brutality and over-reaction if not outright racism? Is it further evidence of a societal breakdown in terms of respect for the law within certain American sub cultures? Is it further evidence of our lostness, our inherent depravity, as revealed in the Bible's talk of God evicting us from paradise and into a harsh reality "east of Eden?" Is it evidence that life is absurd, a chaos, and our feeble attempts to rationalize it through our social conventions and norms—such as laws, legal systems and incarceration—is a sham? There seems to be no universal consensus as to what this shooting means, an outcome that should not be surprising if all knowledge is accumulated at the level of each individual creature.

I'm not suggesting an answer to the question of law and order posed above. Rather, I'm suggesting that what reigns today is what has always reigned: subjectivity.

Every person's "truth" of things is just that: the person's truth and no one else's. It might be shared by others. It might be objectively true. It might not be objectively true. The point is, no one knows with objective certainty because of the universal structure of doubt.

People usually get this confused concerning this gap between subjective truth and objective truth. It's natural. Who wants to work hard to finally get a grip on how they believe the world actually "is" only to admit, at the same time, that it's only their view and nothing more? Who wants to admit they might be seeing mere shadows on a wall instead of real people?

* * *

The structure of doubt also involves *contingency*. Contingency means that a future event cannot be predicted with certainty because future outcomes depend upon random chance, that is, variables that are unknown because they are free.

For example, if I really am as free as I argue I am, I can choose tomorrow to either kill myself or not kill myself. The consequences of my decision, for myself and other people, are many and totally dependent upon my decision. In that case, how can anyone know or predict an actual outcome if it all depends upon my future free decision? I argue you cannot. As such, contingency means the future is undetermined. It is open or indeterminate and not closed as it would be with a predetermined future.

I won't repeat previous discussions about determinism versus indeterminism, except to remind readers that this is a theodicy based upon libertarian free will. Libertarian free will means God, our of love and for love, freely subordinated God's sovereign will to creatures as concerns their moral actions. Since God doesn't predetermine future human actions of a moral nature, then future human actions are unknown. Thus, future outcomes are contingent upon unpredictable, free human actions. Likewise, I've argued that the physical world has been designed to match and mimic human free will such that it, too, is not fully determined.

A question arises of just how contingent or undetermined is the world? Of course, God can limit or determine any outcome in the world that God wants to limit or determine, but my understanding of what vests reality with great heft and meaning is that there is no limit to contingency in the world. The future is open, undetermined and contingent upon the interaction of unknown variables.

Process theology suggests that not only the world's, but even God's, future is open and contingent. Open theism parts with process theology on this point. Open theism argues God is a necessary truth and not a contingent truth. That is, God is a fact that cannot be otherwise, and is true in all circumstances and all possible worlds. While God is affected by events within the world, such as an act of loving faith, and thus is mutable and movable, God's essence and nature never changes. God always "is." If the entire universe evaporated, God remains. God is the eternal "I am" while the world is finite, with beginning and end. God has no beginning and end.

I argue that, theoretically, life on earth could end. But that doesn't mean life in the cosmos ends. If the scientists are correct, and the number of stars and planets in the universe/multiverse are as mind-numbingly numerous as suggested, then the possibility of life elsewhere seems highly probable.

If this earth were the only place in the cosmos with sentient life, then I hope and expect God would somehow limit the contingencies such as to preserve life on earth for a very long time. But, if there are untold other planets with sentient life, then there seems to be no reason that a world-encompassing, life-ending cataclysm couldn't strike this planet at any moment, say a super-volcano or a massive meteor or comet strike.

This thought is obviously disturbing. But the book of Revelations promises an end time to the physical world.

If this disturbing thought shakes someone out of the complacency of their ordinary lives, of just marking time, engaged in distraction or addiction—*mailing in their life*, so to speak—and gets them to start taking seriously the reason for creation and the reason for their life, then it, like all thoughts in an ambiguous world, has a positive value.

* * *

In addition to consciousness, subjectivity, and contingency, the previously discussed *structures of free will* and ambiguity also invite and *require doubt*. Once again, free will requires choices which ambiguity provides, and those choices depend upon one's morality. Because there is moral value, positive or negative, in every choice (e.g., self interest or self sacrifice for another's self interest) there is risk in action.

Doubt, therefore, is an element of faith. Doubt is implied in free will and ambiguity. And doubt is inherent in subjectivity, consciousness and contingency.

Maturity in Christ requires many things. One of them is doubt. Doubt makes us reach, risk, and leap. Faith is an act of courageous love. Courageous love requires doubt. *Certainty robs faith of its love and courage.*

* * *

This issue of doubt, of subjective and objective truth, has caused great division within the body of the church. Many Christians are deeply troubled by this claim that we cannot objectively access truth. The problem usually arises between liberal Christians and fundamentalists Christians.

An excellent example of this tension within the body of the church can be found in dueling books of American pastors and writers: Brian McLaren's *A Search for What Makes Sense* (2007) and John MacArthur's *The Truth War (2007)*.

The headnote quotes to this chapter illustrate this division. McLaren would be labeled, for lack of a better term, more liberal, and MacArthur, more fundamental. Each represents a different approach on how to treat and understand faith.

McLaren (2007) suggests we should admit the obvious: that our human knowledge, and, hence, our faith beliefs, are limited by many factors, one factor being that knowledge is gained subjectively. He does not suggest that what we subjectively believe in our spiritual and cognitive centers is false. Rather, he suggests that we cannot objectively prove to another the truth of the object of our faith. He then seems to argue this should temper an arrogant, militant zeal. Rather, it should foster humility and tolerance. And he suggests it both reflects reality and helps bridge the enormous gulf between other religions and even atheism, through loving tolerance.

MacArthur (2007) sees this "relativism" as "...not authentic Christianity. Not knowing what you believe...is by definition a kind of unbelief. Refusing to acknowledge and defend the revealed truth of God is a particularly stubborn and pernicious kind of unbelief. Advocating ambiguity, exalting uncertainty, or otherwise deliberately clouding the truth is a sinful way of nurturing unbelief." (p. xi)

Anticipating fundamentalism's response, British minister Steve Chalke wrote in the introduction to McLaren's book (2007): "Many people crave certainty. They don't want to have to think, agonize, or grapple with life's difficult questions for themselves. Instead they want dogma. They want guaranteed answers. They want shoot-from-the-hip certainty. This book is not for them." (p. 11)

I side with McLaren on this issue but certainly appreciate and understand the natural urge of Christians to want their subjective faith to be objectively true. However, the obvious question then becomes: *given our need for objective truth—for certainty—why then is God veiled from reality, partly revealed, partly hidden?* Why were we evicted from paradise and, thus, separated from God? Why do we live in a world of different religions and among atheists who doubt God exists? If God were an obvious, objective reality beyond all doubt—if God were as certain as MacArthur suggests God is—then why don't we all believe the same thing?

This very issue of inherent doubt, and what many see as the divine reason for God's partial hiddenness, is part of my argument. And it has many perceived advantages for this theodicy. First, the structure of doubt seems to reflect the reality of how the world actually is designed. That is, all knowledge is acquired at the individual level and, hence, is subject to limits, the most obvious being the inability to objectively prove the truth of the objects of one's beliefs.

A consensus that human knowledge is limited by an inherent unknowability is so wide spread today that it largely explains and fuels postmodern narratives of the world such as feminism, post-colonialism, relativism and many other world views which see the past as dominated—not by the truth of things—but by the sheer, subjective power of white, male dominance. Which leads to another perceived advantage of this theodicy: it works today in a postmodern, relativistic world. It accepts subjectivity and the limits of human knowledge.

Even accepting postmodernism dogma, I argue this theodicy does not in any rational way undermine the Gospel message. On the contrary, the Gospel message is advanced by postmodern thinking in the sense that Kierkegaard suggested: that God works at the individual level and not the collective level. God wants a loving relationship with you, personally. A person's subjective experience/encounter/belief in God is faith's link to the Holy.

Tillich provides some comfort that the structure of doubt, caused by subjectivity, can be largely mitigated by the power of divine revelation. He argues (1967) that a "miracle" occurs when a person subjectively receives divine revelation (the objective truth of the world):

> Revelation always is a subjective and objective event in strict inter-dependence. Someone is grasped by the manifestation of the mystery; this is the subjective side of the event. Something occurs through which the mystery of revelation grasps someone; this is the objective side. These two sides cannot be separated. If nothing happens objectively, nothing is revealed. If no one receives what happens subjectively, the event fails to reveal anything. The objective occurrence and the subjective reception belong to the whole event of revelation. Revelation is not real without the receiving side, and is not real without the giving side. The mystery appears objectively in terms of what traditionally has been called 'miracle.' It appears subjectively is what has sometimes been called 'ecstasy.' (v. 1, p. 111)

Subjective doubt, it would seem, disappears—for all practical purposes—in revelation. This explains that, even though the experience of revelation is subjective, doubt fuels a faith of courageous love, even unto death on the cross, due to the power of its revealed truth.

One only needs to consider two Bible stories to illustrate this power of revelation to strengthen our subjective faith. One is the conversion of Paul on the road to Damascus. He turned his life around on the spot and proceeded to dedicate the remainder of his life to Christ, even unto death.

Likewise, is the remarkable conversion of Christ's original disciples. They went from doubters of Christ's claims—distancing themselves from Him during his arrest, trial and crucifixion, with Peter denying three times to Roman inquisitors that he even knew Christ. And yet, after Christ's resurrection event, all the disciples recommitted to

Christ's journey, task and message to bravely march forth into a hostile mission field, even to their sure death (which most of them suffered for their faith).

These behaviors cannot, to me, be understood absent a belief that divine revelation robs subjective doubt of its power to influence our decisions. God's reality, though it still could not be objectively proven by Paul or the disciples to others, was so certain in their hearts and minds that they were willing to devote their life and face almost certain persecution and death for this belief.

Scriptural Support

We have been talking about doubt in relation to objective certainty, that is, the truth of the world independent of human thought. Scripture tells us that God is the way and the truth. And that the "Truth shall set you free" (Jn 8:32) with "Truth" being the truth of the Gospel message.

The Scripture does not speak of subjectivity, consciousness, contingency or ambiguity. However, everyone who came to the Truth in Scripture came to it personally. And everyone who came to the Truth personally, went forth and witnessed unto others what had been revealed to them.

The disciples did not try to objectively prove the truth of the object of their faith. They merely witnessed to others, revealing their subjective experience of the Truth.

Christ performed miracles and that created a feeling of certainty, of objective truth, during His ministry. However, Christ's greatest miracle—the resurrection—is shrouded in doubt. And this major fact, alone, speaks volumes about God's design of reality.

This major fact was dramatically used in Dostoevsky's novel *The Brothers Karamazov* (1990). Ivan tells his brother, Alyosha, about a dream he had where Jesus came back to earth during the brutal and bloody period of the Spanish Inquisition.

The Grand Inquisitor tells Christ he'll be killed, burnt at the stake, because he gave humans more than they could cope with when he gave them freedom. The Inquisitor chided Christ about his earthly death by refusing to come down from the cross at the moment of death and thereby remove all doubt that Christ was, in fact, the Son of God. By not coming down from that cross in front of the whole world, Christ left humanity with uncertainty and doubt, left them armed only with a free will to believe or not believe Christ is the Lord.

Chalke's introduction to McLaren's work(2007) addresses this charge by Dostoevsky's Inquisitor:

> One thing that the old Inquisitor was right about in his assessment was Jesus's consistent refusal to do things that would force people into believing in him. Instead, he always allowed room for doubt and presented people with the opportunity to explore the question. He never pushed, forced, bludgeoned, beat, coerced, cajoled, manhandled, or manipulated people into faith—he never threatened them with 'an offer they couldn't refuse.' (p. 10)

Christ did reveal his resurrected self to various people within his circle of close followers following burial. The visions of the resurrected Christ differ. In John and Luke an unknown ordinary man (the gardener or a traveler) is later recognized as Jesus. Again in Luke and John, a spirit mysteriously enters the apostles' residence despite the locked doors. The ghost later becomes a stranger with flesh and bones, who says he is Jesus and invites the apostles to touch him and eat with them.

Whatever the post-death encounter, one things is certain: the encounter by the apostles was so overwhelmingly powerful that, seemingly overnight, they converted from cowards at Christ's execution to committed, fearless advocates. They marched forth into the world, proclaiming the Good News of the Gospel, knowing it would lead to their sure death and possible crucifixion. Which, in almost every case, is exactly where their venture into the hostile mission field led them.

British scholar specializing in the history of Jesus, Geza Vermes (1924-2013) provides six explantations for what happened after Christ's death and the empty tomb was discovered in *The Resurrection* (2008). His theories are: the body removed by someone unconnected with Jesus; the body stolen by His disciples; empty tomb was not Jesus's tomb; Jesus was buried alive and later left the tomb; the migrant Jesus; and resurrection was spiritual not bodily. (p. 141-148)

Vermes did not include "two extremes that are not susceptible to rational judgement, the blind faith of the fundamentalist believer [belief in a bodily resurrection] and the out-of-hand rejection of the inveterate skeptic [unbelief in a bodily resurrection]." (p. 141) After concluding that none of his six theories "stands up to stringent scrutiny" (p. 148) he concludes that what happened was a resurrection in the hearts of the disciples.

Vermes concludes that something miraculous happened immediately after Christ's death that exerted a life-altering influence on His disciples, a Resurrection that continues today in the hearts of believers:

> What matters is that within a short time the terrified small group of the original followers of Jesus, still hidden from public gaze, all at once underwent a powerful mystical experience in Jerusalem on the Feast of the Weeks (Pentacost). Filled with the promise of the Holy Spirit, the pusillanimous men were suddenly metamorphosed into ecstatic spiritual warriors." (p. 149)

While Christ's actual bodily resurrection defies physical laws and, thus, can never be verified or falsified—because it is a supernatural event—the post death lives of Christ's disciple's have historical verification.

Something happened after Christ's death that defies rational explanation; something other than one of Vermes' six *rational* theories.

The apostle Paul proclaimed that "If there is no resurrection of the dead, then not even Christ has been raised. And if Christ has not been raised, our preaching is useless." (1 Co 13, 14)

I believe Paul is correct. The Word of God would surely not have been disseminated to the world but for the work of Christ's disciples. And, as Paul notes, those disciples would not have spread the gospel but for Christ's resurrection.

Most defenders of the faith who use logic to defend the faith (apologists), point to the historical fact of the post-death actions of the disciples to prove or at least render probable the fact that Christ rose from the dead.

My purpose in exploring the resurrection story in this theodicy is to illustrate God's purpose in weaving doubt into the equation of life. The resurrection story is the central story of Christianity. Paul is correct: all of Christianity hinges upon Christ's resurrection, an ancient historical event shrouded in mystery.

Did it happen? Was it bodily or, as Vermes suggests, a spiritual Resurrection within the hearts of people? And does it matter either way?

Science cannot prove Christ had a bodily resurrection. History cannot prove Christ had a bodily resurrection. No finite way of knowing can verify or falsify a supernatural event. Christ's bodily resurrection will always be shrouded in doubt. And here, let me repeat, it is objective doubt and not subjective doubt I am talking about.

Christ's resurrection lacks objective certainty(verification) but is overcome by subjective faith. This pestering *objective* doubt is one more essential ingredient necessary to make a person's leap of faith one of courageous love.

Would God want it any other way?

* * *

Finally, we have the pre-resurrection story of Christ on the cross.

What should we make of Christ's death on the cross? Of His inability/refusal to defy death and crawl down from that cross so as to remove all doubt that He is, in fact, the Savior sent by God for humanity's redemption? Could it be that Christ's refusal to defy death, as Dostoevsky's Inquisitor thought would be the reasonable thing to do, reflected His "consistent refusal to do things that would force people into believing in him. Instead, he always allowed room for doubt and presented people with the opportunity to explore the question."?

What should we make of His cry in dereliction before dying: "My God, My God. Why hast though forsaken me?" (Mt 27:45; Mk 15:34)

Christ seems to be telling us that the condition of sin creates negative or evil consequences, such as His physical and emotional suffering: a sense of abandonment, uncertainty and doubt. "Why" Christ called out. "Why?" At that moment, Christ did not know why; Christ was in doubt.

By absorbing all the sins of the world at the moment of death, Christ seems to be telling us from the cross that doubt is a condition of sin, of us being estranged, necessarily, from God. Otherwise, how do we understand his *cry in dereliction*?

* * *

The Bible contains stories of miracles, being events that defy natural or scientific laws. Christ's resurrection—the foundational claim of Christianity—is one such miracle. Since these miracles defy natural or scientific laws, they cannot be objectively verified or falsified. Faith in them necessarily includes doubt—objective doubt. Being subjective faith, belief in Christ's resurrection requires a courageous, loving faith.

The presence of doubt in Biblical revelation is not a sign that faith in Christ is necessarily irrational or mystical. Doubt can be understood, logically, as necessary for humans to grow in Christian maturity. If God's reality was objectively certain, then love, courage, faith, and other consequential acts of moral goodness would be impossible.

Scripture indicates that God wants a love based upon loving faith. Doubt is an inherent element of faith and a requirement for courageous love. Humans knowing God exists, without any objective doubt, robs God of accomplishing God's plan because it robs the act of love of God of its power and beauty gained through a courageous commitment in faith.

3.3.4. ANXIETY

Anxiety is the dizziness of freedom.
Soren Kierkegaard, *The Concept of Anxiety*

*The fundamental human question seeking theological response
has to do with anxiety in confronting our finitude. Such anxiety is the
product of an 'existential shock' at the contemplation of the
possibility of our not-being, that is to say, our contingency.*
Paul Tillich, *Jesus: The Complete Guide*

*...man, being both free and bound, both limited and limitless,
is anxious. Anxiety is the inevitable concomitant of the paradox of
freedom and finiteness in which man is involved. Anxiety is
the internal precondition of sin....The ideal possibility is that faith in
the ultimate security of God's love would overcome all
immediate insecurities of nature and history....The freedom from
anxiety...is a possibility only if perfect trust in
divine security has been achieved.*
Reinhold Niebuhr, *The Nature and Destiny of Man*

*...anxiety is the fuel of psychopathology; that psychic operations,
some conscious and some unconscious, evolve to deal with anxiety;
that these psychic operations (defense mechanisms) constitute
psychopathology; and that, though they provide safety, they
invariably restrict growth and experience.*
Irvin D. Yalom, *Existential Psychotherapy*

Overview

Anxiety is the state of *full awareness of the condition of sin* (being separated from God) and realizing what existence means without God.

When we stare into the dark abyss of nothingness with its suggestion of annihilation and an absurd meaningless for each of our lives, we know what a creation without God is like. It is death, not life. This should impart knowledge and appreciation of, and love for God as life.

Anxiety is a structure of being needed for our Christian maturity. Without it, we might remain prideful, self-reliant, thinking we don't need God. We might think that even adrift in an ambiguous, subjective and uncertain world, armed only with our freedom, we can overcome the limitations of the world.

This is a fool's errand, not unlike the ancient Babylonians who thought they could build a ziggurat to heaven on their own, without God's help. The parable of the Tower of Babel, suggests otherwise. (Ge 11)

The point of creation is not for us to be God or self-rescue ourselves. There is no rescue from the tragic consequences of the world without a transcendent possibility (God). Therefore, human pride with its hubris and the thought we don't need God is, perhaps, the greatest sin. Anxiety serves to jolt us from this sinful attitude.

Premises

P13: Anxiety is a prime driver of human behavior.

P14: Anxiety is the natural outcome of conscious individuals having to freely choose among ambiguous choices within a world of doubt.

P15: Anxiety is the state of sin (of being separated from God).

P16: Anxiety illuminates not only the possibility of no God but, also, the possibility of God.

P17: Confronting anxiety requires confronting the givens of existence (the human condition).

P18: Confronting the givens of existence leads to the realization of our need for God.

Definition

Anxiety is not ordinary fear, such as fear of spiders or snakes or heights. Fear is an unpleasant emotion, usually caused by anticipation of something not wanted, harmful, or dangerous. The object of fear can often be overcome. Perhaps the object can be destroyed, such as by stepping on a dreaded spider. Or perhaps the fear can be mitigated by desensitization techniques, whereby we might overcome, say, our fear of crowds by slowly being exposed to increasingly larger groups of people.

In this theodicy, anxiety is the human condition that, according to Yalom (1980), arises from "a conflict that flows from the individual's confrontation with the givens of existence." (p. 8) And the givens of existence cannot be destroyed or easily mitigated through desensitization.

Yalom goes on to list those *givens of existence*: death, freedom, isolation and meaninglessness. He argues all maladaptive behavior arises from our failure to confront and somehow accommodate the challenges presented by these givens of existence.

We usually fail to accommodate these *givens* for two reasons. One reason is the great difficulty in confronting the givens of life since they create anxiety. The other is that the givens of existence do not easily (if at all) lend themselves to solution. For example, there is no escape from our freedom, though escape we try. There is no finite solution to death.

"Existential tragedy", as used in this book refers to the condition of living in despair (without hope). If there is no transcendent possibility, then there is no hope for our lives surmounting the limits of finitude. Yalom says (1980): "Each of us craves perdurance, groundedness, community, and pattern; and yet we must face inevitable death, groundlessness, isolation, and meaninglessness." (p. 485) The negative consequences of sin ultimately win—without a transcendent possibility.

A "transcendent possibility" refers to a possibility that transcends the physical world, is not of this world (supernatural) such as heaven or God.

This is not to suggest that there are no people who see a life without a transcendent possibility as a tragedy. Rather, it applies to people who hope for eternal union and a life of enduring meaning.

Good Reason for Structure of Aanxiety

Full awareness and loving appreciation of God and God's plan for creation requires awareness of the possibility of there being no God. The possibility of no God suggests our nonbeing; that our life is both meaningless (in the eternal sense) and doomed to eternal annihilation through death.

In other words, anxiety serves to acknowledge our hopeless condition in finitude if there is no God. This state of *anxiety can lead us to God* as the as only possible antidote to our existential malady.

The *Christian message provides the answers to our existential tragedy* of being in the world. It provides the antidote to anxiety through union in Christ. Through union in Christ we: conquer death; have eternal meaning in our lives; find a solid foundation and direction for our freedom; and enjoy loving union.

This realization of sin, of being alone, apart from God, humbles us, undermines our hubristic notions of self-salvation, opens us to the realization that our status is one of complete need—we are nothing without God. In this humble state, we become open to the possibility of God.

What is the possibility of God? God is the possibility left when all other possibilities are extinguished. It is the moment of hopelessness, of total despair. As Kierkegaard stated the proposition in his book, *The Sickness Unto Death (1989)*:

> ...but the decisive moment only comes when man is brought to the utmost extremity, where in human terms there is no possibility. Then the question is whether he will believe that for God everything is possible, that is, whether he will have faith....Salvation, then, is humanly speaking the most impossible thing for all; but for God everything is possible! This is the struggle of faith, which struggles insanely, if you will, for possibility. For only possibility saves....in the end, that is, when the question is one of having faith, the only thing that helps is that for God everything is possible. (1989, p.68, 69)

As many Christian theists agree, from Barth and Kierkegaard to modern apologists like Lewis, it is precisely at the moment we stare into the abyss—the dark void of non-being, of meaninglessness, of absurdity—that we are most open to the reality of God. The transformative mechanism that opens our hearts to the possibility of God is the existential dilemma we are trapped in: an ambiguous world, armed only with our free-will to react in doubt, alone and anxious.

In this sense, *anxiety* is a back door to God, *an anti-epiphany of no God*. All roads lead to God, and the important point being made here is that a paralyzing anxiety born of utter despair and separation from God can be a road to God. In fact, it may be the main road most people travel to find God.

Necessary Cost of Evil for Structure of Anxiety

The experience of anxiety is terrifying. Tillich (2000) says: "It is impossible for a finite being to stand naked anxiety for more than a flash of time. People who have experienced these moments...have told of the unimaginable horror of it." (p. 39)

If sin is defined as separation or estrangement from God, and evil is defined as the negative consequence of sin, then anxiety is one of those negative consequences. *Anxiety can be thought of as pure evil.* Yet, in our ambiguous world, even pure evil serves a divine good. The negative experience of anxiety defines, illuminates and promotes the opposite, positive quality of sin: union with God.

Once again, we find a polarity: sin and salvation, or separation and reunion. Each defines the other. Each is meaningless without the other.

To know, appreciate and love God, we need to know what it feels like if there is no God. The experience of anxiety, therefore, is ambiguous: both good and evil.

Discussion

What is the function of anxiety? Is our behavior driven by the need to deny or suppress the anxiety that arises from our confrontation with the *givens of existence*? Does everyone suffer anxiety?

Let me begin by describing my episodes of anxiety. The first episode was late at night, in rural Kentucky, walking back to my car from my cabin in the woods for some object I had forgotten.

I stopped in the road, looked up at the clear night sky, full of stars, listening to the sounds of the forest and lake echoing through the trees. And then I was suddenly and without warning overwhelmed with terror. My heart raced, my chest tightened, I became dizzy and felt totally alone and disconnected from the world, even myself. My sudden realization was that life made no sense, was absurd, and no conscious scenario made any sense—not time unending, not time ending. All was absurd and meaningless.

I was shaken to my core and fought hard to regain some sense of proportion, some sense of normalcy. My defense mechanisms had all failed. I suddenly had no grand rationalization for what was happening, nor could I deny what I was experiencing. It was as if for the first time in my life I was staring at reality, realizing nothing made sense, and all the sense I previously imagined was just a fabricated, cognitive construct for the mental sanity necessary to go on living with purpose and hope.

Later in life, I occasionally had similar anxiety attacks marked by total terror, the wake-up-in-the-middle-of-the-night-and-scream terror. It was almost always at night, as I fell asleep and was in that twilight zone where my defense shields, so to speak, were down, allowing this sudden realization of meaningless absurdity to flood in and over me.

I would roll out of bed, fall on my knees, and yell, out loud, "Oh no, Oh God, no." My wife would wake and ask if I was okay. I caught my breath, regained some mental footing and told her I'd had a nightmare. Later I admitted to anxiety attacks.

It got worse. I was eventually able to bring on the attacks during the day when the sun was shining and my protective mental weapons were fully armed and operational.

I could bring on the terror reactions by the contemplation that life was meaningless and absurd.

Of course, I grappled with this most powerful of experiences. One observation was that it was always better when I was with people and not alone with my thoughts. Clearly, I concluded, this is one of the most powerful reasons we are social animals and probably largely explains why so many people need to be in an almost permanent state of stimulation through music, video, gaming, social media, sports or other grand distractions.

I realized that in this state of anxiety, God was not there. Missing, for example, was the closeness I felt to God when baptized as a teenager, or in prayer. When I read Tillich's definition of sin as the condition of being estranged from God, I agreed and began to understand the wisdom of that observation. I understood then that one of the conditions of sin was an overwhelming dread of a meaningless existence which ends in annihilation upon death.

I also discovered that my experience of this anxiety attack—what I call an *existential epiphany* (a sudden realization of nothingness)—was not that uncommon.

* * *

What did these terrifying experiences mean? What did they imply? There are many ways to analyze them. Here, I briefly look at science's explanations, primarily *depth psychology, evolutionary theory,* the philosophy of *existentialism as well as a view from art and literature.*

* * *

For *depth psychology,* Yalom's book (1980) relates a similar experience of a patient. Recounting the treatment of a "highly successful, hard-driving executive," Yalom noted:

> At the age of twelve he was sleeping outside, looking at the sky, and suddenly felt himself separated from mother earth and drifting between the stars. Where was he? Where did he come from? Where did something (rather than nothing) come from? He felt overcome with aloneness, with helplessness, and with groundlessness. (p. 359)

Another patient of Yalom's (1980) "had a recurrent nightmare that dated back to early childhood and now, in adulthood, resulted in severe insomnia—in fact, in a sleep phobia, since he was terrified of going to sleep...[In his dream] his world melted away, exposing him to nothingness." (p. 355)

Yalom quotes from the patient's experience of the dream:

I am awake in my room. Suddenly I begin to notice that everything is changing. The window frame seems stretched and then wavy, the bookcases squashed, the doorknob disappears, and a hole appears in the door which gets larger and larger. Everything begins to lose its shape and begins to melt. There's nothing there any more and I begin to scream. (p. 356)

Yalom (1980) calls this experience "existential isolation" and describes it as "an unbridgeable gulf between oneself and any other being. It also refers to an isolation even more fundamental—a separation between the individual and the world." (p. 355)

To Yalom's definition I would add that existential isolation (or alienation) can also be a separation from oneself. This helps explain the terror of death. Not only does death suggest alienation from others and the world, it suggests separation from self: we lose our consciousness, our memories, and whatever else we consider our self.

Yalom (1980) proceeds to describe a phenomenon he labels "defamiliarzation," wherein we constitute a "world fashioned in such a way as to conceal that we have constituted it":

Not only do we constitute ourselves but we constitute a world fashioned in such a way as to conceal that we have constituted it. Existential isolation impregnates the "paste of things," the bedrock of the world. But it is so hidden by layer upon layer of worldly artifacts, each imbued with personal and collective meaning, that we experience only a world of everydayness, of routine activities, of the "they." We are surrounded, "at home in," a stable world of familiar objects and institutions, a world in which all objects and beings are connected and interconnected many times over. We are lulled into a sense of cozy, familiar belongingness; the primordial world of vast emptiness and isolation is buried and silenced, only to speak in brief bursts during nightmares and mythic visions. (p. 358)

Yalom's viewpoint seems confirmed by the work of Churchland

(1988) who describes how we go about understanding not only the world but ourselves:

> ...the mind/brain is a furiously active theorizer from the word go. The perceptual world is an unintelligible confusion to a newborn infant, but its mind/brain sets about immediately to formulate a conceptual framework with which to apprehend, to explain, and to anticipate the world. Thus ensues a sequence of conceptual inventions, modifications, and revolutions that finally produces something approximating our common-sense conception of the world. (p. 80)

Yalom and Churchland (and, as will be discussed, the existentialists) believe that the world is an unintelligible chaos, without intrinsic meaning or purpose. It simply is the "brute fact" or, in the words of atheist Bertrand Russell, simply "is."

Given this view, it's understandable that the human mind sets about furiously organizing the chaos into patterns that suggest meaning and purpose and direction for future action.

Yalom (1980) cites decades of empirical research that show we crave meaning and furiously find patterns, even where none exist: e.g., we see a complete circle when only a partial is shown; we see patterns when shown random dots on a wallpaper. (p. 462)

Yalom (1980) notes that we don't do well if we don't find pattern and meaning:

> When any of these stimuli or situations do not lend themselves to patterning, one feels tense, annoyed, and dissatisfied. This dysphoria [state of unease; opposite of euphoria] persists until a more complete understanding permits one to fit the situation into some larger, recognizable pattern.
>
> The implications for such meaning-attribution tendencies are obvious. In the same way we face and organize random stimuli and events in our daily world, so too we approach our existential situation. We experience dysphoria in the face of an indifferent, unpatterned world and search for patterns, explanations, and the meaning of existence. (p. 462, 463)

In an observation that seemed to reflect my personal experiences, Yalom (1980) quotes Kurt Reinhardt who describes what drives the terror:

> Something utterly mysterious intervenes between him [a person in a 'desert place'] and his fellowmen, between him and all his 'values.' Everything which he had called his own pales and sinks away, so that there is nothing left to which he might cling. What threatens is 'nothing' (no thing), and he finds himself alone and lost in the void. But when this dark and terrible night of anguish has passed, man breathes a sigh of relief and tells himself: it was 'nothing,' after all. He has experienced 'nothingness.' (p. 359)

* * *

I assume *evolutionary theory* would see anxiety as having survival function. Without anxiety, for example, early humans would not have defended against or fled from predators. They would not have taken great pains to protect the family or clan/tribe.

In other words, if mere survival is the driving force behind evolutionary behavior, then the specter of death would be anathema to survival and create anxiety. Anxiety is a basic fuel for survival. A species would not stay alive very long without it.

As for humans mitigating the anxiety of meaningless and chaos through having Yalom's *meaning-attribution tendencies*, such as finding patterns where none exist, those tendencies also reasonably relate to survival chances. Having a schema of meaning—that life matters and has a purpose—should promote an attitude of thriving, of wanting to live. Likewise, seeing patterns within the chaos would seem to reasonably promote one's positive, hopeful attitude towards life. If there are discernible patterns to life, then that suggests meaning and purpose. Otherwise, there would be meaningless chaos which would have no patterns.

The wisdom of depth psychology seems consistent with evolutionary theory. We do best, thrive best, achieve best when we believe our lives, our efforts and our hopes rest upon a life of meaning, purpose and comforting patterns. Insofar as anxiety drives these outcomes, it is a central structure of being.

* * *

From the *philosophy of existentialism*, we find that anxiety is a common theme, both from within atheistic existentialism and theistic existentialism. On the theistic side, Kierkegaard teaches that anxiety is the "dizziness of freedom." To that, I might add anxiety is the dizziness of freedom within an ambiguous, subjective world of doubt.

In other words, if we possess libertarian free will, and we are compelled to exercise the will in an ambiguous and uncertain world, without objectively certain guideposts, then being anxious seems a natural state of being.

Scottish philosopher, theologian and Anglican priest (and theistic existentialist), John Macquarrie (1919-2007) argued (1973): "For freedom means possibility, and to stand on the edge of possibility is rather like standing on the edge of a precipice." (p. 129)

Here we find the terror of freedom. Standing on the proverbial precipice, we realize we can leap to our death. Or we can shove another to their death. Nothing can stop us. Freedom has that possibility. Coupled with that thought is the realization that, because we possess this awesome power, we are responsible for our actions, especially for the moral consequences of our actions, and for self-constituting ourselves.

The realization that we have led a life of some wrong, some bad, perhaps some horrible choices, for which we are responsible, is crushing. This is one reason, for example, that one of the biggest hurdles in getting someone to admit their addiction is to admit personal responsibility. *There is no escape from responsibility because there is no escape from freedom.*

In author and philosopher, Jean-Paul Sartre's (1905-1980) view (2004, Marino) not only are we free, but we are condemned to be free: "Condemned because he did not create himself, yet, in other respects, he is free; because, once thrown into the world, he is responsible for everything he does." (p. 350) We are forced to respond, to choose: "...choice is possible, but what is not possible is not to choose. I can always choose, but I ought to know that if I do not choose, I am still choosing." (p. 360)

Yalom argues (1980) "Both to constitute (to be responsible for) one-self and one's world and to be aware of one's responsibilities is a deeply frightening insight." (p. 221) It is so frightening, that many people flee from freedom through many techniques: addiction; compulsion; denial, or, as Yalom suggests, seeking "structure, authority, grand designs, magic, something that is bigger than oneself." (p. 222) Thus, Yalom advises that "children are upset by freedom and demand limit setting; panicky, psychotic patients exhibit the same need for structure and limits." (p. 222)

Existentialists relate freedom to choice and responsibility. With our freedom we choose and are responsible for those choices. This ushers in the possibility of loss, guilt, shame, and embarrassment that arise from poor choices. We can't escape that dynamic of freedom: choice and responsibility. If we refuse to act—just stand there, stare into the sky and do nothing as if we are not part of this world—that is an action, a response for which we are responsible.

An existentialist might argue (as Sartre did) that it is wrong to say that there's nothing a person can do about some tragic situation in the world. Take mass starvation in Africa. There is always one or more of the following possible actions: you could send every penny you have to fund food programs; you could travel to Africa and dedicate your life to service in their cause. The authentic response is to say that there are people starving in Africa and I choose to not do all I can to alleviate that starvation.

Viewed in this way, a person's freedom is frightening and naturally causes anxiety. It unmasks the old excuse: *but what can I do?*

There are other themes from existentialist atheists that point to anxiety as a natural outcome of being in the world. One of those themes is that *life is absurd*. This was a favorite theme of French philosopher and writer Albert Camus (1913-1960) who argued life was absurd because it was meaningless. Given that life was meaningless, Camus argued the only real question in life is whether or not to commit suicide (based, we can infer, on Camus's atheism which negates the possibility of a

God to provide eternal meaning and direction to life). This outlook is bleak and should produce anxiety, if true.

Other existentialist themes include one's sense of alienation—the notion we don't belong in the world. Another theme is subjectivity—the notion that there are no objective guideposts of absolute truth *out there in the world* to guide our personal decision-making.

Existentialism does not believe in determinism; in fact, the philosophy largely arose from Kierkegaard's disdain for Hegel's determinism: a dialectic that proposes life was spiraling toward perfection. Thus, existentialism believes in contingency, in an open, undetermined future, in other words, in radical freedom. This thought of our contingency creates anxiety.

Finally, as stated, Tillich sees the passage (from the Fall to eviction from paradise) as a passage from innocence to sin—from potential to actualization. Anxiety is the awareness of sin, of being separated from God and primordial innocence. It is the state of actualization, of being alive in the world, forging our moral soul.

* * *

Various attempts have been made within **art and literature** to describe/portray the human condition of and response to anxiety.

Within art, for example, we have Norwegian painter Edvard Munch's (1863-1944) 1893 painting "The Scream", an expressionist painting of a person on a bridge, holding his head in his hands, mouth wide open in an apparent scream of terror. Done in vivid, swirling colors, the image is disturbing. Though panned at the time by art critics, today it's considered iconic—as an image defining an age of anxiety and uncertainty.

One art critic, K. Shabi (2021), referred to Munch's diary entry concerning this painting's personal meaning: "I was walking down the road with two friends when the sun set; suddenly, the sky turned as red as blood. I stopped and leaned against the fence, feeling unspeakably tired. Tongues of fire and blood stretched over the bluish black fjord. My friends went on walking, while I lagged behind, shivering with fear. Then I heard the enormous infinite scream of nature."

Shabi concluded that "for Munch it was a moment of existential crisis. In what sounds like a panic attack, Munch describes feelings of exhaustion while overwhelmed by an almost violent wave of anxiety. Like most panic attacks, Munch's experience by the fjord was a lonely internal struggle, as his two friends walk on without him, completely unaware of the artist's upset."

Within literature, we have Camus's protagonist's (Meursault) famous scream at the end of the novel *The Stranger* (1989). Meursault is in prison for murder and soon to be executed. The gravity of the situation finally settles into his consciousness. At that moment of mortal awareness, Meursault snapped and, in his own words, he "started yelling at the top of my lungs....I grabbed him [the chaplain] by the collar of his cassock. I was pouring out on him everything that was in my heart, cries of anger, cries of joy." (p. 121).

Finally, in the "dark hour before death," and thinking of departing "a world that now and forever meant nothing to me." Meursault, sensing the "blind rage had washed me clean," looked up into the stars, and "opened myself to the gentle indifference of the universe." (p. 122)

* * *

But, we must ask: *Does everyone despair?* All of what I said is fine except for whether or not it's true that a base anxiety inhabits every person's central psychic core.

Perhaps no one suffered this anxiety (or despair or angst) more than the Kierkegaard, who, like me, assumes everyone must confront their anxiety. But some say *that's just Kierkegaard.*

In Alastair Hannay's introduction to Kierkegaard's classic work in anxiety, *The Sickness Unto Death*, (1989) he cites Austrian philosopher Ludwig Wittgenstein (1889-1951) as skeptical of the universality of Kierkegaard's despair.

Now many people, though not perhaps the habitual Christians whom Kierkegaard castigates, might agree at least to the extent of allowing that Kierkegaard has discovered that need [for relief from torment] in himself. They may even agree that the need in question was not altogether untypical of certain kinds of people with certain kinds of background. Something like this is expressed by Ludwig Wittgenstein when he remarks that the Christian religion "is only for the man who needs infinite help, that is, for the man who experiences infinite torment," and that, as he sees it, "the Christian faith...is a man's refuge in this *ultimate* torment." (p. 18)

There is no way to objectively prove or disprove the claim that anxiety resides deep within everyone. Wittgenstein might be correct that only sufferers of *infinite torment* need God, and not everyone suffers infinite torment. But Sartre argues Wittgenstein is wrong (Marino 2004):"Of course, there are many people who are not anxious; but we claim that they are hiding their anxiety, that they are fleeing from it." (p. 347)

Yalom's entire understanding of behavior is that the middle of the proverbial onion—the driver of all behavior—is not Freud's repressed sexual conflicts, but anxiety based upon confrontation with the givens of existence. Yalom would say that if you deny your basic anxiety, you are deep within the delusion of your self-made, paper-thin construct of reality, protected only by an array of psychological defense mechanisms.

In *Denial of Death (1997)*, Becker argues that what drives all behavior is fear of death (one of Yalom's *givens of existence*); not just fear, but a failure to courageously confront it because it causes deep anxiety.

Quoting Pascal, Becker argues: "Men are so necessarily mad that not to be mad would amount to another form of madness." (p. 27) Then, Becker expands on Pascal's thought:

> *Necessarily* because the existential dualism makes an impossible situation, an excruciating dilemma. *Mad* because...everything that man does in his symbolic world is an attempt to deny and overcome his grotesque fate. He literally drives himself into a blind obliviousness with social games, psychological tricks, personal preoccupations so far removed from the reality of his situation that they are forms of madness—agreed madness, shared madness, disguised and dignified madness, but madness all the same. (p. 27)

And the *grotesque fate* Becker speaks of is the truth of our existential dualism: that we are both dreamers of the infinite and also finite animals doomed to die.

By "symbolic," Becker means "He [man] is a symbolic self, a creature with a name, a life history....a creator with a mind that soars out to speculate about atoms and infinity, who can place himself imaginatively at a point in space and contemplate bemusedly his own planet." (p. 26) In other words, Becker suggests we seem to be a "small god in nature." (p. 26) And yet, at the same time, we are worms and "food for worms." That is, we are mere animals, finite, doomed to death like all animals.

In one of literature's most chilling descriptions, Becker (1997) asks:

> What are we to make of a creation in which the routine activity is for organisms to be tearing each others apart with teeth of all types— biting grinding flesh, plant stalks, bones between molars, pushing the pulp greedily down one's gullet with delight, incorporating its essence into one's own organization, and then excreting with foul stench and gasses the residue....Creation is a nightmare spectacular taking place on the planet that has been soaked for hundreds of millions of years in the blood of all creatures. The soberest conclusion that we could make about what has actually been taking place on the planet for about three billion years is that it is being turned into a vast pit of fertilizer. (p. 282, 283)

This image is so terrifying to confront that, Becker observes (1997), "Modern man is drinking and drugging himself out of awareness, or he spends his time shopping, which is the same thing." (p. 284)

This worldview of humanity's existential dilemma leading to denial, repression, projection, and all the other *normal* psychological defense mechanisms, is shared by many within the study of depth psychology and philosophy of existentialism. In other words, our defense mechanisms allow us to function and feel normal. Without them, reality is terrifying, perhaps unbearable.

Jose Ortega y Gasset (1883-1955), Spanish philosopher and essayist, observed much the same in his book *Revolt of the Masses (1957)*:

> For life is at the start a chaos in which one is lost. The individual suspects this, but he is frightened at finding himself face to face with this terrible reality, and tries to cover it over with a curtain of fantasy, where everything is clear. It does not worry him that

his 'ideas' are not true, he uses them as trenches for the defense of his existence, as scarecrows to frighten away reality. (pp. 156-157)

So, do we all suffer the anxiety described above? For those who deny they are driven by anxiety, perhaps they have created a *paper thin* mental construct that is strong and durable. Perhaps they are in denial: lost within an obsession or compulsion, like drinking, drugs, work, sex, or just shopping (i.e., materialism). Or, perhaps they have accepted and stoically steeled themselves against the *givens of existence*.

How would one know, especially if one is loath to confront the issue?

Maybe only some of us suffer existential angst. Perhaps Wittgenstein is correct about Christians. Perhaps we do suffer a torment unique to only certain people and not others.

Perhaps modernity's enrapture today with a secular utilitarian philosophy—with its emphasis on personal and collective happiness—has been quite successful in mitigating infinite torment. It would seem so as evidenced by the drift away from faith and toward secularism in all its forms, especially in Western civilization, especially among the educated elites.

Perhaps acknowledgment of sin today is increasingly rare because of our efforts to suppress the powerful negative emotions associated with sin: shame; guilt; sorrow; anxiety; depression. Perhaps this modern therapeutic approach to suppress anxiety and infinite torment, together with our drift toward artificial intelligence, will usher in a brave new world without sin and anxiety and other negative emotions. We will become like *Star Trek's* Spock: pure reason without emotion. But will we be human in any way we understand humanity? And will we love? Can we love?

* * *

Sociologist, Philip Rieff (1922-2006) extensively wrote of the current downward spiral of western culture because of the rise of secularity. No longer believing in God and God's authority over our behavior, society's secular thought exploded with unbridled hedonism: e.g., sensual pleasure, radical individualism, addictions. The church was replaced by the school as our moral center. The pastor was replaced by the teacher, the theologian replaced by the psychiatrist.

Guilt and shame became irrelevant because moral responsibility to a sacred, transcendent God was gone. We no longer need contrition followed by forgiveness; rather, we need counseling, perhaps a feel good drug.

The problem becomes apparent, according to Rieff, in his book *Charisma; The Gift of Grace, and How It Has Been Taken Away from Us* (2007): "Men will kill for no reason at all—and be acquitted because there will be no reason to convict them. Precisely the 'best' will lack all conviction. If it is for this reason that the revolution to end all revolutions is occurring among the revolutionary rich, among the educated, among the youth; these are the categories who have been most typically without godheads." (p. 209)

When the therapy replaces culture, the "modernist quest for 'meaning' is one animator of the therapeutic, as an ideal figure of hostility to culture in any form. He constitutes the most powerful denial that an action must mean just this, and not that; as an 'ideal' type, the therapeutic is the perfect anti-credal personality, the supreme prophylactic against any denial to man that everything is possible and nothing is true." (p. 205)

Accordingly, Rieff argues that: "The democratization of modern culture consists mainly, I think, of the spread downward, in the social structure, of the cultivated pursuit of pleasure, stripped of the disciples of delay once thought necessary to acquire 'culture' itself. Modern culture is something for which one can shop around: there are bargains to be had and the new ideal is that no ideal could be priced beyond the reach of anyone who wants to have it." (p. 207)

Rieff is a hard read (at least for me). But, what seems to clearly emerge from his thought is that modern society is going to fail in its brave new experiment of removing God from life, of replacing God with secular institutions like the school, the therapist, government. Like Tillich before him, Rieff remains convinced that we don't do well without God.

As reviewer Bruce Ashford said of Rieff's book *Deathworks* (2018):

Deathworks is a devastating critique of modern culture, focusing on our vain Western attempts to reorganize society without a sacred center. According to Rieff, a patently irreligious view of society—which many Westerners desire—is not only foolish and destructive, but impossible. We can no more live without a religious framework than we can communicate without a linguistic framework or breathe without a pulmonary framework. Religion is in our blood, and the more we deny it, the sicker our society becomes. As Rieff surveyed the 21st-century Western world, he perceived the sickness had become nearly fatal.

[Note: Perhaps this abandonment of a *sacred center* in western civilization is why Russia (deeply tied to its Orthodox church) and China (a society dedicated to Marxism that still deeply believes in the notion of authority and the idea of a cultural code) see the Western social model of unbridled personal freedom striving for sensual pleasure as in decline. It's not economic, not militaristic but moral. The West, according to Rieff, seems to have lost is moral center by abandoning the faith-guilt order. There is no sin with its guilt and shame, but only free behavior that can be mediated by the therapeutic.]

Even then, even in a future brave and "perfect" new secular (Godless) world which attempts to eradicate *infinite torment*, the world would remain ambiguous. There will be life and death, good and evil, presence and absence, light and dark. Even then, we will be condemned to freedom. Even then, there will always be doubt and subjectivity deep within a solitary, self conscious individual creature, even a machine. Even then, we will never be able to verify foundational premises underlying every theory of life (e.g., Is there a God or not? Am I experiencing reality?).

The human condition will remain unchanged even if humans are replaced by AI robots. In the movie *Blade Runner* (1982), the robots knew the difference between life and death, had self-consciousness, experienced existential angst, and wondered who created them, for what reason, and why they were programmed to die. Alarmingly, they sought out their scientific creator and killed him.

As long as there are self-conscious, sentient entities—carbon based humans or silicon-based AI machines—the deep recesses of their brains (or digital processors) will ask: What is this all about? Who am

I? What am I to do with my life? And if the failure to find answers to these questions of ultimate concern creates a twinge of anxiety, they can always take a pill. Or a drink. Or go shopping

* * *

Only a stone can avoid the anxiety arising from the great ontological mysteries of existence.

We can deny/avoid/deflect/rationalize our anxiety. We can deny our condition of sin in the world. But the cold, brute, seemingly indifferent world remains: looming dark and foreboding, brimming with existential tragedy.

The argument I make is that everyone has a base anxiety buried deep in their lizard brain that gnaws away constantly, always ready to burst through one's carefully constructed defense mechanisms, to burst through in nightmare fashion, revealing the infinite torment that we are nothing, bound for nothing. As Gingerich states we are merely "specs in an abyss of space and time...in this tiny backwater of the cosmos, overwhelmed by a sea of space and time...lost and insignificant." (Gingerich, 2003, p. 59)

I argue this terrifying anxiety has divine attributions. It is the unvarnished emotional state of sin. It is indeed evil, per se, in the sense it is the ultimate negative consequence of sin. And, yet, in the elegance of God's ambiguous design, it serves to illuminate God as being life, not death, being something not nothing, being infinite God not finite animal. The path to God runs through anxious awareness.

Scriptural Support

The most powerful expression of existential terror, in my opinion, is found in the Bible. It is found on the cross, just moments before Jesus dies. At that moment, Christ cries out: "My God, my God, why have you forsaken me?" (Mt 27:46; Mk 15:34)

This *cry of dereliction* has met with much confusion. Why, for example, would God abandon His Son? In trinitarian logic, how can the Father be separated from the Son if they are one and the same?

And, most troubling, if Christ was here to convince humankind that He was, in fact, the Son of God, how does his death on the cross and this cry of dereliction advance that cause? Logically, it would seem to do just the opposite; it should convince the skeptics that he was just flesh and blood, prone to death, agony, doubt and anxiety like everyone else.

Obviously, this cry has been met with many interpretations. One interpretation I like can be found in *Cross Purposes (2007) by* James Kennedy (1960-2007) and Jerry Newcombe, American pastor and writer, and author, respectively:

> As the time came for his death, Jesus began to feel the worm of sin in the very marrow of His bones. Sin was poured out upon His very body and soul. Jesus Christ, the pure, spotless Son of God, became the greatest sinner who ever lived. All the guilt of the world was piled upon Him. Christ became the arch-criminal of the universe. God looked down upon His beloved Son and saw sin and therefore turned His back on Him. Jesus was abandoned by His Father.
>
> ...He was forsaken by God and abandoned by His Father. There He hung, quivering with all the loathsomeness and vileness of sin—alone and abandoned by God. (p. 80, 81)

To me, Christ's cry of dereliction upon the cross perfectly illustrates just what sin is and what the negative consequences of sin are. When Christ absorbed all the sin of the world unto Himself, He absorbed all the terror of realizing what life is without God. And if that terror was overwhelming to me that dark night in Kentucky so many years ago, I cannot imagine what it would feel like for one person to absorb everyone's despair and terror.

When Christ screamed out "My God, my God, why have you forsaken me?" He exhibited all the hallmarks of awareness of sin. He felt abandoned and alone, estranged from God, which is the state of sin. He felt anxiety which is a negative consequence of sin. He felt doubt ("why?") another negative consequence of sin.

Christ displayed for us just what sin feels like the moment he absorbed all of our sins unto Himself. What a precious gift, not only to absorb our sin but also to both show us the pain of sin, and how it is remedied. The pain of separation is remedied through faithful union with God.

If you are happy with life, content, never feeling anxiety or worry—perhaps taking medication to be happy, engaging in a grand distraction—e.g., all-consuming work, wealth accumulation, materialism, constant sexual gratification or substance abuse—then you deny Christ His sacrifice.

You deny Christ's sacrifice on the cross because he painfully absorbed your despairing condition of sin that you deny or suppress. How can anyone understand and appreciate Christ's loving gift if they don't realize the price He paid and the victory they gained?

It is deep in pain and suffering that we often come to Christ. Understanding Christ's death, suffering, anxiety and humiliation on the cross, is key to understanding why we suffer in life. We suffer in life because we live in a state of sin. This condition of sin carries profound negative consequences, just as it carries the hope of profound positive consequences.

In Christ's painful death on the cross, we see clearly the negative consequences of sin, one of which includes anxiety caused by estrangement from God. In Christ's resurrection from the tomb, we see clearly the positive consequence of sins from anxiety through reunion with God.

3.3.5 SELF-CONSCIOUSNESS: INDIVIDUALS AND THE WORLD

Consciousness is an unusual phenomenon to study scientifically. It is defined as a subjective, first-person phenomenon, and science is an objective, third-person endeavor.

Aaron Schurger and Michael Graziano, *Consciousness Explained or Described*

Without its world the self would be an empty form. Self-consciousness would have no content, for every content, psychic as well as bodily, lies within the universe....The self without the world is empty; the world without a self is dead.

Paul Tillich, *Systematic Theology*

But consciousness or sentience, the raw sensation of toothaches and redness and saltiness and middle C, is still a riddle wrapped in a mystery inside an enigma. When asked what consciousness is, we have no better answer than Louis Armstrong's when a reporter asked him what jazz is:"Lady, if you have to ask, you'll never know."

Steven Pinker, *How the Mind Works*

Overview

The structures of being that we have discussed above are structures that serve to shape, channel and limit creaturely behavior through experiences and inferences from those experiences. *Those structures need a structure for actualization.* That basic structure is a world and self-conscious or sentient humans that inhabit the world.

Tillich (1971) calls this "the basic ontological structure: self and world." (v. 1, p. 168): two centered structures—the objective world and the subjective mind of sentient creatures contemplating not only the world but oneself's relation to it.

Tillich argues (1971) that "man occupies a pre-eminent position in ontology, not as an outstanding object among other objects, but as that being who asks the ontological questions and in whose self-awareness the ontological answer can be found....Man is able to answer the ontological questions himself because he experiences directly and immediately the structure of being and its elements." (v. 1, p. 168, 169)

By *ontology*, I mean the branch of metaphysics dealing with the nature of being, becoming, existence, reality. Specifically, I focus on the philosophers of being (e.g., existentialists) who were consumed by what it means to be alive, especially the phenomenon of qualia (the internal and subjective component of sense perceptions, arising from stimulation of the senses by phenomena).

By *ontological questions* I mean questions concerning the phenomenon of existence such as: Why am I here?; What am I?; What am I to do?; What does it mean to exist?

In other words, if God wanted loving relationships, God would need to create another thing capable of engaging in a loving relationship, and by *relationship* I mean the way in which two or more concepts, objects, or people are connected, or the state of being connected.

I argue that *another* capable of engaging in a loving relationship would need to possess not only consciousness (awareness of things, such as others and the world) but also self-consciousness (awareness of not only others and the world but also of oneself as a conscious thing existing in the world).

Such *another* could become aware not only of God but also of oneself. Then, they could engage in a relationship, knowing they were a thing among things, capable of both receiving love and giving love. A stone cannot do this.

Self-consciousness is our ladder to the divine, while the world is the place where each of us is shaped and channeled (by the structures of being) through concrete experiences that enable learning, appreciating, loving and being morally consequential.

Premises

P19: Self-consciousness enables humans to come to know, appreciate and love God.

P20. Humans possess self-consciousness.

P21. The self without the world is empty; the world without a self is dead.

Definition

As indicated, I understand *consciousness* to mean awareness of things, such as other people and the world. I understand the term *self-consciousness* to mean the ability to be aware of one's own existence as a thing (a unique self) in the world. Canadian-American cognitive psychologist Steven Pinker feels consciousness includes self-consciousness, arguing (1997) that anything conscious of the world can be conscious of itself. He also equates consciousness with sentience (subjective experience, phenomenal awareness). (p. 134-135) (Hereafter, when I merely say "consciousness" that includes self-consciousness.)

In Blackburn's *Oxford Dictionary of Philosophy (2005) it says* one's consciousness "provides the theatre where my experiences and thoughts have their existence, where my desires are felt where my intentions are formed." (p. 74)

Pinker (1997) says consciousness is "typically defined as 'building an internal model of the world that contains the self,' reflecting back on one's own mode of understanding." (p. 134)

Consciousness, therefore, is the foundation for learning, loving, dreaming, acting, for everything we value as being human. For Christians, consciousness is also a ladder to God, connecting awareness of self to others and God.

We are not stones—inert, unthinking, unfeeling things—rather, we are Augustine's horse that can run away if it so chooses.

By "world," I mean all of nature the finite world of time and space, matter and energy. This includes not only the known universe but any additional theoretical universes (e.g., the theoretical multiverse). The world is the physical home where the theatre of one's consciousness has its existence. A physical world provides concrete experiences with others and nature that individuals need for growth in Christian maturity.

Good Reason for Structure of Self-Conscious Individuals and the World

God's good reason for creating a world populated by self-conscious creatures is love. If God's love were narcissistic self-love, God would not need others to share love with. But, if God's love is selfless, charitable love, God would reasonably and naturally express love to others.

I assume that a foundational need for God's plan Y is to create a network of others. Thus, there is a need for a structure of otherness. God didn't create one humongous unitary blob to love. Rather, God created infinite space and otherness, including humans, to populate the structure of otherness. God's love, being selfless, naturally wants to be shared as greatly as possible. As the old child gospel song—*This Little Light of Mine*—God didn't "hide" His light "under a bushel;" God wanted it to "shine."

Creating individuals—billions here on Earth, and who knows how many in the universe/multiverse—generates an immense array of receptors for God's boundless love.

For those "receptors" to grow and mature into a person capable of understanding and appreciating this gift of love, the person needs to be a self-conscious individual.

It is not enough for the individual to have mere consciousness. Individuals must also be aware of themselves. Only when they sense they are some thing, distinct from other things, can they reciprocate God's love in like kind.

True, there is disagreement about what *self* means and whether, given how we evolve and change during our lifetime, there is such a thing as a self. I argue each individual is a self. Though we change and mature through experience over time, a self exists as an entity that can trace its line of thought and experience backwards in time and also project its hopes forward into the future.

Every person is a dynamic, evolving, learning, growing, changing self. And that is a central point of this theodicy: God intentionally placed us in a harsh, ambiguous place separate and apart from God so that, armed with a free will and the ability to learn, change and mature, we can—through ambiguous experiences—increasingly appreciate and love God. The entire paradigm requires an ever-changing, growing self. And that self, whatever else it is, is enough "self" to enjoy a loving relationship with God.

Necessary Cost of Evil for Structure of Individual and the World

Being a self-conscious individual means a person is aware of the existential situation of existence they find themselves enmeshed within.

Conscious creatures are also aware something is going on in the world. Humans, being self-consciousness, are aware of ourselves (a self) as being a thing among things, with our consciousness itself being a yet another thing among things.

It is not uncommon to hear people talk of the surreal awareness of a mind-body disconnect when they contemplate being aware of one's physical self. For example, hold out your arm and wiggle your fingers vigorously, then imagine the relationship between this physical appendage and your mind contemplating that arm, those wiggling fingers, are yours. It can be quite dizzying, perhaps alarming, this self-awareness of self as both physical body and a mind contemplating said body, and even one's mind contemplating one's mind (thinking about thinking). This sense of a mind-body disconnect can create anxiety.

Through self-consciousness we are also aware that we are standing in a stream of time flowing somewhere, but we know not where. We realize we occupy space somewhere within a seemingly infinite space without beginning or end. At the same time, we are aware of our physical body: that we are a finite creature wearing down, aging, doomed to death and decay, and possible eternal annihilation. Yet we also dream of paradise and eternal life in our minds that soar to the heavens. This duality creates a tension, an anxiety driven by ambiguity and uncertainty.

Of this, Kierkegaard (1844) said:

Man's anxiety is a function of his sheer ambiguity and of his complete powerlessness to overcome that ambiguity, to be straightforwardly an animal or an angel. He cannot be heedless of his fate, nor can he take control over that fate and triumph over it by being outside the human condition.

The spirit cannot do away with itself [i.e., self-consciousness cannot disappear]....Neither can man sink down into the vegetative life [i.e., be wholly animal]....He cannot flee from dread. (p. 40)

We also realize that we have the power—through freedom of choice—over how to respond to the ambiguous situations life forces upon us. We have the awareness that we, being captains of our freedom, are responsible for our choices. This ushers in fear of failure and attendant guilt and shame. It ushers in realization that life is a colossal risk. It means awareness of one's potential to do evil, to kill others, even ourselves, for example.

Yalom argued (1980) that freedom, fully understood, is chilling. It, along with fear of meaninglessness, death and alienation, creates a base line anxiety that drives/underlies all human behavior, especially maladaptive behavior. Consider Yalom's observation on freedom and responsibility:

Therefore, *to be a self-conscious individual is also to be anxious.* This all creates a negative cost to the structure of self and the world, which many consider evil. Some philosophers/writers have even mused that the cost of self-consciousness is so great that it would have been better not to be born at all.

The Greek philosopher, Sophocles (c. 496-406 bc) allegedly said that not to be born is, beyond all estimation, best. And after great suffering, even Job—who God called "My servant....There is no one on earth like him; he is blameless and upright"—"cursed the day of his birth" (Job 3:1).

Discussion

What exactly is self-consciousness? Where did it come from? What is it's function? Do we need a world? Finally, does the existence of so many people in the world, within such a vast universe (or multiverse) that might house an almost infinite number of other sentient creatures, undermine the notion that we are special to God?

* * *

Science knows little about self-consciousness, and philosophy calls it the "hard problem." Even if science ever did understand conscious, I think it is doubtful any one person could ever know the *qualia* of another person's subjective felt experience in a given situation.

Blackburn's *The Oxford Dictionary of Philosophy* (2005) defines qualia as "the felt or phenomenal qualities associated with experiences, such as the feeling of a pain, or the hearing of a sound, or the viewing of a color. To know what it is like to have an experience is to know its qualia." (p. 302)

A common example given for the mystery of consciousness involves a bat. We can study a bat extensively and know absolutely everything about a bat that can be known from outside observation. But, even then, we can never know what it feels like to be a bat.

Some say science will soon conquer this *hard problem*, that more sophisticated brain scans (e.g., functional magnetic resonance imaging or fMRI, and the new, emergent technology of functional near-infrared spectroscopy, or fNIRS) will read our minds and see our thoughts in action. Human consciousness is within science's cross hairs, some scientists argue. Perhaps, but, even then, will we know what it's like to be a bat?

Despite these limitations, we can make some observations about consciousness's features. Consciousness is subjective, transparent, and intentional.

By saying consciousness is *subjective*, I mean the experience of conscious awareness is unique to the experiencer (person) and no one else. For example, the conscious experiences of a bat are unique to that bat. If consciousness were objective, we could know what it feels like to be a bat.

By saying consciousness is *transparent*, I mean that we are always aware of and know the work of our consciousness. When we look at a red rose or hear a train whistle, we know what is occurring: we, the subject, are interacting directly with the object of our encounter.

By saying consciousness is *intentional*, I mean it is always directed towards something; it has the structure of a subject and an object. Every conscious experience we have is directed outward, always the result of an encounter with other phenomena. Consciousness doesn't function without interaction with an object; even self-consciousness itself (the subject), for example, is directed toward awareness of oneself (the object).

We're back to Descartes: I think therefore I am. There's something (I, the subject) thinking about something (the object). It's subjective because, as far as "I" know, I'm the only I thinking. It's transparent because, whatever "I" am, I'm aware of thinking. And it's intentional: "I" am directing thought toward whatever my thinking suggests "I" am. And because I'm thinking about anything, means I exist, even if it's merely a self-reflecting exercise of thinking about thinking.

True, my encounter with otherness might result in false knowledge. Perhaps, because I'm color blind, the red rose is really a blue rose. Or I could be dreaming everything, perhaps hallucinating from drugs or a psychosis. I could be deluded, or lost in a digital matrix. It doesn't matter because I am conscious of something. Consciousness enables us to be aware of some thing in the world while self-consciousness enables us to be aware that we are some thing having an encounter with some thing. Self-consciousness unites self with the world.

* * *

Fine, but what are the theories as to consciousness's creation and purpose? Here, I look to *evolutionary biology*, thoughts from *naturalism/neuroscience*, and a *Christian perspective*.

One theory from *evolutionary biology* is that consciousness is "selected" because of the survival benefits that arise from being aware of one's environment and one's place in that environment.

Those animals/species that had no conscious awareness of their environment—say they weren't sensitive to the negative implications of being killed by predators—probably had a low survival rate. Creatures who were conscious of others and conscious of self were *selected* for survival because of this positive attribute. That is: because they were aware a predator (another) could kill them (self), and aware of the negative implications of that possibility (death and danger), their consciousness promoted survival.

One could say consciousness was chosen by necessity—the necessity of survival—and that the evolutionary imperative of selecting for survival has a direction over time that indicates *progress* (given the premise that survival is life's sole goal).

Wilson argues in his book *The Social Conquest of Earth* (2012) that "Consciousness, having evolved over millions of years of life-and-death struggle, and moreover because of that struggle, was not designed for self-examination. It was designed for survival and reproduction." He argues that "thinking about thinking" was not consciousness's purpose. (p. 8, 9)

Here, he's suggesting that the full expression of consciousness today (e.g., thinking about thinking; self-reflecting on our purpose and meaning in life) isn't necessary for evolution. And if we exhibit some of these qualities unrelated to mere survival, then they are behaviors that arose for no reason, or are suboptimal adaptations, even maladaptive. They are meaningless.

In *The Origins of Creativity (2017)*, Wilson suggests humanity's development of *consciousness is purely biological: the product of a large brain*. He argues humans are different than their nearest evolutionary kin, chimpanzees and bonobos. Specifically, we have a much higher rate of socialization, but the "signal event was a massive increase in brain size, mostly entailing the frontal lobe." (p. 16, 17)

According to Wilson (2012), "Starting about three million years ago, the cranial capacity of our prehuman ancestors grew from that close to chimpanzees at 400 cubic centimeters (cc) to 600 cc in the habilines (*Homo habilis*), then by a million years ago to 900 cc in our direct ancestors *Homo erectus*, and finally by the modern level (around 1,300 cc) in Homo sapiens." (p. 16, 17)

Wilson admits he does not know the nature of consciousness but only its functional reason for its selection. In *Origins*, he concludes: "At the base, we need to explore even more deeply the meaning of humanity, why we exist as opposed to have never existed on Earth before. The grail to be sought is the nature of consciousness, and how it originated." (p. 197)

However, evolutionary biologist Stephen Jay Gould (1941-2002) disagrees with the traditional evolutionary belief that biological change is a gradual, smooth predictable and progressive process driven by necessity to survive (which suggests evolutionary determinism). Rather, throughout his many writings, Gould has advanced a theory of *punctuated equilibrium* which proposes that most evolution is characterized by long periods of evolutionary stability, infrequently punctuated by swift periods of branching speciation.

Throughout his many writings, Gould sees evolutionary change as often abrupt, due to pure accident or chance. He argues there are unintended consequences from the higher functions of the larger human brain [e.g., self-consciousness] which undermines traditional evolutionary theory. Thus, Gould suggests evolution displays as much indeterminism as determinism, which argues against some slow predictable march to *progress*.

In *Dinosaur in a Haystack: Reflections in Natural History* (1995), Gould argues that "Humans are not the end result of predictable evolutionary progress, but rather a fortuitous cosmic afterthought, a tiny little twig on the enormously arborescent bush of life, which, if replanted from seed, would almost surely not grow this twig again, or perhaps any twig with any property that we would care to call consciousness." (p. 327)

In a 1989 interview with the LosAngeles Times, Gould labeled the rise of the human as "an afterthought...a little accidental twig" and calling consciousness "a lucky afterthought."

Therefore, Gould argues our *consciousness is just a cosmic accident,* nothing more, the result of a cataclysmic collision of an extraterrestrial object with the earth some 65 million years ago.

The transformative event is thought to be the impact of an asteroid or comet approximately 7 to 50 miles wide that struck Chicxulub, Mexico, where it remains buried beneath the Yucatan Peninsula. It was a violent mass extinction event, wiping out the dinosaurs and some 75% of all plant and animal species on earth.

Gould notes that this allowed the tiny mice-sized mammals who lived underground to emerge, prosper and eventually evolve into humans. Gould argues that before this extinction event, the dinosaurs that ruled the land, with their tiny brains, showed no proclivity toward consciousness, at least not the type today where we wonder about God and experience existential angst.

Evolutionary theory, therefore, argues human consciousness arose in one of two ways: as the result either of a deterministic necessity for survival or reproduction, which suggests some logic and direction to the evolutionary process; or as the result of indeterminate pure chance, driven by unknown and uncontrollable contingencies of existence, which suggests little logic or direction.

This illustrates a difference within evolutionary theory: some scientists argue that all behavior has evolutionary function, while others believe that many human features and functions might have no evolutionary function. That is, they emerged and survived not as the result of a logical and inevitable course of events but from a succession of random, contingent events. Some functions are just *there*, having nothing to do with survival. One of those functions that might have slipped through the evolutionary net is human self-consciousness.

For example, Wilson argues he understands the function of thinking (consciousness) as having survival and reproduction necessity. But he admits he has no idea what the evolutionary function of thinking about thinking (self-consciousness) possesses. Evidently, evolutionary thinking cannot fully explain, for example, our sense of existential angst or of obsessively worrying about who we are, what happens when we die, why are we here. Perhaps thinking about thinking has no evolutionary function. Perhaps its function is divine.

* * *

In his book *The Big Picture (2016)*, Sean Carroll, a theoretical physicist and philosopher argues from the perspective of **naturalism** (the philosophical belief that reality is limited to natural properties and processes). Being a naturalist, Carroll believes reality is limited to physical properties and processes, and that supernatural properties and processes don't exist. Accordingly, Carroll indicates (2016) that "One view is to argue all these so-called qualia or inner experiences simply *don't exist*—they are illusions." (p. 361)

Carroll argues another perspective is "a strong form of reductionism that insists that subjective experiences simply are physical processes happening in the brain. They exist, but they can be identified with specific neural correlates." (p. 361).

Carroll concludes by saying that conscious experiences exist and are real, but "They are not part of the fundamental architecture of reality, but they serve as essential pieces of an emergent effective theory. The best way we have of talking about people and their behaviors makes important reference to their inner mental states; therefore, by the standards of poetic naturalism, those states are real, existing things." (p. 361)

To a scientist who embraces the philosophical notion of naturalism, self-consciousness can be traced to a atoms reacting chemically to stimulus within the structure of the nervous system. It's all physical brain stuff.

Self-consciousness and free will are inextricably linked in the sense that free will can only be actualized by a person self-consciously being the instigator of the future action. Another way to phrase it is to argue that if we're not free, then how can our self-conscious serve any meaningful function? Therefore, neuroscience's views on free will seem to equally apply to self-consciousness. Let's briefly restate the range of views within neuroscience.

The determinism view of many neuroscientist is that we don't consciously create actions; actions are created/determined unconsciously or, as some say, preconsciously based upon past causal inputs external to our will.

The indeterminism view—where our actions are not determined by factors external to our internal will—suggests free will. Determinist critics argue that since uncaused behavior, such as mindlessly wiggling your fingers around, is simply random, uncaused behavior and, therefore, is in no way willful caused (as should happen with free will). It seems a paradox.

The solution to the seeming paradox is that our actions are, in fact, determined not just by factors external to our will, but also by our will. If the brain can set criteria for future mental activity, through, say, planning, imagining, and setting goals for future outcomes, such that certain neural synapses are given greater weight in determining action in, say situation A, then that future action can be seen as caused by our will. True, our will as we find it at any given time is a product of past causal inputs. But, the point is that our will is dynamic and can exert influence on our brain's programming for action such that it is a determining input.

There is scientific evidence that we can become braver, more loving, more caring, if we work at it. Our will can be a causal input for action. Our self-conscious reflection on who we want to be, and how we want to act and live our lives, finds expressions through our free will. We can be authors of our future actions.

There is scientific evidence of conscious will activity prior to the brain's activity of action and which suggests our will can be a causal input for action, which suggests free will. Which suggests the role and reality of self-consciousness, which suggests our conscious free will can manipulate neural receptors in all their forms and states—their magnitude, order of importance or weight, etc.—to be an original causal input.

Today, I feel I can say with confidence that no scientists knows what it feels like to be a bat. Question; How could they ever prove the hypothesis that they know the qualia of a specific bat? Nonetheless, their faith that they can and will eventually do it is strong, so strong, as to be almost like a religious faith. Likewise, they cannot deny human consciousness and free will and how they intertwine to create morally consequential behavior. The brain is too complex and the instruments to measure behavior too crude.

In like fashion, no neuroscientist can know what it feels like to be seized by God's love.

* * *

One *Christian perspective* is that the function of consciousness is to *be aware of the possibility of God*. Self consciousness presents the possibility of communion with God as an intentionally chosen act.

Here, I might add the notion of self consciousness, being subjective, marries up quite well with Kierkegaard's notion that God interacts with us subjectively, at the level of each person.

Kierkegaard stressed personal subjectivity, arguing Christianity is a matter of individual subjective passion, His idea was that God operated at the intimate level of the individual. And, at the level of the individual, all knowledge is subjective, and, like consciousness, is unique to the experiencer and no one else.

This idea was described by Alastair Hannah in his introductory notes to Kiekegaard's *The Sickness Unto Death* (1989):

> Kierkegaard writes that 'the whole development of the world tends in the direction of the of the absolute significance of the category of particularity.'...In this sense it is indeed true that Kiekegaard's world was bound for an absolutization of the particular, away from the universal....particularity is 'precisely the principle of Christianity'. What this suggests is that the exigencies of this development force upon people that state of particularity where, divested of any coherent social identity, they find themselves in the lonely situation

that enables them, as single human beings, to stand directly before God. (p. 8, 9)

By comparison, since no one knows what it's like to be a bat, no one knows what it feels like when Christ seizes another person's heart in love. No one knows what Paul's conversion experience felt like on his road to Damascus, except Paul. (See: Ac 9) We can only imagine that, based upon the sudden changes in Paul's life, the experience was life-altering, ecstatic, overwhelming, passionate.

Being seized by God's love, therefore, is a mystery unreachable by science, because it involves a person's subjective conscious experience of the encounter. A scientist, no matter how polished their reductionist skills, can never reduce a revelatory conversion experience beyond showing us images on an MRI that lights up this or that part of our brain.

* * *

Self-conscious awareness unfolds within a *world*. There is a function in suffering physical effects from worldly experience. They help shape, channel and limit human behavior.

Existentialists refer to *concrete experience:* the physical world delivering hard felt experiences that have a profound impact on one's emotions, well-being—physical and mental—worldview, and attitude.

Theoretically, we could walk through a brick wall without feeling anything, given quantum theory. But, in reality, we suffer pain and injury when we try. And when we do bang into a brick wall, the knowledge gained by experiencing pain and suffering, and failure to pierce through to the other side, over-rides the theory that we should be able to walk through a wall. After all, reductionists have told us a brick wall is merely empty space with some atoms here and there made up of subatomic, purely theoretical particles of seemingly no mass.

In the background of this quantum strangeness lurks the Higgs field. Scientists have build that largest scientific instrument in history (the Large Hadron Collider in Geneva, Switzerland which runs 18 miles long) to prove the existence of the Higg's boson, the so-called "God particle." The God particle is the "molasses" in the universe that provides resistance to all the purely theoretical subatomic stuff whizzing about, thus giving everything mass. Thus making us skin our knees, elbows and noggins when we try to walk through a brick wall.

Why? Why can't we walk through a brick wall? Why is there a brick wall in the first place? Why is it so hard, dense and real when it's actually mostly empty space? Why is there a physical world since it produces such pain, injury, misery and death? Isn't my self-consciousness and God sufficient to form a loving relationship?

The short answer is that the physical world, however insubstantial or seeming ethereal at its core, provides concrete experiences—positive and negative—which, in turn, promotes knowledge and Christian maturity.

These concrete experiences present ambiguously without yielding objective truths about anything. Take water. Surely water is an objective good: we are largely made of water; need water to live; use water to grow necessary food, to bath, even to get baptized. And yet water kills: floods, tsunamis, drownings. The natural world mirrors, and is understood within and through, the structures of being that physically impinge upon all humans. As Paul said "We know that the whole creation has been groaning as in the pains of childbirth right up to the present time." (Ro 8:22)

The life process of a self-conscious individual within a physical world imparts hard-learned wisdom. Our minds want to be free to run through a brick wall but our body tells us we can't. It tells us there are consequences—positive and negative—for decisions and actions. These concrete experiences create opportunities to acquire knowledge, grow in discernment, and make morally consequential choices. *Having a free will within an ambiguous, tension-laden, physical world creates pain and suffering, but it also creates maturity in Christ.*

* * *

But can we say that each of us is a *self*? I can't imagine any argument against the assumption that each human constitutes a self-conscious individual, other than the argument, especially among some existentialists, that the "self" is an illusion.

I feel like a distinct self that has changed over time. To me there exists a clear trail of bread crumbs from the beginning of my life until now, regardless of twists and turns, tragedies and transformations.

At a minimum, I feel I am some thing perceiving myself and other things. Whether I'm perceiving a real world external to my conscious awareness of things, or whether I'm merely experiencing an internal illusion, I cannot know. But I am experiencing some thing. Thus, I'm at least an experiencer, an I, a self.

* * *

In terms of a *Christian perspective* of being a human in a world, another issue is that some Christians feel sentient life is limited to Earth, based upon their Scriptural understanding of Earth as the center of existence. In addition to Scripture, there is the quite natural urge to want to be *special to God*. Thus, the idea of there being *too many individuals in the world*, and *too many worlds* within the universe/multiverse, *creates anxiety* of not being special.

When we once believed that the universe spun around Earth, and we were the center of the universe, this suggested rather strongly that we were special. Scientific discoveries over the centuries have eroded our sense of specialness in the world to the point that we might feel totally inconsequential.

First came the discovery by Copernicus, soon verified by Galileo, in the 16th and 17th century that the earth revolved around the sun and not vice-versa. Then came the emerging concept of the immensity of our universe and the fact that our Milky Way galaxy with its 250 billion stars (plus or minus 150 billion) is but one of 100 billion to 2 trillion other galaxies within our known universe.

This notion of God being present with everyone in the world is staggering given that the universe is incomprehensibly immense. The possibility of sentient life elsewhere is highly probable given the immense number of other possible worlds that may support sentient life in some form.

True, the *Argument from the Fine-Tuning of Physical Constraints* (Goldstein, p.357) suggests otherwise. It points to the highly improbable chances that all the variables necessary for life as we know it can exist within such a narrow bandwidth. And yet they all do exist in what some call a *Goldilocks* range of possibilities. It is incredible, almost impossible. A miracle. Therefore, suggesting uniqueness.

However, British evolutionary biologist and writer, Richard Dawkins' (2006) presents a counter argument to the theory of fine tuning: the Earth's "Goldilocks" conditions for our earth, far from being unique in the cosmos, can be seen as fairly common. Dawkins argued:

> ...as with Goldilocks, the anthropic alternative to the design hypothesis is statistical. Scientists invoke the magic of large numbers. It has been estimated that there are between 1 billion and 30 billion planets in our galaxy, and about 100 billion galaxies in the universe. Knocking a few noughts off for reasons of ordinary prudence, a billion billion is a conservative estimate of the number of available planets in the universe. Now, suppose the origin of life...really was a staggeringly improbable event. Suppose it was so improbable as to occur on only one in a billion planets....And yet..even with such absurdly long odds, life will still have arisen on a billion planets—of which Earth, of course, is one. (p. 137-138)

Even more staggering to the imagination than the size of our known universe is that some scientists theorize there is more than this one universe; in fact, a multiverse of infinite other universes that, in total, constitute the whole of physical reality.

These *numbers are unfathomable* and have been used by *atheists to argue that surely no personal God can exist to care about each and every citizen* of earth given our cosmic insignificance.

Writer Mark Twain (1835-1910) wrote a short book around this very theme: *Extract From Captain Stormfield's Visit to Heaven* (1909). In it he describes a man awakening from being dead "about thirty years" (p. 1) finding himself being whizzed along through space at "about a million miles a minute—it might have been more" (p. 3) on some sort of flying contraption. As he looked out at the vastness of space, he asked the Captain where Earth was.

The Captain "got in a balloon and sailed up and up and up, in front of a map that was as big as Rhode Island." (p. 23) He did this for a few days before finally coming back down and saying "he thought he had found that solar system [ours], but it might be fly-specks. So he got a microscope and went back." (p. 23, 24)

It is hilariously told, in broad comic strokes, this fable of how insignificant humanity and its world is in the intergalactic sense. At its heart, it reflects Twain's increasing bitterness and skepticism, near the end of his life, toward the idea of a benevolent God who cared about humanity.

Twain's skepticism—and the skepticism of many atheists—assumes that God, like the rest of us, is limited to the physical laws and constraints of humanity and finitude. For the rest of us, the reach of space and time does render us quite small and insignificant in the cosmos. But God, infinite creator of finitude, is not so limited. God transcends nature and the laws of physics.

God is omnipresent, an attribute emanating from God's omnipotence. Therefore, God's love can shine as brightly on one lonely person living on the edge of one small, rather insignificant, dying galaxy among 100 billion plus other galaxies, as on the entire multiverse. Instantaneously. For every soul.

Further, this immensity of life is consistent with the boundlessness of God's selfless love. God does not hide his love under a bushel basket, as the old Sunday school song goes. It shines infinitely, radiates beyond our comprehension, yet can focus on each and every one of us as if we were the entire world—which to God each of us is.

If we think of God like us, as a physical thing among physical things, then, yes, these scientific breakthroughs can create anxiety that we are not so special. After all, our common sense asks, How could God ever get around to me, one of 8 billion humans on a tiny planet in a vast solar system, within a vast galaxy of 250 billion stars, in a universe of up to 2 trillion other galaxies, not to mention a multiverse?

Given that God is not a physical *thing* among physical things, and is not limited by nature's physical laws, processes and properties, then we should not be troubled by the march of science that keeps increasing the size and breadth of possible life. *Let science find near infinite worlds to fill the love of our infinite God for each creature and it will never exhaust God's supply of love for everyone.*

If God is omnipresent (everywhere and at all times) then God is present with you now, giving you full attention. You call, God is there. I believe this is one of God's attributes: omnipresence, part of God's omnipotence. Clearly an omnipresent God is a being *that which nothing greater can be conceived.*

This structure of a world and self-conscious individuals supports God's plan Y of exporting boundless love: an immense propagation of being that can yield a network of agape.

To a Christian, self-consciousness might extract a high cost throughout life, such as psychic suffering, anxiety, confusion and doubt. But the cost is a justified necessary cost if it enables us to come to know, appreciate and love God. The secular evolutionary behaviorist might see self-consciousness as a necessary feature promoting survival. Others might see it as evil, preferring never to have been born in the first place. It is up to each individual to freely choose their understanding of their self-consciousness: divine gift or devilish burden?

Scriptural Support

The Genesis story of creation reflects this most basic of structures with the creation of a physical world and of a man and woman, two separate, distinct individual humans. (Ge 1)

God gave them a command to obey and they disobeyed. This shows they had minds and could reason, and that they were both sentient and conscious of God as another entity separate and distinct from them. Further, after they disobeyed and were punished, they felt shame and guilt, cloaking their nakedness with fig leaves. This guilt and shame displays awareness of self.

God said they would "die" if they ate of the tree of knowledge of good and evil. They ate and did die into the ambiguous world of good and evil, into a place separated from God, a harsh place "east of Eden" where joy and pain dance in consort.

In this harsh world the Christian story unfolds around major themes of sin and salvation and of a redeeming love involving humans and God.

The Bible is based upon self-conscious individual humans within a physical world as the structural center of the Christian story.

* * *

As concerns the question of the specialness of humans in the world, certain literal readings of Scripture suggests the earth is, in fact, uniquely special in its relationship to God.

Historically, religious opposition to heliocentrism (the idea that Earth revolves around the sun as the center of our solar system and not vice versa) arose from Biblical references such as: "In the beginning, God created the heavens and the earth." (Ge 1); "God made two great lights—the greater light [sun] and the lesser light [moon] to govern the the night. He also made the stars." (Ge 1:16); "The world is firmly established, it cannot be moved" (Ps 93:1 and 96:10; 1 Ch 16:30). In the same manner, see "He set the earth on its foundations; it can never be moved." (Ps 104:5 NIV) Further, consider "The sun rises and the sun sets, and hurries back to where it rises". (Ecc 1:5).

These passages read literally indeed suggest that the earth is the center of the God's creation. Scientific discoveries since the drafting of Scripture suggest otherwise.

This leaves us with three possibilities: science is wrong; the above passages should be read symbolically and not literally; or science is correct but, even then, earth and its inhabitants are special to God.

Let me stress that I am not a literalist as to everything revealed in Scripture. Some facts I take literally, some allegorically, some metaphorically, some as teaching parables. My overall approach is to render an interpretation that best supports the main themes and goals of Scripture in a most charitable way. I interpret the passages cited above as metaphors to stress that we (the subjects of Biblical revelation on earth) are indeed special to God.

This interpretation supports both science and Scripture's meta theme of God's love for each and every one of us.

I am not a science skeptic. On the contrary, I understand science and its foundations of math, logic, and reason as gifts from God. I highly value these gifts. How we use them is another issue. For example, if we elevate science and human reason above God as our hope for the future as solutions to life's existential tragedies, then we deify science and human reason.

This is sin based upon human pride, hubris—the notion that we do not need God and can solve our problems without God. As Niebuhr said (1996):

> Every effort to identify meaning with rationality implies the deification of reason. That such an identification represents idolatry, and that the laws of reason and logic are incapable of fully comprehending the total meaning of the world, is attested by the fact that life and history are full of contradictions which cannot be resolved in terms of rational principles. Furthermore a mind which transcends itself cannot legitimately make itself the ultimate principle of interpretation by which it explains the relation of the mind to the world. The fact of self-transcendence leads inevitably to the search for a God who transcends the world.

Man is constantly tempted to the sin of idolatry and constantly succumbs to it because in contemplating the power and dignity of his freedom he forgets the degree of his limitations. (v. 1, p. 165-166)

God is our only hope for the future, the only answer to our existential tragedies. Science cannot solve our ontological problem of being in the world. The finite can never prove/disprove the infinite. Science is inherently (and by definition) limited. Science and human reason should be viewed as gifts from God to enable us to come to know, appreciate and love God.

To demonstrate the point that science is limited, I am reminded of a joke about a man hunting for his keys one dark night. Joe sees this man down the street underneath a street light. Joe approaches the stranger and says, "Can I help?" The stranger looks up at Joe and says, "Yes. I'm looking for my car keys which I lost." Joe says, "Did you lose them right about here?" The stranger replies, "No. I lost them further up the street. But the light's better here."

Science only looks where it can see. It doesn't and cannot look where it cannot see. Paul tells us we "live by faith, not be sight." (2 Co 5:7 NIV). Science does not understand that. Nor should it, because then it wouldn't be science.

I argue modern science only makes it seem we are not significant to God by: (1) arguing we evolved from other species; and (2) from being seemingly lost and adrift in an aging solar system on the edge of one galaxy among billions of galaxies.

But I think what science has shown is that God is truly God, beyond comprehension, is truly *that which nothing greater can be conceived.* The more science reveals of the world, the greater God seems to be.

* * *

Without consciousness, no one could even read this book or the Bible. Without self-consciousness, no one would or could relate the Bible's content—the words, arguments, implications, etc.—to their own life as a thing within a world of otherness.

Yes, self-consciousness creates negative outcomes such as tension, uncertainty, worry and fear. However, it's just as true that self-consciousness illuminates the ultimate positives in life that stands in stark contrast to the nothingness that negative experiences portend.

The path to God runs through a world of good and bad concrete experiences within a physical world that powerfully imparts powerful positive and negative behavior- shaping effects. A person's consciousness—the theatre where our experiences and thoughts have their existence, where our desires are felt where our intentions are formed—is the mechanism that connects us to God.

If the Bible can be read in good faith to be consistent with what our gifts of reason, math and logic have revealed of the world as it actually seems to be constituted, then I think reading the Bible in this way is the most charitable way to understand Scripture. I argue that understanding the universe today as science understands it does no damage to the idea of an omnipotent and omnipresent God loving and caring for each and every one of us as if we were God's only child.

The expansion of our notions of reality only seems to expand our notions of God's greatness, glory and boundless love.

- PART 4 -

CONCLUSION

The world is built for (God's) love. God is the Great Cosmic Lover...
He loves and wants to be loved by us.
H. D. McDonald, *The God Who Responds*

It [the Samaritan helping the Jew in the parable of the Good
Samaritan] creates a new kind of fittingness, belonging together,
between Samaritan and wounded Jew. They are fitted together in
dissymmetric proportionality...which comes from God, which is that
of agape, and which became possible because God became flesh. The
enfleshment of God extends outward...into a network, which we call
the Church....it creates links across boundaries, on the basis of...the
kind of love God has for us, which we call agape.
Charles Taylor, *A Secular Age*

...as you know, my friend, a gem is not polished without
rubbing, nor a man perfected without trials.
Earl Derr Biggers, *The Black Camel*

I CONSIDER THIS THEODICY an extension and improvement of exist-ing free will theodicy such as expressed by Hick and Swinburne, in general, and open theism in particular: like taking a one-legged, somewhat rickety stool and adding additional legs to support and stabilize it.

I believe that this theodicy in many ways reflects not only ideas found in other theodicies but also within some traditional Christian responses and defenses to evil. What I hope to have added are the life processes or structures of being that shape and channel us toward knowledge, appreciation and love of God and others, which is God's main good reason for creation. In other words, I focus on God's design of how we experience life (e.g., how we learn, feel, believe, grow and mature, appreciate and love, engage in moral behavior).

I also argue this theodicy is *consistent with science*—in fact embraces and depends largely on the best of scientific thinking. Further, it largely *reflects many concepts found in our current postmodern thinking* (e.g., relativism, subjectivity, contingency, ambiguity) that undergirds new atheism and much of modern secularity.

I find, like Kierkegaard and Tillich and others what I would loosely call Christian existentialists, that much of *postmodern secular thinking* (which is largely founded upon existentialist philosophy) *can be understood to reflect God's plan for creation* as revealed in Scripture just as strongly as it suggests atheism.

Thus, I consider this theodicy *not only scripturally sound but also relevant today, intellectually defensible and ideologically durable*, in the sense of reflecting science and modern concepts of philosophy.

The Word and the world are logically compatible. And that relationship between the world and the Word explains the world as it actually exists and as Scripture speaks to our condition of being in the world.

* * *

In ending, I choose to address Rowe's two examples of evil—*Sue* and *Bambi*—because one deals with moral evil, the other with natural evil, and because they are examples of horrendous evil for which the theist is challenged to demonstrate both God's good reason for and the necessity of these horrible, seemingly gratuitous evil acts

Sue

Once again, Rowe's example of horrendous moral evil is as follows:

> This is an actual event in which a five-year-old girl in Flint, Michigan was severely beaten, raped and then strangled to death early on New Year's Day on 1986. The case was introduced by Bruce Russell, whose account of it, drawn from a report in the *Detroit Free Press* of January 3, 1986, runs as follows:

> The girl's mother was living with her boyfriend, another man who

was unemployed, her two children, and her 9-month old infant fathered by the boyfriend. On New Year's Eve all three adults were drinking at a bar near the woman's home. The boyfriend had been taking drugs and drinking heavily. He was asked to leave the bar at 8:00 p.m. After several reappearances he finally stayed away for good at about 9:30 p.m. The woman and the unemployed man remained at the bar until 2 a.m. at which time the woman went home and the man to a party at a neighbor's house. Perhaps out of jealousy, the boyfriend attacked the woman when she walked into the house. Her brother was there and broke up the fight by hitting the boyfriend who was passed out and slumped over a table when the brother left. Later the boyfriend attacked the woman again, and this time she knocked him unconscious. After checking the children, she went to bed. Later the woman's 5-year old girl went downstairs to go to the bathroom. The unemployed man returned from the party at 3:45 a.m. and found the 5-year old dead. She had been raped, severely beaten over most of her body and strangled to death by the boyfriend. (1988: p.119)

First, there is the crime of rape and murder. *If we are free in the libertarian sense, then such evil actions as rape and murder are possible.* Could God have designed life such that we cannot engage in evil acts? Yes, but then God would be limiting our freedom such that we are not free in the libertarian sense, and love would not be possible.

Could God have designed life so that, while we can commit evil acts, there is a limit to the depth and breadth of evil actions? For example, could God have limited evil acts to property crimes and not crimes of violence? Could God have limited crimes to misdemeanors and not felonies? Could God have limited evil acts to minor wrongs only?

To limit our capacity for evil would mean there would be some sort of standard or bright line of wrong-doing. We would all come to know what that bright line of wrong-doing was because we would notice that we, and others, couldn't cross it.

In terms of limiting the depth of evil, could God, say, have decreased the amount of pain and suffering in life by 90%? Swinburne answers yes, God could do that but then our opportunity for courageous moral action would be reduced by 90%. It would become, according to Swinburne, a "toy world" where moral action was largly unneeded.

Or, let's assume that while we can commit minor crimes—e.g., theft, simple battery, intimidation, breaking and entering— we can never commit crimes of great bodily harm such as rape or murder. There would be no murder, no more rape. Try as we might, we couldn't murder or rape anyone. No one could. There would never be another *Sue* scenario.

Everyone would realize there is this bright-line of evil behavior which none of us could ever cross. What would the effect of this be on our free will and the other structures of being?

I argue one effect of a bright line limit to evil behavior would be that our free choices would no longer be free. The ambiguous possibilities that enable freedom would be not exist. When it comes to murder or rape, there would be no ambiguity, no choice, as murder and rape would not be a possible behavior option. It would be a certainty, a unitary possibility without option, this inability to kill or rape another. We would know that we are not fully free, that something, somewhere restricts our ability to act. And as the certainty of determinism rises, the ability to love diminishes accordingly.

Secondly, what about the structures of doubt and anxiety? Don't they depend upon the uncertainty inherent in the structures of a conscious free individual struggling within an ambiguous world? If doubt is removed, because of certainty, then there is no doubt that God exists because only God could have restricted the range of our possible actions.

Someone might argue, *well, that's a much better world than one with rape and murder, this determined world where freedom is limited and the certainty of God is increased.* Perhaps, but it's also one that vitiates if not eliminates moral behavior such as love, courage and faith.

The scales of life's delicate balance between "God or no God" would be tipped sufficiently that we would know someone or some thing is controlling our behavior, either God or some other supernatural possibility. We would know, at least should know, that we live in a controlled world such that our actions are not free in a libertarian sense.

How much courage, then, would be required for faith? I argue none. Would our faith be founded upon (1) a courageous leap of love or (2) be driven by the certainty of God's reality? Wouldn't Pascal's Wager be a much easier bet, one based upon cool calculations, one even a fool would make?

Or, let's assume another possibility: Could God allow an unlimited range of evil—such as this horrendous case of rape and murder—but limit the type of victim?

Could God not permit the rape and murder of innocent young children? Could God establish a bright line limit on the minimum age for victimhood such that young children never suffer great harm or early death? God could do that but what, then, would be the standard? Should God design life so that no one under, say, 7 years of age would ever suffer death or rape? Would that give everyone enough life before death? If not, how about 21? 40? Or 60?

Perhaps God could also establish an innocence threshold whereby only those with unclean hands, stained by sin, can be victims of evil actions?

After all, many people believe there are some among us who deserve to be murdered. For example, I argue some people would not regret the boyfriend in Sue's case receiving the death penalty.

Would critics be satisfied with God's justice if only elderly evil people for whom no mercy seems warranted are the victims of murder or rape? In the *Sue* scenario, for example, what if Rowe presented a scenario entitled *boyfriend*. In this scenario, Rowe recounts the boyfriend's life of drugs, alcohol and domestic violence, of lying and cheating, and otherwise being a most unpleasant person. Then during a drug deal gone bad, equally depraved dealers from a rival gang beat him to death for trying to cheat them. Question: Does this scenario change anything? Does Rowe still use it as his poster child against the possibility that a good and loving God exists? I argue he wouldn't because nobody would be that outraged.

However, if only elderly, morally reprehensible violent criminals were murdered, but never any one else, what does that do to God's design of being to achieve plan Y? I argue a sense of certainty would rise and with it, doubt, anxiety, freedom and moral consequentiality would correspondingly decline.

The same analysis applies both to our ambiguous, imperfect court system that didn't prevent this human tragedy, and to the frailty of human behavior—e.g., addiction, cruelty, inebriation, jealousy, predatory behavior—that fueled this evil scenario. To limit each dysfunctional dynamic involved in this tragedy, so as to render it less tragic, would compromise those structures of being that leads us to God's love.

Finally, I would argue that God's limiting the possibility for human evil restricts our ability for moral good. That is, morally bad situations present opportunity for growth in Christ through morally good behavior.

*　＊＊＊*

The Sue example is rich with opportunities for morally good action both before, during and after the tragedy. People who knew of the volatile, dysfunctional relationship could have intervened in any number of ways: e.g., call the child welfare hotline; call the police; call known family members; knock on the door and try to convince the mother of the impending danger, etc.

True, the intervention could be futile as drug and alcohol addiction are very difficult to overcome, and people in dysfunctional relationships often resist intervention. But sometimes preventive intervention works. Perhaps just one call or home visit from a concerned neighbor or family member could have saved this five year old's life.

True, becoming involved out of love and for love in such a volatile dysfunctional family situation creates risk for the intervenor. There is risk because the well-intentioned intervenor realizes they are stepping into an ambiguous situation, anxious because of the possibility that they will be harmed or even killed in by intervening.

Love is only love if it's courageously made in the face of doubt about the ambiguity of the choices and the risk involved in the choice. Love without courage is not love. To love your neighbor requires the courage to act. This is the parable of the Good Samaritan, where on the road to Jericho a Samaritan came across a Levite laying by the same road "half dead," the victim of a brutal robbery. Despite the fact Samaritans and Levites were bitter tribal enemies, the Samaritan "took pity" upon the Levite, "bandaged his wounds" and took him to an inn and further cared for him. The next day, the Samaritan gave "two silver coins" to the innkeeper and said "Look after him...and when I return, I will reimburse you for any extra expense you may have." (Lk 10: 25-37)

The parable of the Good Samaritan was given by Jesus when asked "Teacher...what must I do to inherit eternal life?" (Lk 10:25) Jesus recited the parable of the Good Samaritan and told the questioner: "Go and do likewise." (Lk 10:37)

The Good Samaritan parable involved moral evil—a robbery and a beating—but it could have just as easily involved natural evil—e.g., a rock slide; a heart attack. There is no difference between moral and natural evil in responding to the call of Jesus to "Go and do likewise."

People who know of the dangerous situation and do nothing arguably have some moral culpability for the resultant tragedy. After all, refusing to act is an action. Refusing to act when Christ's love calls for action might well be a sin in the sense that when you refuse to do what Christ would do, you are disconnected from God.

Even after a tragedy, there is a need to comfort those mentally scarred by the tragedy. There's a need to help the perpetrator to accept blame, ask for forgiveness, accept salvation, and turn their life around, even in prison. There's a need to provide supportive comfort and restorative love to those emotionally damaged by the evil. There's an opportunity to get more involved—in your family, in the neighborhood, in the world—to hopefully prevent future similar tragedies.

Opportunities abound to live and love like Christ because of the structures of being that present themselves in the midst of great tragedy. There is no wasted motion in life, no shortfall of opportunities to live and love like Christ. Life is pregnant with moral consequentiality. Even non action in the face of tragedy is a moral action. In Sartre's sense, we are condemned to be morally consequential. Refusing to act, denying evil is occurring in front of you, turning your head away, all are moral actions.

Failing everything—that is, finding it impossible to prevent such tragedies, being rebuffed in ministering to the needs of victims, even failing in hope and becoming skeptical and despondent about God's power and love—there is still one more opportunity: the opportunity to turn to God in absolute need. There is the opportunity to see, as Kierkegaard argued, God as possibility when no possibility remains. *Maintaining faith in God when all seems hopeless is an invaluable option and opportunity presented by the despair of helplessness in the face of great evil.*

Christ on the cross never lost faith in God. True, Christ cried out in pain and suffering, in doubt as to this pain and suffering, and in the anxiety of dying, but at all times on the cross Christ was talking to God. Likewise, Job in the depths of his seemingly gratuitous tragedy never lost faith in God. Yes, he was upset with God because Job did not understand "Why?" he was being punished so harshly and unfairly. Job didn't understand "What?" he did to deserve this punishment. But he kept talking to God. He might have been upset with and confused about God, but he believed in God. Eventually both Christ and Job were restored: Christ to reunion with His Father; Job restored with prosperity.

* * *

Thankfully, there are positive moments in life, victories for good in striving to be like the Good Samaritan. Evil doesn't always win for then there would be certainty of evil. Sadly, there are negative defeats in trying. Good doesn't always trump evil for then there would be certainty of good. As Tillich says, life is ambiguous, full of both good and evil, positive and negative, at all times.

God's balance of good and evil in the world might seem disproportionately tilted toward evil, given examples like Sue. However, if it were titled more toward goodness, such that the certainty of God is increased, then doubt and anxiety would be diminished. The subjective would become more objective. Freedom wouldn't be as free and ambiguity wouldn't be as ambiguous.

The power for courageous faith within the human heart, a power fueled by the dizziness of freedom in an ambiguous world of doubt and anxiety, would be detuned. Everything God desires from creation would lose its heft and meaning. Love would be less courageous, less a leap a faith and more a level-headed, rational calculation as to the best course of action. We would all follow Pascal's Wager and go to God, not in love, but in reasoned calculation, a cold-blooded decision of the head and not the heart and soul.

If, as I claim, anxiety reveals an absolute need for God, all the actors in the *Sue* tragedy should know concretely, and without doubt, both the tragic limits of finitude and the need for God. They should all feel the pain and suffering of being in the world. They have touched the terror of das Nichtige, of nothingness, the absurd, the meaninglessness of death. They are deep into the reality of what is not God. They have lost all childish innocence and a childish lack of depth of seriousness. They stand on the razor's edge of nothingness.

It may not seem like a positive outcome for all the participants in the Sue tragedy, nor a good place to be, but they are prepared to cry out for God in a surrender to loving grace. At the end stage of utter despair, we are all left with one possibility when all possibilities are gone. God is always there after we exhaust our finite options.

* * *

Bambi

Here is Rowe's example of horrendous natural evil.

> In some distant forest lightning strikes a dead tree, resulting in a forest fire. In the fire a fawn is trapped, horribly burned, and lies in terrible agony for several days before death relieves its suffering. (1979, p. 337)

Rowe's argument is that the fawn's suffering is pointless, that surely no good reason justifies this suffering, and, even assuming some good reason justifies this suffering, it's not necessary—that is, God could have prevented this suffering without thereby losing some greater good or permitting some evil equally bad or worse.

There are many traditional arguments developed over time to address natural evils such as Rowe's example of Bambi. An excellent discussion detailing ten leading arguments can be found in Chapters 8 and 9 of Boyd's theodicy (2001). Boyd disagrees with all ten arguments, finding some shortcoming in each one, thus developing his own theodicy, in Chapter 10, which blames Satan. As Boyd argues (2001), there "is a class of evils in the world that cannot be explained adequately except by appealing to Satan." (p. 17)

As indicated, I disagree with Boyd's theodicy primarily for this one reason. But I would like to focus briefly on Boyd's theory because many free will Christian advocates I admire in addition to Boyd, (e.g., Plantinga, Lewis, Polkinghorne) suggest that the moral evil of non-human creatures might explain natural evil.

The argument is that fallen angels, such as Satan, were also given free will. Given their turning against God, and given their status as supernatural beings, they can and have used their malevolent ways to wreak great damage on the world.

This may be metaphysically true, but I find it insufficient for theodicy for a number of reasons. One is the illogic of God needing supernatural agents, such as angels, to achieve God's plan, Y. If God is omnipotent, omniscient and omnipresent, God needs no help with creation. He is with each one of us, fully, always, ready to enter our lives if asked.

Another objection is that blaming fallen angels, like Satan, doesn't solve the problem of evil. Rather, it merely shifts the question from: How can evil exist if God is perfectly powerful and loving? to How can Satan exist if God is perfectly powerful and loving? The problem of natural evil becomes the problem of Satan. We get nowhere.

Swinburne agrees (1992) when he argues:

> Many theists have of course claimed that natural evils are really brought about by free agents other than men, viz. fallen angels, and hence that a defense similar to the free-will defense can be used to give the same kind of account of them as of moral evils. But this looks very much like an ad hoc hypothesis added to theism to save it from falsification by evidence which would otherwise falsify it. Although this hypothesis may save theism from formal falsification, it would seem that natural evil still greatly disconfirms theism, if

the only way to save theism from falsification is by adding to it an ad hoc hypothesis. If the fallen-angel defense is to be taken more seriously, we need evidence of the existence of fallen angels, other than that provided by the existence of natural evil. (p. 306)

As concerns Boyd's cited ten traditional arguments against natural evil, I embrace many of them as providing partial answers and invaluable insight. My tack is slightly different than those I embrace, primarily in more fully describing God's good reasons for the structures of being God wove into the fabric of experiential life to achieve those reasons.

My defense against natural evil is not unlike my defense of moral evil, nor any other evil that can be imagined. It is the same in that all evil can be traced to the functioning of the structures of being described in this book.

To illustrate, let's deconstruct the Bambi example to see how we could have a different outcome given the design of life. Let's start with the phenomena of fire. If there had been no forest fire, Bambi would not have been burnt and suffered horribly.

Fire, like everything in life is ambiguous: fire saves life and fire destroys life. In terms of saving life, humanity's mastery of fire is considered one of its greatest advancements. Harnessing nature's fire allowed humans: to produce heat that provides comfort and protection against the cold; a method to cook food; have protection against predators; and fashion advanced tools and products such as steel.

In terms of destroying life, fire can kill if one is caught in its flames, heat or smoke, like Bambi was caught by fire.

Should God have not allowed fire within the world because of its ambiguous nature of both good and evil? Further, if God did allow fire, but only for purposes of good, then wouldn't God have to do the same for every physical phenomena (e.g., water, dirt, wind)? After all, Bambi could have been killed by a flood, a landslide, or hurricane. Would that have changed the power of Rowe's example?

Even assuming God allowed fire within the world with its ambiguous potential of both good and bad, should God have designed the world such that no creature—human or animal—was ever harmed by fire? God certainly has the power to do that. What would be the effect if God allowed fire but, say, made creatures inflammable, or otherwise immune or impervious to the heat, smoke and danger of fire?

Or, should God have made trees inflammable? If so, wouldn't every other natural object be made inflammable? Why just trees?

Or, should God have eliminated lightening from creation such that there would never be a forest fire ignited by lightening to kill Bambi? If God eliminated lightening from nature, what about other sources of ignition for fire? Should he have banned matches, or rubbing sticks together to create enough heat to generate fire?

We could go on and on with suggestions as to how God could have better designed nature to prevent Bambi's suffering. But the point is fairly obvious: God's creation of bright-line limits to suffering—like no forest fires, or no lightening, or say, no innocent children or young animals should ever suffer—destroys the delicate balance of the dynamic operation of the structures of being that lead humans to God.

When can we die and suffer? Should it be when we reach maturity, say age 18 whereby no one dies or suffers until they are 18? Or should the bright-line for death and suffering be after we've enjoyed a fairly good life, say age 60, perhaps 80?

I argue that in limiting nature's evil we limit nature's good, thereby undermining the process of God achieving God's plan (God's good reasons) through humans aquiring "knowledge/appreciation/love maturation" outcomes carved upon the anvil of freedom, ambiguity, doubt, anxiety and self-consciousness.

Let's explore that thought a little more.

* * *

Boyd (2001) has trouble with why God didn't design nature better. While admitting his own premise that "the power to influence for the worse must be roughly proportionate to our power to influence for the better" (p. 23), he argues there should be limits. But arguing his own premise doesn't adequately explain natural evil:

> ...it does not explain why God would tolerate the massacre of little children by a tornado....why could God not have intervened just enough to prevent the actualization of these hazardous potentials?

Even if one maintains that, for whatever reason, the tornado *must* be allowed to occur, why could God not have shifted the tornado several yards in one direction or the other to spare the children? Would God's intervention have undone natural laws and natural objects equivalent to supposing that water lost its capacity to drown creatures or the sun lost its ability to scorch the ground? I cannot see that it would. (p. 279, 280)

It seems so compelling, this argument that it would be simple for an all-powerful God to physically intervene in nature just a little—move a tornado a few feet here or jump over that house there, limit the earthquake's range, stop the plague from spreading so far. Think of the good that can flow from just a little physical intervention.

Boyd finds the notion so attractive that he cannot bring himself to blame God in the sense that God created the world, with its physical laws and natural processes. God is omnipotent and can prevent natural evil and God is wholly good and would want to prevent natural evil—at least horrendous natural evil that takes, say, the life of young child in a tornado or a fawn in a forest fire. It has to be Satan that makes the tornado seem to hit the house and kill the children and incinerate the fawn, he argues.

Of course, as I've argued (apologies for being redundant, but this is a key point) if natural evil were more certain—say, we all notice that no one's house containing little children ever, in the history of tornados, was hit by a tornado because they always skirted left or right several yards or miraculously jumped over it—then we would know something certain about a supernatural controller of the world. We would know there is one. Doubt would be diminished, anxiety would be lessened, freedom would lose its moral power. We could breathe more easily: lean back, relax, not worry because God's in control, and what will happen will happen, and there's nothing we can do about it. It's fate—God's determinist will.

Boyd's concerns about excessive natural evil begs the obvious question: Why does God have to intervene at all? God designed the world, established the laws of nature and physics with all their ambiguous potential for good and evil outcomes, and set into motion the structures of being. Did God goof in this design such that God has to physically intervene here and there, moment to moment, to prevent something God didn't intend? And if God is omniscient, couldn't God have foreseen the tornado heading for a house with children, the 2004 Asian tsunami, and the Holocaust? Can't God foresee and prevent every tragedy?

Of course, God could do that. But God apparently doesn't do that. Or, at least if God does it, God does it in such a subtle, veiled way that there is no discernible pattern that suggests divine intervention in the world. Maybe one innocent child is spared death in a given storm but others aren't. We only see it as random chance. This is possible, but if we knew such selective random acts of divine intervention happened in the world, here and there, wouldn't it seems arbitrary and capricious for God to save only some innocent children but not all innocent children? Only sporadic intervention in nature to, say, prevent tragedy in situation A but not situations B through Z seems incoherent when talking of God's essence.

Natural evil reflects the analysis made earlier of Adam and Eve's Fall. Like the analysis of the Fall as being a fall upward, toward Christian maturity, and not a fall downward into depravity, natural evil cannot be God's negligence, nor wrath, nor indifference and uncaring. *In the Christian scheme of God's essence as perfectly powerful and loving, nature must be a fall upward, presenting creatures with the opportunity to mature in Christ.*

Boyd's objection, like Rowe's, strikes me as being more about where God draws the line in just how much evil is allowed in creation (it's amount and its degree, its breadth and depth), than whether evil, per se, should be allowed at all. Both are deeply troubled by horrendous evil which seems excessive and pointless. God, being God, could eliminate horrendous evil but doesn't. Rowe says this suggests there is no God, while Boyd suggests it must be Satan. I suggest there must be and is a divine good reason.

I would agree that when and if I were suffering under the lash of evil, God's line would always seem to be drawn too much in favor or allowing pain and suffering. *Why me?* I'd moan like Job, *and not that guy down the street who richly deserves suffering more than me?* I would see this state of affairs as unjust, proof God isn't good and loving. In a state of great pain and suffering, I would not appreciate the tight logic of a theodicy.

The subjective experience of great pain and suffering by an individual might always seem to vitiate the probability that God exists. That is the nature of great suffering by an individual. However, it doesn't eliminate the logical understanding that it all makes sense given God's plan for creation. As Tillich observed (1987), "The exclamation has been and will be repeated innumerably: How can an all-powerful God who is, at the same time the God of love, allow such misery? Either he has no sufficient love or He has not sufficient power. As an emotional outburst this question is very understandable. As a theoretical formulation it is rather poor." (p. 148, 149)

That's the argument: if we all suffered exactly the same amount of evil as everyone else in the world, and if the degree of pain and suffering was of the same degree, such that it was seemingly fairly distributed, then we would know for sure there is a transcendent power controlling creation.

To create a world with enough doubt and anxiety to bruise our pride, dent our hope, and bring us to see our absolute need for God, *evil must be asymmetrical in amount, degree and distribution.*

However, none of this means God hasn't designed limits to the amount of pain and suffering any person can endure. There are, for example, the natural laws and laws of physics that limit natural evil. There are also limits on human suffering. As Swinburne (1992) argues:

> The free-will defense does not deny that there must be a limit to the amount of harm which a good God would allow man to do to others deliberately or through negligence. Clearly in our world there is such a limit because there is a limit to the amount of harm which men can suffer. Men only live so long, and if you inflict too much pain on them during their life they become unconscious. It is no way obvious that the limit to human suffering inflicted by other men is drawn in the wrong place—that if there is a God he has given to men too great a control of their own destiny. (p. 305)

Not only are there limits to pain and suffering, there are counter-balancing reasons for hope. There are positive experiences in life (e.g., joys and hopes, love and warm relationships, the thrill of achievement and/or doing morally good things) to counter-balance life's pain and suffering and evil (negatives in life).

Tillich argues (1987) that positives exist, and that the world is balanced in its ambiguity. "Life is not unambiguously good. Then it would not be life but only the possibility of life. And life is not unambiguously evil. Then nonbeing would have conquered being." (p. 151)

If nature were perfect—not free, not ambiguous and imperfect—that would signal a perfection in creation that undermines doubt, lessens anxiety and relieves the tension necessary for moral action such as courageous, loving faith.

Freedom, as argued, needs choices which the structure of ambiguity provides. An ambiguous natural world would provide those opportunities. And, as Peterson argues, natural elements, such as water, both saves and kills.

Water is essential for life: our bodies are composed primarily of water (approximately 65%); we must replenish ourselves constantly (without water, it estimated we can only live 3-10 days); and its use is necessary for the production of food. Yet water kills; it can be a negative element of life. In the 2004 Asian tsunami, over 250,000 people were killed by water. Scripture reveals the same ambiguous nature of water: on the one hand it is a holy symbol (of life, of baptism, of salvation), and yet, the great flood (Ge 7:1-24) was deadly. Water is both creative and destructive, like all elements of life.

If water never killed, that would mean there would be significantly fewer opportunities for moral actions involving courage, faith, and selfless love. The same result would apply to every natural property, such as *lightening and fire*, as in the Bambi example.

Think of it: nature never kills, never harms, never presents an opportunity for humans to live and love like Christ.

Swinburne argues natural evils are a necessary concomitant to free will in that they afford humans opportunities for courage, patience, and tolerance. Further, physical or mental evils brought on by nature motivate empathetic, sympathetic, loving people to action, to alleviate the pain and suffering of others.

Ambiguity not only enables the acquisition of knowledge and the gift of appreciation, and enables love by providing choices to freedom, it also presents opportunities for morally significant actions (i.e., moral consequentiality). My view of ambiguity seems to reflect Peterson's and Swinburne's understanding of nature as "limited" (Boyd's term).

I argue this theodicy also embraces Barth's das Nichtege. Even God needed ambiguous structure (nothingness) to create reality (something). God created reality from nothing: "the earth was formless and empty, darkness was over the surface." (Ge 1:2)

I argue the something that God created from nothing is unknowable without the nothingness to stand over and oppose it. Likewise, nothingness is unknowable without something to stand over and oppose it. It is life's foundational structure of ambiguity: something and nothing (or being and nonbeing).

It forms an axis, in tension, each pole opposed to the other. Boyd, channeling Barth, describes the tension (2001): "According to Barth, when God said yes to creation (that is, when God created this particular world) he necessarily said no to everything he did not create. This *no* is 'the nothingness' that stands over and against creation.... Barth portrays this realm of 'the nothingness' as the 'potent' nonbeing that God must always resist in order to preserve creation." (p. 284, 285)

Boyd (2001) sees Barth's theory as "insightful and useful. The insight that every *this* affirmed by God implies a *that* denied by God helps us understand some aspects of 'natural' evil. It articulates the truth that even God must confront metaphysical constraints in creating any possible world. Hence, we may understand why vulnerability is a necessary feature of creatures' contingency. This truth accounts for some of what we experience as dark in creation." (p. 287)

Think of the implication: even God is subject to the *metaphysical constraints* of ambiguity. Not only might this explain natural evil, but it might offer glimpses into the structures of eternal life.

My preference is to understand natural evil in the same way I understand moral evil: woven into the fabric of creation are structures of being that actualize God's plan by the sheer dynamic of its operational design; said structures actualize God's plan without the need for metaphysical intervention in the world; said structures are not inconsistent with scientific thinking; and said structures reflect the world as it actually exists.

Thus, my argument for the justification for natural evil is much like the above argument for moral evil concerning *Sue*, resting upon the operation of the structures of being.

* * *

Finally, some atheodicists argue *theodicy must explain every type and degree of evil.* For example, a good theodicy must explain animal cruelty, especially species extinction being the lost lives of animals before humans appeared on the scene.

First, I disagree this is necessary. Even if necessary, where would it end? The universe/multiverse is a large place. Say a moon circling some distant planet in a galaxy we aren't even aware of exploded. And say it was an ice moon, its ice mantel covering an ancient ocean rich with organics and complex compounds, perhaps even primitive one-celled microbes. Would theodicy have to explain the evil visited upon those microbes?

If evolution of life over 13.8 billions of year, or so, was God's chosen method of creation, then everything in creation has suffered and will continue to suffer until death.

Secondly, even disagreeing with the need to justify every evil, I argue this theodicy does explain every evil in creation. The negative consequences of the structures of being I have described are universal and not incident specific. They would apply to every sentient life form in the universe/multiverse.

Ambiguity is ambiguity, not only for humans but also for the bird eating the worm (which is good for the bird, bad for the worm) and the hawk swooping in killing the bird but saving the worm (good for the worm but bad for the bird). Life is omnipresently ambiguous, always presenting with good and evil.

Free will is terrifying, with its demand of choosing among ambiguous options armed only with an imperfect knowledge, and being responsible for that choice. There is no escape, for any sentient creature to this structure.

Life is contingent, meaning that not only might there be genocides or world wars or animal extinctions, but also extinction of life on earth—perhaps obliteration of the physical planet, itself is possible. Creation is always in tension with the formless void over and against which it stands.

The anxiety that springs from our conscious awareness of the doubt about our situation in the world—of not having security from harm; of not having a possibility for post-death life; of life not having a transcendent meaning beyond merely surviving in finitude—causes us to deny our contingency, our possibility of non-being. The existential dread is suppressed, denied and dealt with in any numerous psychic adaptations, some maladaptive.

When an epic natural disaster occurs, say a horrific tsunami, or a soul-wrenching moral horror unfolds, say a genocide, our anxiety is stirred. The great tragedies are splashed all over the national news. The disturbing, alarming photos and stories shake our foundations of normalcy. When epic, unthinkable tragedy is literally thrust in our face, we cannot escape confrontation with Yalom's *givens of existence* (our existential tragedy of being in the world).

Yet, every day, everywhere, there are small, individual tragedies: e.g., a baby is killed by a parent angry because the baby won't stop crying; a young couple is killed in a car wreck; a family loses their income when the bread winner is fired without just cause; an innocent person is found guilty by a jury and sent to prison. Everyday there is a *Bambi*. Everyday there is *Sue*. Yet these everyday, individual tragedies don't usually threaten to unmask collective society's *carefully constructed paper thin constructs of reality.*

Individual, small, isolated cases of horror fly beneath our radar of anxiety. Yet, there is no fundamental difference between individual tragedy and epic tragedy. Existential tragedy is existential tragedy, from the macro to the micro, from the horror of world war to the horror of one person's great suffering.

We have been thrust into a harsh physicality, estranged from our Creator, armed only with our freedom to respond to the situation we find ourselves enmeshed within. All our choices are pregnant with different possibilities, and there are no objective guideposts to point the *perfect* way forward. We base our decisions on what we have: our subjective knowledge gained from experiences—both current and historically embedded—and our gift of reason to analyze the possibilities and choose the best course of action.

The doubt and anxiety of our existential situation in the world is crushing, so crushing our behavior is largely designed for psychic safety: for seeing pattern in the chaos; meaning in the absurd; hope in the despair; comfort in union; distraction in addictions and compulsions; even mental illness born of a lack of coping mechanisms to deny the looming abyss of nothingness.

This is the world as it exists. It defines the universally experienced human condition.

This theodicy does not shirk from the reality of our existential tragedy of being in the world. On the contrary, it embraces the structures of being in the world and the givens of existence. In that embrace, it finds God. It finds God on the cross. It finds God in the heart. It finds God is our pain and suffering. It finds God in the experience of evil. It finds God in the experience of love. It finds God in the mercy, courage, compassion, charity, love and faith of others. It finds God when contemplating the nothingness that is not God. It finds God in anxiety, when considering the possibility of our non being. It finds God in the joys of living and the mystery of being. It finds God not just in our heart but also in the rational structure of our mind, as a logical and intellectually satisfying answer to the "Whys?" of the givens of existence.

The architecture leading us to God can be rationally understood. We can begin to not only devoutly believe that God made no mistakes in creation, but we can begin to intellectually comprehend it.

– PART 5 –
APPENDIX

Acknowledgments

Since this work began over twenty years ago, let me apologize to anyone whose help I have enjoyed if I omit you. It is not intentional, merely the cost of passing time on memory.

First, there is my niece, Suzanne Davis who introduced me to theodicy (specifically, in joining a church book study session being Boyd's *Satan and the Problem of Evil*). Being a lawyer as well as a strong Christian, she was quite persuasive.

Thanks also, to my former minister, Scott Zorn, for hosting the book study and helping to guide me through not only the thorny thicket of the problem of evil but also the exciting theological worldview of open theism.

Within the church, I found invaluable insight and assistance from Cecil Smith, a walking and talking encyclopedia of understanding the Bible in its most powerful and accurate (tracing back to his knowledge of both Greek and Hebrew) expression. Cecil also kindly reviewed early drafts of my thinking and provided advice that guided me toward a more mature understanding of God's message.

Thanks to Colleen Lehmann for editorial assistance during my early drafts, and to Katherine Colwell for her outstanding editing job on my finished product. Also thanks to Joe Colwell for suggesting Katherine and for goading and prodding me on to finish the book.

I also appreciated the thoughts of friends whose opinions I highly valued. They include Dr. Roger Beck, Dr. John Best and Dr. Doug Carnine. I should add that none of them identify as Christians, with two being Buddhists. But they are open-minded, generous in their helpful tips and a joy to discuss such important philosophical matters.

A special thanks to Rev. Sheryl B. Peterson, Ph.D., of Colorado (and to whom the Colwells referred this book) for her detailed and insightful suggestions as to how to make it better. I especially appreciated her comments about directing it more clearly either to academic scholars or critically thinking lay people, which I have attempted to do—tilting on the side of critically thinking lay people.

A special thank you to my book designer/publishing consultant Connie King, whose professionalism, talent, wise and kind guidance helped bring this all to completion in a beautifully published book.

My wonderful, kind-hearted, devoted and ever-loyal and supportive wife, Becky, has always been there along the long journey: reading and re-reading different drafts and sections; listening to me bounce off of her my various thoughts and theories; and providing Christian guidance and support along the way. I can't imagine undertaking and completing such a difficult task without her support.

Once again, I apologize to anyone I might have omitted.

Mike Carroll
Tuscola, Illinois

Glossary of Key Terms
and Concepts

Following are key terms and concepts, as I understand and use them, which may or may not already be described in the text.

Scriptural references are from the New International Version (NIV), Zondervan, 1985 edition.

* * *

Atheism. is the disbelief or lack of belief in God or gods.

Atheodicy. is the philosophical discipline of studying the problem of evil with a view toward denying the possibility or probability that an omnipotent, wholly good God exists. Atheodicy also refers to any argument doubting the existence of an omnipotent, wholly good God as not probable, or even not possible. A person who engages in atheodicy is an atheodicist.

Being. is the something (e.g., life) rather than no thing (i.e., not existing), the polarity often called *being and nothingness*. In existentialist thought, being describes every existing thing plus the ground upon which being exists. It also refers to the conscious phenomenon of contemplating existence.

Compatibilism. is the view that determinism is compatible with human free will. That is to say, even though our behavior is determined by some force external to our will (e.g., God or prior causes), we nonetheless have free will as a practical matter.

Contingent. is an outcome that is subject to chance instead of necessity. In philosophy, a contingent truth is one that is true as it happens, or as things are, whereas a necessary truth is one that is logically necessary.

das Nichtige. is the "nothingness" Karl Barth employed to account for evil in creation. Barth argues these are all the possibilities that God did not choose in creating this particular world, which serve to menace God's creation.

Determinism. is the view that human free will does not exist; rather, all our actions are determined by forces external to our will. Theists who embrace determinism argue it is God's will that determines human behavior in the sense God controls it or foreknows it—in either case, we cannot undo what God plans. In secular thought, it is argued that determinism is caused by prior inputs (causal or causation theory) or grand forces external to our will (e.g., Marxism, Freudianism).

Evil. is understood in its relationship to the concept of sin. Sin is both the condition of being separated from God and any actions we take that further that separation. Paul tells us that anything not done in faith to God is sin. (Ro. 14:23) God, therefore, can never sin, by definition.

Evil is the negative consequences of being in a state of sin, often expressed as pain and suffering—either as physical pain or mental suffering—or other unwanted, undesirable experiences and outcomes.

In terms of the type of evil, there is moral evil and natural evil, with moral evil being the evil that comes from human action/inaction (e.g., the Holocaust) and natural evil arising from natural processes (e.g., the 2004 Asian tsunami).

In terms of the degree of evil, there is ordinary, seemingly justified evil (e.g., the pain from a broken bone protects the bone from further damage by limiting movement) and and seemingly unjustified evil (e.g, horrendous evil: disproportionate, excessive, pointless)

Finitude. is state of having limits or bounds, such as the natural world of matter and energy which is limited by space and time and by natural processes (e.g., entrophy) and properties. It is the place we exist, which, like our lives, is limited and bound.

God. is ineffable, that is, too wondrous for words. This is closely related to Anselm's (1033-1109) definition of God—from his written prayer "Proslogion"— as "a being than which no greater can be conceived."

Others prefer to say *than that which nothing greater can be thought,* because the word "being" seems to restrict God to a physical being. Tillich, for example, sees God as the *Ground of all Being*, and not a thing among things.

I understand God as ineffable. But I also understand God wants us to come to know, appreciate and love Him (and, here, I use "Him" not to establish a gender but to reflect traditional terms), even if only through broad, even metaphorical, terms and concepts. Such concepts include seeing God's nature or essence as love, life and creative. We can understand that from our reasoned experience of noting that there is something (life) rather than nothing, and that within life, amazing and new spontaneous things happen (creative), and that our most prized feelings involve being loved (love).

Advancing our understanding, from Scripture, experience and rational inference, we can say (as Christians believe) that God's attributes include omnipotence, omniscience, and omnibenevolence (or being wholly good).

Good Reason: God has a reason (a justification for everything in creation) and God's reason is good (divine motive for advancing God's plan, consistent with God being wholly good).

Indeterminism. is the concept that not all events are determined. Some happen by chance or are contingent upon unknown future events such as human free will.

Incompatibilism. is the idea that human free will and God's will are incompatible; one has to yield to the other. Incompatible free will is the argument that human free will can override God's will, at least as concerns actions or lack of actions having a moral dimension. Theistic determinism, such as found in predestination thought is the idea that God controls the future and, thus, God's will overrides human free will.

Love. Love is both a noun and verb and is commonly understood as both an internal feeling of deep affection as well as a feeling of deep affection projected outward to someone or something.

Here, love is understood with reference within a range of two polar extremes. At one pole lies self-love or narcissism which is love of self— seeking only personal gain— the shallowest range of love. At the other extreme is selfless, charitable love: selflessly broadcasting one's love to others and God—thinking only of the needs of others—even if there is no benefit to self in doing this, and especially if there's risk of loss to self in doing this. This is the deeper expression of love.

If sin is separation from God, then selfish love, with its pride and self-centeredness, is the state of sin. Selfless love, with its charitable emphasis on helping others, is the state of virtue or goodness.

God's perfect love as expressed on the cross of Christ is both the widest and deepest expression of love possible. Christ gave all He could possibly give—His life—to the maximum amount of beneficiaries—all of humankind—and for the most beneficial, loving, generous reason—their salvation from sin.

Metaphysics. is something abstract and theoretical with no connection to physical reality; an idea, doctrine or posited reality beyond human sense perception.

Metaphysically true. is the ultimate reality as partly or wholly transcendent of perceived actuality and experience; the ultimate truth of things that lies beyond the natural world and our ability to know it through our five senses.

Objectively true. is a statement that has a definite correspondence to reality, independent of anyone's feelings or biases; facts that apply to everyone in every situation, and can be proven to be true through scientific experiments.

By comparison, subjective truths are just that: subjective. That is, they are based upon a person's internal perceptions, observations, thoughts and opinions. Thus subjective truths may not be true for everyone at all times.

Omnibenevolent or omnibenevolence. means being wholly good or perfectly good, which, in turn, usually means *being incapable of moral wrong*, and/ or being *perfectly loving.*

Omnipotence. Omnipotent or omnipotence means being able to do all things. Some (including me) limit the term to God being able to do all logical things. God, for example, could not both exist and not exist.

Omnipotence would include every other power imaginable, such as the ability to be present everywhere at all times (omnipresence). It importantly includes the ability to forego a power. God, for example, could relinquish foreknowledge (omniscience) of our future moral actions to enable love to flourish.

Omniscient. Omniscient or omniscience means being able to know all true things, including future things.

Under the classical understanding, God eternally exhaustively foreknows the future. There are no contingent or indeterminate outcomes unknown to God. God is never surprised.

The issue in theodicy is whether or not God voluntarily relinquishes this power of omniscience to some limited degree, say, to allow humans the freedom to choose to love God or not love God.

Naturalism. A philosophical viewpoint according to which everything arises from natural properties and causes. Accordingly, supernatural or spiritual explanations are excluded or discounted. Thus, philosophical naturalism reflects atheism and is associated with similar non-faith worldviews such as materialism and scientific materialism.

Necessary and contingent truths. A necessary truth is one that could not be otherwise; that it must be true in all situations and all possible worlds. A contingent truth is one that is true in a particular situation but could have been false in another situation; that is, a contingent truth depends upon how things are at any given time.

If, for example, the future is preordained by God, then all unfolding truths will be necessary truths. It cannot be otherwise. But if, for example, God foregoes some degree of His omnipotence and omniscience and allows for creaturely free will to unfold, undetermined by His sovereign will, then at least some future truths are contingent because they will depend upon undetermined human choices and actions.

Sin. is the condition of both being separated from God within the world and doing acts that promote separation instead of union with God.

Subjectivity. refers to decisions that are influenced by personal bias, prejudices, opinions, emotions. It refers to beliefs and perceptions that exist within a person's mind instead of the world.

Supernatural. means something beyond nature; a thing unobservable by sense perception; beyond scientific understanding and the laws of nature.

Sufficient reason. The principle of sufficient reason holds that for every state of affairs or true proposition, there is an explanation of why it is the way it is.

Theism. is the belief in the existence of a god or gods, especially belief in one god as creator of the universe, who cares about creation and, in some fashion, participates in creation.

Polytheism refers to the belief in many gods, such as is found in Hinduism or in ancient Roman culture.

Monotheism is the belief that there is only one god. Judaism, Islam and Christianity are all monotheistic religions, each tracing genesis to the ancient story of Abraham and his family, each believing their god is the one true god.

Deism is a belief in a god, but one who does not intervene or participate within creation.

Pantheism is a belief in god who literally is the universe or at least the universe is a manifestation of god.

Theodicy. is the theological discipline of studying the problem of evil with a goal of defending the possibility, even probability, that such a God exists. Theodicy also refers to any argument that defends the existence of an omnipotent, omniscient, wholly good God given evil in the world. A person who engages in the discipline of theodicy is known as a theodicist.

Transcendent. means beyond the range of human experience. God, for example, is not subject to the limitations of the material universe, but transcends it.

Ultimate or ultimately true. A necessary truth that exists within all possible worlds and that is not limited to human perception or the natural world and its properties and processes. It exists in the world independent of the human mind and encompasses all transcendent, metaphysical possibilities. It is the truth upon which all life stands, finally and at the end.

References

Adams, M. (1986). "Redemptive Suffering: Christian Solution to the Problem of Evil," as cited in Peterson, M. (2011) *The Problem of Evil*. Notre Dame, Indiana: University of Note Dame Press.

Augustine, St. (2009). *The City of God*. Peabody, MA: Hendrickson Publishers

Augustine, St. (1991). *Confessions*. Translated by Henry Chadwick. Oxford: Oxford University Press.

Augustine, St. as quoted in Plantinga, A. (1977). *God, Freedom, and Evil*. Grand Rapids, Michigan: Wm B. Eerdmans Publishing.

Barth, K. as cited in Boyd, G. (2001). *Satan and the Problem of Evil*. Downer's Grove, Illinois: InterVarsity Press.

Becker, E. (1997). *The Denial of Death*. New York: Free Press Paperbacks.

Berra, Yogi.(1998). *The Yogi Book: I Didn't Say Everything I Said*. Workman Publishing.

Blackburn, S. (2005). *Oxford Dictionary of Philosophy*. Great Britian: Oxford University Press.

Boyd, Gregory A. (2001). *Satan and the Problem of Evil*. Downer's Grove, Illinois:InterVarsity Press.

Campbell, Joseph (1991). *The Power of Myth*. New York: Anchor Books.

Camus, A. (1955). *The Myth of Sisyphus*. (J. O'Brien, Trans.) New York: Vintage Books.

Camus, A. (1989). *The Stranger*. (M. Ward, Trans.) New York: Vintage International: Vintage Books.

Carnine, D., et. al. (2004). fourth edition, *Direct Instruction Reading*. Upper Saddle River, N.J.: Pearson Education, Inc..

Carroll, S. (2016). *The Big Picture: On the Origins of Life, Meaning and the Universe Itself*. New York, N.Y.: Dutton.

Churchland, P. (1988). *Matter and Consciousness*. Cambridge, MA: A Bradford Book.

Dawkins, R. (2006). *The God Delusion*. Boston: Houghton Mifflin Company.

Dennett, D. (2014). [Review of the book *Reflections on Free Will*, by Harris, S.] at https://www.samharris.org/blog/reflections-on-free-will.

Dennett, D. (2006). *Breaking the Spell*. New York: Penguin Books.

Dostoevsky, F. (1990). *The Brothers Karamazov*. New York: Farrar, Straus and Giroux.

Englelmann, S. & Carnine, D. (1991). *Theory of Instruction: Principles and Application* (Rev. Ed.), Eugene, OR: ADI Press.

Engelmann, S. and Steely, D. (2003). *Inferred Functions of Performance and Learning*. London: Psychology Press.

Gasset, O. (1957). *The Revolt of the Masses*. New York: Norton.

Gingerich, O. as quoted in Kurtz, P. (2003). *Science and Religion: Are They Compatible?*: Amherst, New York: Prometheus Books.

Goldstein, R.N. (2010). *36 Arguments for the Existence of God*. New York: Pantheon Books.

Godel, K. as quoted in Dawkins R. (2008). *The Oxford Book of Modern Science Writing*. Oxford: Oxford University Press.

Gould, S.J. (1995). *Dinosaurs in a Haystack*. New York: Harmony Books.

Gould, S. J. (1989). "The Cosmic Lottery: As Stephen Gould Sees It, Human History is a Tale of Random Luck," Los Angeles Times: Nov. 28, 1989. at https://www.latimes.com/archives/la-xpm-1989-11-28-vw-322-story.html

Harris, S. (2006). *Letter to a Christian Nation*. New York: Knopf.

Hasker, W. (2008). *The Triumph of God Over Evil*. Downers Grove, Il.: Inter-Varsity Press.

Haught, J.A. (2005, April-May, Vol. 25, No. 3). "Why Would God Drown Children?" *free inquiry*.

Hick, J. (1978). *Evil and the Love of God*. San Francisco: Harper and Row.

Hick, J. (1981). "An Irenean Theodicy," in *Encountering Evil*, ed. S. David. Atlanta: John Knox Press.

Hitchens, C. (2007). *god is not Great: How Religion Poisons Everything*. New York: Twelve.

Huxley, A. (1962). *Brave New World*. New York: Bantam Books.

Kant, I. (1999). *Critique of Pure Reason*. Cambridge: Cambridge University Press.

Kant, I. (1783). *Prolegomena to Any Future Metaphysic*, transl. Jonathan Bennett, Early Modern Texts, at www.earlymoderntexts.com.

Kasper, C.G. (1986). *The God of Jesus Christ*. New York: Crossroad.

Kennedy, W.K. and Newcombe, J. (2007). *Cross Purposes*. Colorado Springs, Colorado: Multnomah Publishers.

Kierkegaard, S. (1989). *The Sickness Unto Death*. England: Penguin Classics.

Kierkegaard, S. (1957). *The Concept of Dread*. (W. Lowrie, Trans.) Princeton; University Press ed.

Kornhuber, H.H. and Deecke, Luder (2012). *The Will and Its Brain: An Appraisal of Reasoned Freedom;* Maryland: University Press of America.

Lewis, C. S. (2001). *The Problem of Pain*. SanFrancisco: HarperSanFranscisco.

MacArthur, J. (2007). *The Truth War*. USA: Thomas Nelson.

Mackie, J.L. (2011). As quoted in Peterson, M., *The Problem of Evil*. Notre Dame, Indiana: University of Notre Dame Press.

Macquarrie, J. (1973). *Existentialism*. Middlesex, England: Penguin Books Ltd..

Marino, G. (2004). Paperback Ed., *Basic Writings of Existentialism*. Modern Library Classic.

Martin, M. from *The Modern Schoolman* 58 (March 1981), St. Louis: Saint Louis University.

Maslow, A.H. (1943). *A Theory of Human Motivation. Psychological Review*, 50(4), 370-96.

McLaren, B. (2007). *A Search for What Makes Sense*. Michigan: Zondervan.

McDonald, H.D. (1986). *The God Who Responds*. Minneapolis: Bethany House.

McDowell, J. (1972). *Evidence That Demands a Verdict*. USA: Campus Crusade for Christ.

Moore, G.E. (1953). *Some Main Problems of Philosophy*. London, George Allen and Unwin.

Musser, G. (2015). *Spooky Action at a Distance*. New York: Farrar, Strauss and Girous.

Neiman, Susan. (2002). *Evil in Modern Thought*. Princeton University Press.

Niebuhr, R. (1996). *The Nature and Destiny of Man*. (Vol. 1 and 2) Louisville: Westminster John Knox Press.

Nietzsche, F. (2012). *Thus Spake Zaruthra*. New York, N.Y.: Sterling and Ross.

NIV Study Bible (2002). Zondervan. Grand Rapids, Michigan: Zondervan.

Pascal, B. (1958). Pascal's Pensées. New York :E.P. Dutton.

Pinker, S. (1997). *How the Mind Works*. New York: W.W. Norton.

Pinnock, C. (2001). *Most Moved Mover: A Theology of God's Openness*. Grand Rapids, Michigan: Baker Academics.

Plantinga, A. (1977). *God, Freedom, and Evil*. Grand Rapids: Wm B. Eerdmans Publishing.

Plato. (1971). *Timaeus and Critias*. (D. Lee, Trans.) Penguin Classics. Harmonsworth Middlesex: Penguin books LTD.

Polkinghorne, J. (2005). *Exploring Reality: The Intertwining of Science and Religion*. New Haven: Yale University Press.

Rieff, P. (2007). *Charisma: The Gift of Grace and How it Has Been Taken Away From Us*. Pantheon Books.

Rieff, P. (2018). Vol 43, issue 1. [Review of book *Dreamworks*, by Ashford, B.] "The Gospel Coalition." at: https://www.thegospelcoalition.org/themelios/article/a-theological-sickness-unto-death-philip-rieff-prophetic-analysis/

Rovelli, C. (2016). *Reality is Not What it Seems: The Journey to Quantum Gravity*. (Carnell and Segre, Trans.). New York: Riverhead Books.

Rovelli, C. (2023, December 30-31, p. C8). Carlo Rovelli: The author, most recently of "White Holes: Inside the Horizon." *The Wall Street Journal*.

Rowe, W.L. (1979). "The Problem of Evil and Some Varieties of Atheism," *American Philosophical Quarterly* 16: 335-41.

Rowe, W.L. (1988). "Evil and Theodicy," *Philosophical Topics* 16: 199-32.

Sartre, J-P. (2007). *Nausea*. (L. Alexander, Trans.) New York, N.Y.: A New Directions Paperbook.

Sartre, J-P. (2004). "Existentialism and Human Emotions" as quoted in *Basic Writings of Existentialism*, by Marino, G., New York.: The Modern Library.

Sapolsky, R.M. (2013). *Determined: A Science of Life Without Free Will*. New York: Penguin Press.

Shabi, K. (2021, Oct. 6). *Legomenon*, "Meaning of the Scream," at: https://legomenon.com/meaning-of-the-scream-1893-painting-by-edvard-munch.html

Smedes, L. (1978). *Love Within Limits*. Michigan: Wm. B. Eerdmans Publishing Company.

Smolin, L. (2008). As quoted in Dawkins R, *The Oxford Book of Modern Science Writing*. Oxford: Oxford University Press.

Stephenson, N. (2015). *Seveneves*. New York: William Morrow an imprint of HarperCollins.

Sterrett, T.N. (1974). *How to Understand Your Bible*. Downer's Grove, Illinois: InterVarsity Press.

Strathern, P. (1997). *Kierkegaard in 90 Minutes*. Chicago: Ivan R. Dee.

Swinburne, R. (2013). *Mind, Brain and Free Will*. New York: Oxford University Press.

Swinburne, R. (1988). "Does Theism Need a Theodicy," *Canadian Journal of Philosophy*, 18:287-312.

Swinburne, R. (1998). *Providence and the Problem of Evil*. Oxford University Press.

Swinburne, R. (1992). "Natural Evil" as cited in Peterson, M. L., *The Problem of Evil: Selected Readings*. Notre Dame, Indiana: University of Notre Dame Press.

Taylor, C. (2007). *A Secular Age*. Massachusetts: The Belknap Press of Harvard University Press.

Thuesen, P. (2009). *Predestination*. Oxford: Oxford University Press.

Tillich, P. (1971). Vol. 1-3. *Systematic Theology*, Chicago:University of Chicago Press.

Tillich, P. (1954). *Love, Power and Justice*. Oxford: Oxford University Press.

Tillich, P. (1963). "The Ambiguity of Perfection." *Time*, 17 May 1963, p. 69.

Tillich, P. (1987). As quoted in Church, F. *The Essential Tillich*, New York: Collier Books.

Tillich, P. (2000). *The Courage to Be*. New Haven: Yale University Press.

Tse, P. (2013). *The Neural Basis of Free Will*. Boston: MIT Press.

Twain, M. (1909). *Extract From Captain Stormfield's Visit to Heaven*. New York and London: Harper and Brothers.

Vermes, G (2008). *The Resurrection*. New York: Doubleday.

Ware, B (2000). *God's Lesser Glory*. Wheaton, IL: Crossway Books.

Wesley, S. (2009). As quoted in Thuesen, P., *Predestination*. Oxford: Oxford University Press.

Willard, D. (1998). *The Divine Conspiracy: Rediscovering Our Hidden Life in God*. San Francisco: Harper San Francisco.

Wilson, E.O. (2017). *The Origins of Creativity*. New York: Liveright Publishing Corp.

Wilson, E.O. (2012). *The Social Conquest of Earth*. New York: Liveright Publishing Corp.

Wilson, E.O. (2014). *On Free Will*, Harper's magazine, Sept. 2014.

Wykstra, S. (1984). *The Human Obstacle to Evidential Arguments from Suffering: On Avoiding the Evils of 'Appearance'*."International Journal for Philosophy of Religion 16.

Yalom, Irvin D. (1980). *Existential Psychotherapy*. Basic Books: A division of HarperCollins Publishers.

Author

 Michael Carroll, a graduate of the University of Illinois School of Law, has been studying theodicy for more than twenty years. He is a retired Illinois Judge, served as a State's Attorney, City and Township attorney, and private attorney during his forty-year legal career. During this time, he was also a real estate developer, newspaper columnist, art shop owner, antique dealer, and writer.

Prior to these expansive career endeavors, he was an officer in the U.S. Army and a research specialist with the Army's Corps of Engineers designing innovative building-delivery models.

He currently lives in his hometown of Tuscola, Illinois, with his wife, Dr. Rebecca Cook, retired Special Education professor.

www.ingramcontent.com/pod-product-compliance
Lightning Source LLC
Chambersburg PA
CBHW030912120626
46554CB00001B/117

9798218462116